Animal Miscellany

Books by Vernon Coleman include:

The Medicine Men (1975)
Paper Doctors (1976)
Stress Control (1978)
The Home Pharmacy (1980)
Aspirin or Ambulance (1980)
Face Values (1981)
The Good Medicine Guide (1982)
Bodypower (1983)
Thomas Winsden's Cricketing Almanack (1983)
Diary of a Cricket Lover (1984)
Bodysense (1984)
Life Without Tranquillisers (1985)
The Story Of Medicine (1985, 1998)
Mindpower (1986)
Addicts and Addictions (1986)
Dr Vernon Coleman's Guide To Alternative Medicine (1988)
Stress Management Techniques (1988)
Know Yourself (1988)
The Health Scandal (1988)
The 20 Minute Health Check (1989)
Sex For Everyone (1989)
Mind Over Body (1989)
Eat Green Lose Weight (1990)
How To Overcome Toxic Stress (1990)
Why Animal Experiments Must Stop (1991)
The Drugs Myth (1992)
Complete Guide To Sex (1993)
How to Conquer Backache (1993)
How to Conquer Pain (1993)
Betrayal of Trust (1994)
Know Your Drugs (1994, 1997)
Food for Thought (1994, revised edition 2000)
The Traditional Home Doctor (1994)
People Watching (1995)
Relief from IBS (1995)
The Parent's Handbook (1995)
Men in Dresses (1996)
Power over Cancer (1996)
Crossdressing (1996)
How to Conquer Arthritis (1996)
High Blood Pressure (1996)
How To Stop Your Doctor Killing You (1996, revised edition 2003)
Fighting For Animals (1996)
Alice and Other Friends (1996)
Spiritpower (1997)

How To Publish Your Own Book (1999)
How To Relax and Overcome Stress (1999)
Animal Rights – Human Wrongs (1999)
Superbody (1999)
Complete Guide to Life (2000)
Strange But True (2000)
Daily Inspirations (2000)
Stomach Problems: Relief At Last (2001)
How To Overcome Guilt (2001)
How To Live Longer (2001)
Sex (2001)
We Love Cats (2002)
England Our England (2002)
Rogue Nation (2003)
People Push Bottles Up Peaceniks (2003)
The Cats' Own Annual (2003)
Confronting The Global Bully (2004)
Saving England (2004)
Why Everything Is Going To Get Worse Before It Gets Better (2004)
The Secret Lives of Cats (2004)
The Cat Basket (2005)
The Truth They Won't Tell You (And Don't Want You To Know) About The EU (2005)
Living in a Fascist Country (2006)
How To Protect and Preserve Your Freedom, Identity and Privacy (2006)
The Cataholic's Handbook (2006)
Animal Experiments: Simple Truths (2006)
Coleman's Laws (2006)
Secrets of Paris (2007)
Cat Fables (2007)
Too Sexy To Print (2007)
Oil Apocalypse (2007)
Gordon is a Moron (2007)
The OFPIS File (2008)

novels
The Village Cricket Tour (1990)
The Bilbury Chronicles (1992)
Bilbury Grange (1993)
Mrs Caldicot's Cabbage War (1993)
Bilbury Revels (1994)
Deadline (1994)
The Man Who Inherited a Golf Course (1995)
Bilbury Pie (1995)
Bilbury Country (1996)
Second Innings (1999)
Around the Wicket (2000)
It's Never Too Late (2001)
Paris In My Springtime (2002)

Mrs Caldicot's Knickerbocker Glory (2003)
Too Many Clubs And Not Enough Balls (2005)
Tunnel (1980, 2005)
Mr Henry Mulligan (2007)
Bilbury Village (2008)

as Edward Vernon
Practice Makes Perfect (1977)
Practise What You Preach (1978)
Getting Into Practice (1979)
Aphrodisiacs – An Owner's Manual (1983)

with Alice
Alice's Diary (1989)
Alice's Adventures (1992)

with Donna Antoinette Coleman
How To Conquer Health Problems Between Ages 50 and 120 (2003)
Health Secrets Doctors Share With Their Families (2005)

Animal Miscellany

Donna Antoinette Coleman
& Vernon Coleman

Illustrations by Vernon Coleman

Published by Blue Books, Publishing House, Trinity Place, Barnstaple, Devon EX32 9HG, England.

ISBN: 978-1-899726-12-7

A catalogue record for this book is available from the British Library.

Printed and bound in Great Britain by
CPI Antony Rowe, Chippenham, Wiltshire

Dedicated

To the animals
And to those who care

Basic Definitions

Animal (n): a living being with sense organs, able to move voluntarily; any such being other than a human.

1. Tame animals were once wild but have been captured (as individuals) and adapted by humans.
2. Domestic animals have been bred and reared by humans for a number of generations. They have been altered by association with humans. A domestic animal has been selected and bred by humans in order to satisfy specific requirements. Dogs are bred for appearance or temperament. Farm animals are bred for their ability to grow muscle or produce milk. The animals which most satisfy our demands are used for breeding. The animals which don't meet our needs are (barring inevitable accidents) removed from the breeding chain.
3. Feral animals were once domestic but have become wild. A feral animal is an animal which was once domestic (and therefore bred artificially) but which has reverted to the wild and is now breeding according to the basic rule of natural selection: the survival of the fittest.
4. Wild animals are not and never have been trained in any way. A wild animal is a result of natural selection. Only the individuals most suited to their environment will have survived and bred. The less well-adapted will have disappeared from the gene pool. Genetically speaking, a wild animal is a wild animal wherever it may be. A lion is a wild animal in a zoo just as much as it is roaming free on the African plains. The space on our planet which is available for wild animals is shrinking. More than a third of the earth's animal and plant species live on just 1.4 per cent of its surface.
5. Herbivores have teeth adapted for cutting and grinding-up vegetation, enzymes for breaking down plant cell walls and micro-organisms in their guts to help the digestive process.
6. Carnivores have strong, sharp teeth for tearing flesh from bones, and special enzymes for breaking down meat into useful constituents.

Foreword

It's surprisingly difficult to obtain real facts about animals. Much of what we read, and think we know, owes more to imagination than to science. Rumour, gossip and folklore have, over the years, taken the place of solid research.

Our knowledge about animals is limited (and our ignorance far greater than we like to think) for several reasons.

Many people (including some scientists who really should know better) make the mistake of assuming that science is an exact subject where facts are all agreed upon by everyone. The truth is that science (and this is true of all branches of science – not just biology and zoology) is a work in progress, and there are endless confusions and disagreements. New discoveries may change our view about the ancestry of some animals.

But sometimes, scientific disagreements are a result of political pressure rather than genuine scientific ignorance.

So, for example, some experts classify the orang-utan as a member of the Hominidae family while others say it is a member of the Pongidae and yet others say that one is a synonym for the other.

Now if you can't even decide which family an animal is a member of you really cannot call your subject 'exact' in the way that most people think it should be.

(This difference isn't just academic. It has all sorts of practical, legal and even moral complications. If an orang-utan is a member of the Hominidae family then, in some countries, it must, in law, be treated quite differently from other animals. Indeed, it is possible to argue that this might explain why some so-called scientists, probably under political pressure, insist on putting it in the Pongidae family.)

One reason for excluding animals such as the orang-utan from the Hominidae family is to make it easier for vivisectors to experiment on them without having to face all sorts of searching questioning from animal rights lovers and whichever politicians can be embarrassed into taking an interest.

Surprisingly, little accurate research has ever been done into the way animals live and behave.

In the case of wild animals this is not, perhaps, too surprising. Studying wild animals properly would require following them for years in the wild (a difficult if not impossible task which would require superhuman dedication and would, in the end, produce research of questionable value because the very presence of the outside, human observer might well alter the behaviour of the animals). Studying 'wild' animals in the entirely unnatural conditions of the laboratory, zoo or safari park is as likely to provide useful information about the way animals naturally behave as studying prisoners would provide useful information about human behaviour. One thing we do know for certain is that wild animals kept in captivity behave very differently to wild animals living in their natural habitat.

It should, of course, be much easier to observe farm animals. Cows, pigs, sheep and other domesticated animals are easy enough to watch. And since the observer need not alter the animals' routines, the observations should be of value.

But, very few proper studies have been carried out on farm animals either, and vets and farmers are invariably quite mistaken in their beliefs about animals such as sheep and cows.

The truth, sadly, is that little or nothing of value has been written or broadcast about pigs, cows, sheep and other farm animals (though they are just as interesting as wild animals) because the various parts of the meat industry don't want us to know that the animals which are reared and killed for us to eat are sensitive, thoughtful and intelligent.

Farmers and butchers have a financial interest in perpetuating and strengthening the myth that animals (particularly farm animals) are stupid.

We don't like to eat dogs or cats because we recognise that they have intellect and personality. (There is, needless to say, a vast amount of information available about household pets.) But, if we knew the truth about the capabilities of pigs, sheep and cows, the market for meat would collapse. It is inconvenient to know that sheep are sensitive and intelligent creatures. And so tame academics (a large and malleable group) happily help to endorse the 'farm animals are stupid and so don't matter' myth.

Surprisingly, even many vets are largely ignorant about farm animals. We have, for example, met vets who believed that sheep are stupid (not true) and that they have only short-term memories of 20 minutes or so (also not true). But we have not met many who realise that sheep hate getting wet (true).

In writing this book, we have done our best to isolate the real facts and to expose – rather than perpetuate – myths and misunderstandings. We have used hundreds of textbooks, journal articles and (where we could satisfy ourselves as to their reliability) websites; we have talked to trustworthy experts and we have done a good deal of our own original research. It took us three years to research this book, and another year to check and edit the material we collected. In writing our book, we have done our best to ensure that you can trust what you read on these pages. Where we are not entirely sure about something (because of conflicting evidence) we've made it clear.

The result will, we hope, enable you to glory in the marvellous world of animals: there is more variety than most of us realise. Animals possess a wider range of skills, and more surprises, than you might imagine. The one thing humans have that animals don't have is the conceit, the arrogance, to assume they are wiser and in some way better than all other animals and, consequently, entitled to do as they will with other members of the animal kingdom. All animals are special and all are worthy of our awe and respect.

Sadly, that respect is the one thing our relationship with animals usually lacks. Maybe this book will help put it back.

Vernon Coleman and Donna Antoinette Coleman, January 2008

Note: All the good bits in this book were written by Donna Antoinette Coleman. The mistakes were made by Vernon Coleman.

ANIMALS EXHIBIT ALTRUISTIC BEHAVIOUR

- Animals don't just show love; they frequently exhibit behaviour that can only be described as altruistic. Animals can suffer, they can communicate and they can care. There are numerous well-authenticated stories of animals putting their own lives at risk in order to save their loved ones.
- Elderly lionesses who have lost their teeth and can no longer hunt and who are too old to have young are, theoretically, of no value to the rest of the pride. But, nevertheless, the younger lions will share their kills with them. An older lioness may spend her old age – 20 years or more – being looked after by younger females.
- A three-year-old chimpanzee is able to recognise when an adult chimpanzee (even one who is a complete stranger) needs help. And he will provide the required assistance even when there is no benefit to be gained – without expecting a reward or praise of any kind. The young chimpanzee helps simply because it wants to. For example, young, agile chimpanzees will climb trees to fetch fruit for their older relatives. Old age brings respect. Older male chimpanzees are only rarely threatened by younger animals and are tolerated without aggression. Older chimpanzees are given more grooming than they get.
- Foxes have been observed bringing food to adult, injured foxes. When one fox was injured by a mowing machine and taken to a vet by a human observer, the fox's sister took food to the spot where the injured fox had lain. The Good Samaritan sister fox made the whimpering sound that foxes use when summoning cubs to eat (even though she had no cubs).
- Whales have been observed to ask for and receive help from other whales.
- Author J. Howard Moore described how crabs struggled for some time to turn over another crustacean which had fallen onto its back. When the crabs couldn't manage by themselves they went and fetched two other crabs to help them.
- A gander who acted as a guardian to his blind partner would take her neck gently in his mouth and lead her to the water when she wanted to swim. Afterwards he would lead her home in the same manner.
- Pigs will rush to defend one of their number who is being attacked.
- When wild geese are feeding, one will act as sentinel – never taking a grain of

corn while on duty. When the sentinel goose has been on watch for a while, it pecks at a nearby goose and hands over the responsibility for guarding the group.

- When swans dive, there is usually one which stays above the water to watch out for danger.
- Time and time again dogs have pined and died on being separated from their masters or mistresses.
- Author Konrad Lorenz described the behaviour of a gander called Ado when Ado's mate, Susanne-Elisabeth, was killed by a fox. Ado stood by Susanne-Elisabeth's body in mourning. He hung his head and didn't bother to defend himself when attacked by strange geese. How would the animal abusers describe such behaviour other than as sorrow born of love? There is no survival value in mourning. It can only be a manifestation of a clear emotional response – love.
- Coyotes form pairs before they become sexually active – and then stay together. One observer watched a female coyote licking her partner's face after they had made love. They then curled up and went to sleep.
- Geese, swans and mandarin ducks have all been described as enjoying long-term relationships.
- One herd of elephants was seen to be travelling unusually slowly. Observers noted that the herd travelled slowly so as not to leave behind an elephant who had not fully recovered from a broken leg. Another herd travelled slowly to accommodate a mother who was carrying her dead calf with her. When the herd stopped to eat or drink, the mother would put her dead calf down. When they started travelling, she would pick up the dead calf. The rest of the herd was accommodating her in her time of grief.
- Vampire bats will regurgitate blood into the mouth of a sick bat.
- Gorillas, like elephants, have been seen to travel slowly if one is injured and unable to move quickly.
- When animals die, their relatives and friends will often bury them. A badger was seen to drag another badger which had been killed by a car off the road, along a hedge, through a gap and into a burial spot in nearby woods. Elephants won't pass the body of another elephant without covering the corpse with twigs, branches and earth. After scientists and park officials culled elephants in Uganda, they cut the ears and feet off the dead animals and stored them in a shed ready to sell for handbags and umbrella stands. But during the night, a group of elephants broke into the shed and buried the ears and feet. Elephants have even been seen burying dead buffalo and dead lions.
- If adult foxes are killed (for example, by a hunt) and they leave behind an orphaned cub, relatives of the slaughtered foxes will look after the cub. They take on responsibility as though the cub were their own.
- Penguins keep warm in groups. When the birds on the outside begin to feel the cold they go into the centre of the group to get warm while the warm birds, who have been huddled inside, take their turn on the outside.

- Geese fly in changing formations to protect one another
- Grooming, picking fleas, bugs and mud from each other's hair, is an essential part of family life for gorillas.
- A dwarf mongoose in the Taru desert of Kenya was badly injured. Her group stayed around her, grooming her and bringing her food until she was able to walk again.
- Elephants will pull one another to their feet if they are having difficulty in getting up.
- Elephants have been known to rescue captured elephants in hunting raids.
- Swiss researchers studying rats at the University of Bern discovered that rats demonstrate altruism towards strangers in much the same way that people sometimes do. People are more likely to lend a hand to a perfect stranger if they have benefited from kindness in the past, and rats are just the same. Curiously, this discovery did not convince experimenters that rats (and other animals) are sentient creatures who deserve to be treated with respect and consideration.
- A researcher from the University of Parma, has shown that in Rome, where there are 350,000 stray cats in 2,000 separate colonies, male alley cats let the weakest individuals in their colony – small female cats and their kittens – eat first. The researcher concluded that the male, feral cats, although normally aggressive, recognise that the weaker females and the young kittens need more food and need to be given precedence in order to survive. Of course, the cats may just have surprisingly good table manners. Whatever the explanation may be, their actions can undoubtedly be described as altruistic.

Armadillos

- Armadillos belong to the family Dasypodidae, and live mainly in South America. The armadillo's habitat includes: arid desert, savanna, thorn scrub and forests.
- The armadillo is stout with short legs and long, sharp claws; it has a tough body armour (called a carapace) which consists of very strong, bony plates covered in scales. The bony plates are separated by bands of flexible tissue.
- Different species of armadillo have a different number of flexible bands across the carapace. Some species are named by the approximate number of bands they have, such as the nine-banded armadillo and the six-banded armadillo.

- There are around 20-21 species of armadillo.
- The giant armadillo is the largest of the species. It can weigh 66lb (29.93kg) or more and grow to 39.37in (100cm) in length
- The smallest of the species are the fairy armadillos. There are two species of fairy armadillo, with the smaller of the two species being around 6in (15.24cm) long.
- Armadillos are related to sloths and anteaters.
- Although they have a tough exterior, armadillos are not exempt from natural predators. Bobcats, mountain lions, coyotes and alligators are just some of the armadillo's predators.
- Most armadillos have poor eyesight but a well-developed sense of smell and hearing, which they use to detect their prey. The armadillo's sense of smell is so good that it can detect its prey as far as 8in (20.32cm) underground.
- The armadillo's diet includes: vegetation, fungi, insects, worms, lizards, snakes, small mammals and carrion.
- The northern naked-toed armadillo, which can be found in Central and South America, eats insects. And just like the anteater, it licks up insects with its long, sticky tongue.
- Armadillos can devour up to 40,000 ants in one sitting.
- Most armadillo species living in the wild produce one to four young in a litter. The giant armadillo usually gives birth to one to two young and has a gestation period of around four months. The nine-banded armadillo, which can be found in North, Central and South America, always gives birth to quadruplets of one sex: either four female babies or four male babies.
- The nine-banded armadillo is capable of delayed implantation. For example, one captive nine-banded armadillo gave birth several years after copulation.
- In some male species of armadillo, the penis extends a staggering two-thirds of its body length.
- The hairy armadillo has coarse hair all over its thick armour.
- For self-defence, some species of armadillo burrow into the ground and wedge themselves really tightly into the earth so that predators will have great difficulty in dislodging them. If the armadillo hasn't completely buried itself, it will just

Ten Animals Discovered In The Last 150 Years

1. Grevy's zebra
2. Andrew's beaked whale
3. Mountain gorilla
4. King cheetah
5. Okapi
6. Emperor tamarin
7. Golden bamboo lemur
8. Mountain nyala
9. Giant forest hog
10. Mexican banana bat.

leave the armour on its back exposed. The armadillo will stay in this position until danger passes. When threatened, the three-banded armadillo (of which there are two species) is capable of rolling itself into a tight ball to protect its vulnerable underside.

- The southern naked-tailed armadillo walks on the tips of its claws on its front feet and on the soles of its back feet.
- Armadillos live up to 20 years in captivity.
- The word 'armadillo' is Spanish for 'little man in armour'.
- The nine-banded armadillo is capable of filling its whole body with air, including its intestines, just by taking in a deep breath. It will usually do this if it has to swim across a large stretch of water to get away from danger. The air inside the armadillo's body helps to keep it afloat so that it can swim safely to land. If the air is released, the armadillo will sink like a stone. The nine-banded armadillo is capable of holding its breath underneath the water for up to six minutes.
- Armadillos are usually solitary animals, and all species of armadillo are nocturnal.
- The nine-banded armadillo is the most commonly seen of the species.
- Nine-banded armadillos in Louisiana and Texas can catch human leprosy whereas nine-banded armadillos residing in Florida cannot.
- Armadillos don't have any enamel on their teeth. The giant armadillo has nearly 100 teeth.
- Sadly, in some parts of America, armadillos are killed for their meat and body plates.

Animals Have A Sense Of Fun

Human beings are not the only animals to have a sense of humour and fun and to enjoy playing games.

Masson and McCarthy, in *When Elephants Weep,* report that foxes will tease hyenas by going close to them and then running away. Ravens tease peregrine falcons by flying closer and closer to them. Grebes tweak the tails of dignified swans and then dive to escape. A monkey has been seen to pass his hand behind a second

Ten Of The Cleverest Mammals In The World

1. Chimpanzee
2. Gorilla
3. Orang-utan
4. Baboon
5. Gibbon
6. Monkey
7. Small toothed whale
8. Dolphin
9. Elephant
10. Pig

monkey so that he could tweak the tail of a third monkey. When the third monkey remonstrated with the second monkey, the first monkey – the practical joker – was clearly enjoying himself.

We have watched lambs play their own versions of king of the castle, tag and many other games customarily played by children.

When scientists examined the dung of lions, the lions dug up the latrine the humans had been using and inspected their contents.

Ants, fish, birds, cats, dogs, sheep, horses, monkeys, porpoises and many other creatures have been observed playing games.

Badgers (Eurasian Badger)

- Badgers belong to the family Mustelidae. Eurasian (also known as European) badgers can be found in Europe to East Asia. Badgers are widespread throughout Europe, from arctic Finland to Spain. Although not so prevalent in some parts of the country, the Eurasian badger can be found in every county in the British Isles.
- Badgers have wedge-shaped bodies; short, thick necks; elongated snouts; strong limbs; short tails; small, white-fringed ears and small eyes. The Eurasian badger also has striking black and white facial markings. The stripes, on both sides of its face, extend from its ears, crossing over the eyes and down to its nose.
- Badgers can grow to 35in (89cm) or more in length and weigh 15lb-29lb (6.8kg-13kg). A badger's weight depends on the amount of food that is available.
- Badgers tend to occupy both unforested grassland and woodland.
- The male badger is called a boar. The female badger is called a sow. The baby badger is called a cub.
- The badger's main diet consists of earthworms (they can devour as many as 200 in an evening). Badgers also like to eat: slugs, amphibians, fruits, bulbs, roots, grain, birds' eggs, small mammals and carrion (as long as the flesh is relatively fresh). Badgers are amazingly adept at retrieving earthworms from the soil intact – only about 25 per cent of earthworms are not in one piece.
- Badgers have long, powerful claws and are expert diggers. Badgers sometimes use their long claws to dig out wasps from their nests.
- Badgers have poor eyesight and rely on their acute sense of smell and hearing when foraging for food. Badgers are opportunistic feeders and will eat anything edible that comes their way.
- Badgers are extremely powerful animals and can be vicious when they feel threatened. So if you come across an injured badger, do not attempt to help it yourself but call for specialist assistance from a vet or other expert.
- Badgers store fat on their bodies in the autumn. They rely on this fat store if food becomes scarce during the winter months.
- Eurasian badgers live together in groups or clans. But there are exceptions. In

southern Spain, for example, they either tend to live in pairs or alone, probably because of a lack of food supply. A clan may include as many as 12 or more badgers.

- ☞ Badgers in a group usually scent each other (known as 'musking') repeatedly with their secretions. This is believed to serve for personal recognition and to differentiate them from other badger clans living nearby. When musking, the badger presses its tail end against the other badger's body and squirts a strong smelling secretion from its anal and/or subcaudal glands.
- ☞ Eurasian badgers avoid parasites by building large underground chambers known as setts. The building of a sett can take many years.
- ☞ A sett is made up of a complex labyrinth of underground chambers and tunnels. A sett may have several entrances, depending on its size (for example, one extremely large sett was reported to have had over 100 entrances). Within their sett, badgers move around from chamber to chamber so that parasites die off before they go back.
- ☞ Grass, bracken and leaves are usually used to line the chambers of the sett for bedding. Badgers also use fresh green material such as bluebell leaves and wild garlic as bedding. They pick material for its aromatic, antibacterial and insecticidal properties, and are especially careful when preparing bedding for their vulnerable young. Badgers regularly bring their bedding to the surface for a day or two before taking it back underground. They do this because sunlight helps to kill any bugs with which their bedding might be infected.
- ☞ Badger setts are often passed down from generation to generation; some setts have been used for hundreds of years. For instance, one sett in England is known to be at least 200-years-old.
- ☞ Badgers are known to keep their setts meticulously clean, and to frequently change their bedding.
- ☞ In some countries, destroying or obstructing badger setts is against the law.
- ☞ Badgers usually like to follow the same routes within their territories, creating well-defined pathways.
- ☞ Eurasian badgers can be very territorial and may fight viciously with any unrelated badger who intrudes upon their territory. Badgers leave dung pits to mark their territories as a warning to trespassers to keep away.
- ☞ Badgers are largely nocturnal animals.
- ☞ Badgers tend to mate any time between February and October. However, delayed implantation means that females do not become pregnant until midwinter.
- ☞ The female badger has seven to eight weeks of normal gestation before her cubs are born.
- ☞ Female badgers usually give birth to two or three cubs.
- ☞ Cubs are normally born in a breeding chamber in the sett, where they will stay for the first two months of their lives.
- ☞ Cubs are about 4.7in (11.94cm) long when they are born.
- ☞ Badger cubs are weaned at around 12-weeks-old.

- ☞ Badger cubs usually stay in their natal groups for the rest of their lives.
- ☞ Badger cubs' enemies include: owls, birds of prey, wolverines and wolves.
- ☞ Adult badgers scream on occasions: eerie long-drawn out screams. Nobody really knows for sure why they do this.
- ☞ Adult badgers purr for pleasure.
- ☞ Road accidents are the main cause of death among adult badgers.
- ☞ Badgers can contract the muscles in their ears to stop dirt and dust particles getting into them while they are burrowing.
- ☞ In captivity, badgers can live up to 25 years.
- ☞ The trademark black and white striped face of the Eurasian badger is believed to differ slightly between each individual.
- ☞ Although Eurasian badgers spend days or weeks of inactivity during the winter, they only hibernate in colder climates.
- ☞ If you wish to prevent badgers from coming into your garden, you should get your dog to urinate along the badger's known routes. If you do not have a dog, you could always get the human male of the house to urinate in the garden instead. Females urinating in a garden have proved ineffective at deterring badgers from the area.

'All animals except man know that the ultimate of life is to enjoy it.'
SAMUEL BUTLER (1835-1902)

ENDANGERED ANIMALS

OVER THE CENTURIES, HUMAN BEINGS HAVE KILLED MILLIONS OF ANIMALS for food, for clothing and in self-defence.

Only in the last 400 years, however, since the development of modern agricultural methods led us into changing huge swathes of the planet, has man destroyed animals in such large numbers that some have become extinct and many others are in danger.

North America has the blackest record of all.

The North American bison was massacred in huge numbers in the 18th and 19th centuries, and in the same period (early 18th century to 1870) the population of the pronghorn antelope, one of America's oldest inhabitants, was reduced from 40 million to 19,000.

By 1914, Americans had completely exterminated Arizona elk; Easter elk; eastern forest bison; giant sea mink; the California, Texas and plains grizzly bears; eastern puma; plains grey wolf; Badland bighorn and many birds including: the great auk, passenger pigeon, heath hen and Carolina parakeet.

ANIMAL ADJECTIVES

We all know that someone who is catlike is feline and that someone who resembles a bull (or a cow) can be described as bovine. But how would you describe someone who reminded you of a boa constrictor or an armadillo?

Here's a list of the appropriate adjectives:

AARDVARK	edentate
ALLIGATOR	eusuchian
ANT	myrmicine
ANTELOPE	alcelaphine
APE	simian
ARMADILLO	dasypodid
BADGER	mustelid
BAT	vespertilian
BEAR	ursine
BEE	apiarian
BISON	bisontine
BULL	bovine
BUZZARD	cathartine
CALF	vituline
CAT	feline
CHIMPANZEE	simiid
COW	bovine
DEER	cervine
DINOSAUR	diapsidian
DOG	canine
DOLPHIN	delphine
DORMOUSE	myoxine
DRAGON	draconic
ELEPHANT	pachydermic
ELK	cervine
FOX	vulpine
FROG	ranine
GIRAFFE	artiodactylous
GOAT	caprine
GOLDFISH	cyprinid
GORILLA	pongid
HARE	leporine
HORSE	equine
KANGAROO	macropodine
LEECH	hirudinoid
LIZARD	saurian
MOLE	talpoid
MONGOOSE	viverrine
MONKEY	pithecoid
MOUSE	musine
OTTER	lutrine
OWL	strigine
OX	bovine
OYSTER	ostracine
PEACOCK	pavonine
PORCUPINE	hystricine
RABBIT	leporine
RAT	murine
RATTLESNAKE	crotaline
RHINOCEROS	ceratorhine
SEAL	phocine
SHEEP	ovine
SHREW	soricine
SKUNK	mustelid
SLOTH	xenarthral
SLUG	limacine
SNAKE	anguineous
SQUIRREL	sciurine
SWAN	cygnine
SWINE	porcine
TOAD	batrachian
TORTOISE	chelonian
WEASEL	arctoidean
WHALE	cetacean
WOLF	lupine
WORM	helminthic
ZEBRA	zebrine

These creatures are all gone for ever.

In numeral terms, the slaughter of the passenger pigeons was the most extraordinary. Billions inhabited eastern North America in the early 19th century. Single flocks of passenger pigeons used to number 2,000 million birds. The passenger pigeons would cloud the skies for three days at a time when flying south. But the birds were shot, netted and destroyed in huge numbers. Farmers would drive their pigs 100 miles (160.93km) to fatten them on the carcasses of the passenger pigeons. Men slaughtered the birds in huge numbers and shipped them in trainloads to sell in city meat markets. The birds were eventually finished off by the destruction of the forests they needed for food and shelter. Martha, the last passenger pigeon, died in Cincinnati Zoo in 1914.

Some Of The Animals Threatened With Extinction

All the animals below are close to extinction. The common factor causing their extinction is, of course, man. In many cases, human beings are the only factors endangering these animals. Traditionally, some animals are threatened because they are hunted for their tusks or their skin (or to be sold as pets). But the biggest threat is the cutting down of the forests and draining of wetlands to create land to grow biofuels.

1. Bornean and Sumatran orang-utan
Spend most of their time in trees, but the Indonesian rainforest (where they live) is disappearing because of biofuel plantations. Habitat loss resulting from palm oil plantations means that the orang-utans are, as a species, on the critical list. (The word 'orang-utan' originally meant 'person of the forest').

2. Rhinoceros
Five species are left and three, the black rhino, Javan rhino and Sumatran rhino are endangered.

3. Asiatic lion
Lives in just one forest in India and is threatened by hunters and disease.

4. Red wolf
Hunters have almost destroyed the red wolf.

5. Tiger
Hunted for their skins. Body parts are used in Chinese medicines. Three kinds of tiger are already extinct and three more are on the critical list.

6. Leatherback turtle
Many types of turtle are in danger of disappearing as their natural habitats are destroyed.

7. Giant ibis
One of the world's largest birds. The ibis is threatened because its habitat – the wetlands of Cambodia and Laos – are being drained to turn into farmland.

8. Mountain gorilla
Forest clearances and poaching have endangered the mountain gorillas.

9. Iberian lynx
The most endangered cat in the world. It is hunted for its fur.

10. Orange-bellied parrot
Originally lived in Tasmania, Australia but there are now very few left.

11. Yangtze river dolphin (or Baiji)
Pollution, fishing and habitat loss mean that this freshwater dolphin may already be extinct.

12. Great hammerhead shark
Killed so that cooks can make soup out of their fins. Also endangered because they often get entangled in fishing nets.

13. Gharial crocodile
Loss of natural habitat in India and Nepal has cut numbers by two thirds in recent years. The gharial crocodile could be extinct very soon.

Some other animals classified as endangered include: African wild dog, black-faced impala, blue whale, golden lion tamarin monkey, Indian elephant, red panda, snow leopard, wild water buffalo, woolly monkey and the volcano rabbit.

'All animals are equal, but some animals are more equal than others.'
George Orwell (1903–1950)

Seven Animals Which Are Extinct In Britain

1. Brown bear
2. Wolf
3. Reindeer
4. Elk
5. Wild boar
6. Beaver
7. Wild ox

Animals Damaged By Their Environment

Global warming, chemicals used in agriculture and other environmental problems don't just affect people: they affect animals too.

Seals and dolphins have been badly affected by environmental damage. The biocidal butylins which are used to protect the hulls of ships from barnacles don't just keep barnacles at bay. They also damage mammalian immune systems and consequently lower their resistance to cancers and infectious diseases. The pollution of their breeding grounds has produced a global epidemic of mysterious tumours. Porpoises in the seas around England have been made ill and killed by high concentrations of polychlorinated biphenols and mercury.

Some amphibians have become extinct, killed off by fungal infections created by environmental pollution which affect both disease resistance and development.

Bats (Common Pipistrelle)

- The common pipistrelle (Pipistrellus pipistrellus) belongs to the family Phyllostomidae, and can be found in Europe, Africa and Asia.
- The pipistrelle weighs approximately 0.8oz (22.68g). Including its tail, the pipistrelle can grow to approximately 3.34in (8.5cm) long.
- The pipistrelle bat has a mouse-like body; a very dark face and ears; short, triangular ears; a tail and dark brown, leathery wings.
- The pipistrelle's fur is normally reddish-brown with paler fur underneath its body.
- The pipistrelle bat has a wingspan of 8.7in (22cm) or more.
- The bat's wings are made up of a thin membrane of skin which consists of muscles, elastic tissue and blood vessels. The wings are supported by enormously elongated digits with a hooked thumb on each wing.
- To help them detect prey and navigate, bats use an echolocation system. Sound waves are emitted which are then reflected back from the objects they hit. Bats are then able to interpret the distance of the object, the object's size and texture. The pipistrelle's echolocation calls can be measured at around 45kHz.
- The pipistrelle's main diet includes: moths, mayflies, midges and caddisflies. Moths, which are able to hear the echolocation calls of bats more than 100ft (30.48m) away, try to avoid getting caught by flying in a zigzag pattern or by diving rapidly to the ground.
- The pipistrelle is reputed to eat as many as 3,000 insects in an evening.
- Like nearly all species of bat, the pipistrelle usually roosts during the day and feeds at night.
- Contrary to popular belief, bats are not blind.

- Pipistrelles tend to use high-pitched squeaks when calling to one another, especially before they go hunting. Humans with good hearing can detect their sounds.
- The pipistrelle prefers to occupy urban areas, marshes, rural woodlands and farmland.
- The pipistrelle likes to roost in buildings. When it does this it usually roosts in roof spaces. It will sometimes also roost in hollow trees.
- The pipistrelle roosts by hanging upside down – using the claws on its feet to grip onto its perch – with its wings neatly folded by its side. Just before sunset, pipistrelle bats emerge from their roosting places and take to the skies. They come out of their roosting places in large numbers to try to scare predators who might be waiting for them.
- When hunting, pipistrelles have rather jerky flight movements. This is because they are constantly changing direction, twisting and diving to seek their prey.
- Pipistrelles hibernate for part of the winter, usually from mid to late November to the end of March. They wake up several times during this period.
- Mating usually takes place in the winter with delayed fertilisation occurring in the spring.
- During the summer months, female pipistrelles gather in groups called 'nursery roosts' or 'nursery colonies' to have their young. Nursery roosts may include over 1,000 adult females.
- The pipistrelle's pregnancy usually lasts up to 44 days.
- When giving birth, the pipistrelle hangs to the surface the right way up (instead of its usual upside down position). The mother will use its interfemoral membrane (a piece of skin extending from one foot to the other) as a pouch to catch the baby as soon as it is born. The pipistrelle usually gives birth to one baby.
- In recent years, the number of pipistrelle bats in many areas has declined. The decline in numbers has been blamed on farmers who use sprays to kill off insects. Fewer insects mean less food for bats. The destruction of habitat such as trees and hedgerows has not helped.
- The pipistrelle's predators include: birds of prey, owls, members of the weasel family, cats and rats.
- In recent years, the common pipistrelle has been identified as two species. The other species is the soprano pipistrelle, which is so named because its echolocation call is at a higher frequency than the common pipistrelle's. The frequency of the soprano's echolocation call is around 55kHz.
- Bats are incapable of walking far because of their poorly developed hind limbs.
- More than one fifth of all mammals are bats.

- It is a myth that bats get entangled in human hair; a bat's echolocation system is so good that it is highly unlikely to bump into anything – let alone a human head.
- On average, bats live four to five years.
- Bats are the only mammals capable of true flight. The flying squirrel does not fly – it glides.

Bears (Brown Bear)

- There are eight different species of bear: American black bears, Asiatic black bears, spectacled bears, sloth bears, sun bears, giant pandas, polar bears and brown bears. 
- The brown bear (Ursus arctos) belongs to the family Ursidae, and is commonly found in northern Europe, Asia and North America. The brown bear's habitat includes: grassland, forest, mountains and dry desert.
- The brown bear's scientific name 'Ursus arctos' means 'bear bear'. 'Ursus' means 'bear' in Latin. 'Arctos' means 'bear' in Greek.
- Of all the species of bear, the brown bear is the most widely distributed.
- There are a number of brown bear subspecies. The North American brown bear or 'grizzly bear' (Ursus arctos horribilus) is the best known of the subspecies.
- The brown bear has a large head; small, round ears and a thick coat. Although usually brown in colour, the brown bear's coat may vary from blond to black. The bear's coat is made up of two types of fur: short, fine underfur and long, coarse guardhairs. The bear's coat helps to insulate the bear from the heat as well as from the cold.
- All subspecies of brown bear have a distinctive shoulder hump (which is made up of fat and muscle) called a 'roach'.
- The brown bear can grow over 9ft (2.74m) long (or tall when standing up) and weigh 2,200lb (998kg) or more.
- The brown bear's average lifespan is around 25 years in the wild.
- Brown bears who live in cold climates go into a form of hibernation throughout the winter period. Body temperature is dramatically reduced in most hibernating animals, but the bear is different – the brown bear's body temperature only

drops by a few degrees. Unlike most hibernating mammals, brown bears do not eat, drink, defecate or urinate during the hibernation period. During hibernation, the brown bear lives entirely on its stored fat reserves. The brown bear spends its hibernation period in a cave or den.

- The brown bear's diet includes: insects, fish, small and large mammals, carrion, frogs, birds' eggs, honey, roots, bulbs, grasses, nuts and berries. Although the brown bear is classified as a carnivore, its diet is more herbivorous than carnivorous. However, some coastal populations of brown bears spend much of their time at waterfalls during the summer catching salmon who are travelling upstream from the ocean to the rivers to lay their eggs. Of all the bear species, it is the polar bear that is primarily carnivorous.
- The brown bear can eat as much as 35lb (15.87kg) of food in one day.
- The average age at which the brown bear gives birth is between five and ten years of age.
- Mating usually occurs in May or June.
- The brown bear's pregnancy lasts for approximately nine weeks (this excludes delayed implantation). The cubs are born in a den, and will spend the first few months of their lives in their mother's lair.
- The brown bear's litter contains one to four young: two cubs are usual.
- At birth, cubs weigh less than 1lb (0.45kg) and they are weaned at around four-months-old.
- Baby cubs' predators include: wolves, cougars and adult bears.
- Female brown bears give birth approximately every two to five years.
- The cubs may stay with their mother for two to four years.
- Brown bears can reach speeds of over 30mph (48km/h), but only over short distances.
- It is a popular myth (and potentially dangerous) that bears cannot run downhill; bears can run very well downhill.
- The male brown bear's home range can be up to 800 sq. miles (2,072 sq. km): the female's is half that.
- A bear standing on its hind legs is not necessarily an aggressive stance. Bears usually stand on their hind legs if they want to get a better view of their surroundings or if they want to smell the air to pick up any nearby scent.
- Although generally quiet animals, the adult brown bear's vocal repertoire includes: roars, growls, snorts and grunts.
- Adult brown bears are solitary animals. However, a female with young offspring may occasionally meet with another female with offspring to share responsibility of the cubs. Also, bears will tolerate one another in an area providing plenty of food, such as a stretch of river containing lots of salmon.
- As with all the species of bear, the brown bear has five toes on each foot. Its curved claws are non-retractable.

- The brown bear is a shy animal and does its best to avoid contact with humans. It will only usually attack if it is startled or if its cubs are threatened. The brown bear will also become aggressive if defending a carcass. Sometimes, the brown bear makes bluff charges by running as if going to attack and then stopping before it gets to its trespasser, hoping that a bluff charge will be enough to scare the person or animal away.
- Bears are good swimmers.

- Occasionally, males can be aggressive with one another, for instance, if they are competing for food or competing for a female in oestrus. When a fight does ensue, it can be rather vicious and may result in death.
- Some of the main dangers bears face include habitat destruction (by man) and poaching for body parts (by man). The bear's body parts are used in the preparation of some medicines.

Strange But True (Part 1)

- King penguins living on remote islands have been reported to fall down with shock after catching sight of a human being.
- A guide dog for the blind is incapable of telling the difference between a red light and a green one at the pedestrian crossing. The dog makes his judgement on whether it is safe to lead his master across the road by the flow of traffic.
- In 4,000 years, not one animal has been incorporated into our livestock.
- Unbelievably, old tomb paintings have shown that Egyptians used to brand their cattle 4,000 years ago.
- There are forty thousand muscles in an elephant's trunk.
- The hardy cockroach can live for nine days without its head.
- A honeybee (not a bumblebee, which can sting as many times as it likes) can sting only once and then it dies. The honeybee queen can sting as many times as she wants. This is because the honeybee queen's sting is designed not to be left behind in its victim's flesh.
- Ants will not cross a line of chalk.
- About ten per cent of rams are gay.
- Dogs deposit around 10 tons (10.16 tonnes) of faeces on the streets of Paris every day.
- Bugs Bunny was originally called 'Happy Rabbit'.
- The largest dog show in the world, 'Crufts Dog Show' held in London, has been going since 1886.
- Henry III of France (1551-89) owned 2,000 dogs.
- A Zebra is white with black stripes – not the other way around.
- The male western grey kangaroo is nicknamed the 'stinker' because of its odour, which apparently smells of curry.
- The female knot-tying weaverbird will refuse to mate with a male who has built a scruffy nest.
- Every lobster community is dominated by an alpha male. Subordinate males constantly challenge the alpha male for his high status position. To make sure that the males in the community know who's in charge, every night the alpha male chucks the other males out of their homes and – not content on doing just that – beats them up. Female lobsters are attracted by this exhibition of brutality.
- Animals reduce their anxiety levels by grooming, hugging and stroking themselves or one another. In times of great stress, they can calm themselves this way.
- A newborn rat will not attach itself to its mother's nipples unless the nipples are covered in the mother's antiseptic saliva. The antiseptic protects the newborn rat from harmful bacteria which may be on the mother's nipples.

- Hunts which used to hunt foxes often used to breed foxes especially for hunting. It was, therefore, a nonsense to claim that hunts were essential to keep the fox population under control.
- The silkworm has eleven brains.
- A camel's pupils are square.
- Sharks never get ill. They are immune to every known disease including cancer. If they lose teeth they grow new ones in 24 hours.
- A rat can manage without water longer than a camel can.
- Laika, the Husky dog, was the first living creature to orbit earth. Russia sent Laika into space aboard Sputnik II in 1957.
- Rats who live in the city grow to be twice as big as rats who live in the country.

- Ragwort is extremely toxic to cattle, sheep and horses. The plant is so toxic that you should never handle ragwort without wearing gloves.
- Thirteen seconds is the longest recorded flight of a chicken.
- It is illegal to catch mice without a hunting licence in Cleveland, Ohio.
- Tennis balls are a common cause of choking in dogs.
- In an average year in America, around 5 million people are officially recorded as having been bitten by dogs.
- Birds roll in dust to soak up excess feather oil. This helps by making their skin dry and less hospitable to mites. When birds lift their wings, they are doing so to expose the underside to sunlight and, thereby, kill bacteria.
- Capuchin monkeys sometimes wash themselves with their urine. They do this because urea (a main component of urine) is an antibacterial and antifungal and has a stronger cooling effect than water alone. A healthy individual's urine is sterile and antiseptic.
- An oyster changes its sex several times (and more) during its lifetime.
- Toads will only devour moving prey.
- In the United States, there are over 100 million cats and dogs.
- Tannin-rich plants are astringent, they make the mouth feel dry and they don't taste very nice. Most grazing animals avoid them. But tannin-rich plants are antiseptic, antibacterial, antifungal, antidiarrhoeal and antihelmintic. And so

animals which are ill will often choose to eat these plants in order to treat themselves.

- The contraceptive pill works on gorillas.
- Chimpanzees who have intestinal parasites will do three things to help themselves. They will chew plants which contain multifunctional compounds. They swallow folded up hairy leaves which catch worms and speed their expulsion. And they eat termite mound soil which has the medicinal properties of clay and is able to secret antibodies too.
- A birdbath should contain two and a half inches of water. Any more water will make birds nervous. Any less water will make it difficult for birds to bathe.

'Nature teaches beasts to know their friends.'
SHAKESPEARE (1564-1616)

Camels (One Hump Or Two?)

- The Camelidae family consists of six members: the llama, the guanaco, the vicuna, the alpaca, the Bactrian and the dromedary. It is the dromedary and the Bactrian camels that give the family its name, Camelidae.
- The dromedary (or Arabian or one-humped) camel has one hump. The Bactrian (Asian or two-humped) camel has two humps. To remember which species of camel has two humps, try visualising the capital 'B' in 'Bactrian' lying on its back – you then have what looks like two humps sticking upwards.
- The Bactrian camel can be found in desert and cold, flat grasslands in Asia. The dromedary camel can be found in desert in Asia and Africa. There are feral populations of dromedary camels residing in Australia where they were introduced in the 1800's.
- The dromedary camel is a breed of camel trained for racing or riding.
- Bactrian and dromedary camels have small heads; small fur-lined ears; long muzzles; long, curved necks; slender, long legs and thick coats to keep out the heat during the day and to conserve body heat during the cold nights. The Bactrian camel grows a long, shaggy coat in time for the harsh winter months, which it then sheds in time for the summer. The hair on the Bactrian camel's winter coat may be over 10in (25.4cm) long on various parts of its body.
- Besides being important beasts of burden, camels are also valued for their meat, hide, milk, wool and dung.
- There are two types of Bactrian camel: one domesticated and one wild. Wild

Bactrian camels are thinner, have smaller humps and shorter hair than domestic Bactrian camels. Wild Bactrian camels are considered to be an endangered species.

- Measured at the hump, camels may grow to over 7ft (2.13m) in height.
- A camel's hump contains fat – not water. The camel's hump helps to increase its survival rate when food is scarce. If a camel doesn't eat, its hump will shrink.
- The fat in the camel's hump helps to protect the inner organs from the harsh sun. And the fat in the camel's hump allows the rest of its body to have little fat, which helps the camel to lose heat more easily in the hot desert.
- Camels can live 50 years or more.
- When it rains in the desert, camel owners tend to have difficulty keeping their animals under control. Camels rely heavily on people to draw water for them from the wells. So when it rains, camels believe that they don't need people any more and will make a bid for freedom. Some camels come back to their owners afterwards – others do not.
- Without camels, people would not be able to inhabit certain areas of the desert. People rely completely on camels to carry them from place to place.
- Camels are very smelly animals.
- The camel has an extraordinary ability to close its slit-like nostrils to help keep the desert sand out during sandstorms.
- The camel has a double row of long eyelashes to keep the sand and dust out of its eyes.

- Camels also have a third eyelid which sweeps from side to side, very much like a windscreen wiper on a car, to wipe away the sand and the dust. The camel's third eyelid is transparent enough for the animal to be able to see through it. So when the desert storms become too bad, the camel is able to close its third eyelid and still see where it is going.
- Camels have broad feet (with two toes on each foot), which help to spread their weight and provide stability on the soft sands of the desert. The camel is equally well-equipped for walking in the snow.
- Camels are ruminants, which mean that they chew the cud.
- Camels feed on vegetation growing in the desert that is unpalatable to other animals. They will even eat thorny bushes.
- Camels are very intelligent and shy animals.
- Just like people, camels can also be bad-tempered at times. If a camel has a temper tantrum, some camel owners have a good method of calming down their animals. The camel owner will take off the coat from his back and give it to the camel. The camel will then chew the item of clothing to pieces in a fit of rage using its sharp teeth. Afterwards, having had something on which to vent its anger, the camel will be much calmer.
- In order to conserve their body fluid levels while out trekking in the hot desert sun, camels excrete dry faeces and very concentrated urine or, sometimes, no urine at all.
- Camels can carry loads weighing 595lb (269.88kg).
- Depending on the circumstances, camels can endure up to ten months without drinking any water. Camels obtain a fairly adequate amount of water from the vegetation they consume.
- Camels will usually refuse to drink water that is dirty.
- The camel can drink 30 gallons (136 litres) of water in one sitting.
- Camels are social animals and – under normal circumstances – live in small herds, usually containing half a dozen females (depending on the species of camel), their offspring and one dominant male. Less dominant males are either solitary or live in bachelor herds. Sometimes, during the breeding season, one of the less dominant males will break away from its bachelor herd to challenge a dominant male. When this happens, a fight may ensue with lots of biting and neck wrestling. Also, both males may inflate the insides of their mouths to extrude a balloon-like sac with which to intimidate each other. This balloon-like sac is known as a 'goulla'.
- Camels spit. They project a combination of saliva and stomach contents at any object which annoys or threatens them.
- The camel is capable of varying its body temperature. For example, the camel will raise its own body temperature to adapt to the heat in the desert sun so that it sweats very little. Having the ability to vary its body temperature prevents the camel from losing too much fluid through panting and sweating.

- During really hot weather, the camel will normally face towards the sun so that the vast area of its body is dramatically protected from the sun's rays. This helps the camel to conserve water in its body by not becoming too hot and losing vital fluids through sweating.
- Air is moistened through the camel's nostrils when it inhales, and air is cooled when the animal exhales. This amazing ability is to help conserve water in the camel's body.
- Camels can run at 20mph (32km/h) or more.
- A camel's pregnancy can last up to 410 days.
- Camels usually give birth to one young.
- At birth, the baby camel weighs 66-88lb (29.93-39.91kg).
- The baby camel is able to walk properly within 24 hours of birth.
- You will sometimes hear camels being referred to as 'ships of the desert'. This nickname is probably due to the way camels walk by moving their front and back legs simultaneously on each side of their body in turn, which gives the camel a sort of 'swaying' appearance just like a ship. They probably also acquired the name in recognition for their tireless work of carrying people and goods long distances.
- Some of the camel's vocalisations include: roars, rumbling growls, loud bellows, high-pitched bleats and moans.

'Wild animals never kill for sport. Man is the only one to whom the torture and death of his fellow creatures is amusing in itself.'

JAMES ANTHONY FROUDE (1818-1894)

CHERNOBYL – THE UNLIKELY WILDLIFE PARK

THE ACCIDENT AT THE CHERNOBYL NUCLEAR POWER STATION in the Ukraine (in the former Soviet Union) is the worst in the history of nuclear power generation. In April 1986, technicians tried an experiment which caused the chain reaction in the core to go out of control. The lid of the reactor was blown off and a great deal of radioactive material was released into the atmosphere. There was also a partial meltdown of the core. There was an attempt to cover up what had happened but Swedish monitoring stations reported unusually high levels of radioactivity, and the Soviet Government eventually admitted what had happened. In the immediate aftermath of the accident there were 32 deaths, but doctors expect cancer deaths and other types of radiation-induced illness to occur for decades. The Chernobyl accident is still used as a reason not to use nuclear power.

Twenty years later, Chernobyl's exclusion zone remained off limits to human beings. The area around the former power station is still regarded as unsafe.

Ironically, the land has become one of the world's most robust wildlife sanctuaries. Numerous endangered species can be found there and the area is full of moose, roe deer, foxes, river otters, wolves, eagles and black storks.

The worst nuclear power plant accident in history has produced a wildlife sanctuary.

No one really knows whether or not the radiation is harming the animals. But excluding humans from this highly contaminated ecosystem has significantly outweighed the dangers created by the radiation leakage.

Animals And The Foods They Eat

★ Animals living in the wild are very good at adapting to their surroundings and ensuring that they have a balanced diet. They adapt their diet according to what is available and in order to obtain the essential nutrients their bodies need.

★ Fallow deer eat grass in the summer and browse on fruits such as acorns in the autumn. During the winter they eat ivy, holly and brambles. Then, in the spring, when the grass starts to grow again they start eating grass once more.

★ Wildebeests migrate from the lush grass of the north of the Serengeti Plains of Tanzania when they have calves. They go to the southern plains and to the foothills of volcanoes where they eat grass growing on ash-rich soils. The grass there is rich in calcium and phosphorus (both of which are necessary for lactation).

★ In California, desert tortoises travel long distances to find calcium which they consume in vast quantities. They need the calcium to keep their shells strong.

★ Rats need extra calcium in pregnancy and lactation. So they deliberately eat more calcium-rich foods. Their bodies help by absorbing more calcium from the food available.

★ Similarly, reindeer, who also need calcium and phosphorus for antler growing (as well as for milk production), will chew on old antlers. They will also eat soil from around decayed bones and lick rocks.

★ Camels and giraffes (both of which are, like moose and reindeer, vegetarian) have been known to eat the bones of dead animals in order to obtain essential minerals.

★ In the jungles of Malaysia, elephants have been seen drinking water from the bottom of a spring pool because there was more sulphur there.

★ In Scotland, reindeer have been known to lick and chew at salt-preserved canvas tents.

★ In Africa, buffalo have been seen licking other buffalo which were sweating, in order to replenish their salt supplies.

★ Dogs and other animals which live with humans, will lick toilet bowls to obtain the salt in the urine.

★ Biologist and author, Lyall Watson, reported seeing a herd of cattle eating and licking at the bark of a tree. When he examined the tree, he found that the tree had a copper nail embedded in the bark. The cattle were all copper deficient.

★ Sheep, which have access to a fully varied diet, can adjust their feeding to make sure that they have the right mixture of protein and carbohydrate. They can also adjust their diet to ensure that they repair any mineral deficiencies.

★ Animals don't just eat foods their bodies need. They will sometimes flavour their foods to increase their enjoyment. An Indian elephant living in a zoo used to split an apple into two and then rub the two halves onto the hay to flavour it.

★ Herbivores are very good at avoiding toxic plants. Bracken fern comes in two forms – one of which contains toxic cyanide. Both red deer and sheep avoid the bracken that contains the cyanide but eat the bracken that doesn't. Voles can discriminate between clovers that contain cyanide and clovers that don't. If they have no alternative but to eat the clover with the cyanide in, they just eat less of it.

★ Moose need large quantities of calcium and phosphorus for their antlers. Without the necessary minerals, they are likely to suffer from osteoporosis as their growing antlers take the calcium and phosphorus from their bones. To avoid this problem they chew on old, cast-off antlers to get the minerals they need.

- ★ Moose will eat aquatic plants such as water lilies because they are rich in sodium.
- ★ Animals have a strong tendency to eat a varied diet. If a grasshopper is given only one food item it will try to eat anything else it can find in order to vary its diet.
- ★ Rats increase their consumption of a food if they see other rats eating it, or if they smell that another rat has been around. If they find a new food that no other rats have eaten they will taste it, wait to see if they become ill and if they don't they go back to eat the rest.
- ★ A baby elephant will find out which foods are safe to eat by taking food from its mother's mouth and tasting it.
- ★ Some foods are harmful to mice but if eaten in the right proportions they are safe because the toxins in one cancel out the toxins in the other. Mice manage to adjust their diet to ensure that they get the balance right.

Cats (Domestic)

- ➢ Domestic cats belong to the family Felidae. The Felidae family comprises 37 recognised species of cat in four genera – including the big cats such as the lion and the tiger, and the smaller cats such as the lynx and the puma.
- ➢ Recent findings suggest that all modern domestic cats are descended from a small family of wild cats who lived in the Middle East around 130,000 years ago.
- ➢ The male cat is called a tom. The female cat is called a queen, especially when breeding.
- ➢ Domestic cats can, today, be found almost anywhere in the world.
- ➢ Cats are carnivores and are perfect hunting animals. They have powerful jaws; long, sharp teeth and retractable claws. They also have excellent hearing and eyesight. Their eyesight is particularly good in the dim light just before dawn and just after dusk – the best periods for hunting. When hunting, cats either lie in ambush to pounce on their prey or stalk their prey until they get quite close and then attack with a final rush. Even though domestic cats are often well-fed at home, their strong survival instincts force them to continue hunting.
- ➢ Cats are solitary by nature and usually prefer their own company. However, if necessary, they do show a remarkable degree of sociability and will tolerate cats of the same litter reasonably well.
- ➢ Cats sleep on average 16 hours a day.

Newborn kittens usually spend even longer sleeping. A ten-year-old cat will have spent more than six years sleeping.

- A domestic female cat is typically six to eight months old when she first comes into oestrus. Oestrus usually lasts up to ten days and occurs every two to three weeks around the spring and summer months. In a lit and heated environment, oestrus can occur throughout the year.
- When the female comes into oestrus, she will 'call' to the male whose territory she has chosen. Other males nearby will also respond to the female's 'calling' as well as to her sexual odour. The female will then excite the males further by writhing and rolling around on the ground. There is much howling and wailing amongst the males as they squabble for their chance to mate with the female. However, it is the female who often exerts control of the situation and decides which male or males she will mate with. The male mates the female by grabbing her by the scruff of the neck with his jaws and then mounting her. After copulation has finished, which is always brief, the female will turn around to try to attack her mating partner. The male has to get away quickly in order to avoid her claws. The female tries to attack her mating partner because the withdrawal of the tom's penis is extremely painful; this is due to the backward-pointing spines that cover its organ.
- Oestrus in females can be so intense that, in some cases, females who are kept or trapped indoors have been known to jump from windows to get to a tom.
- A cat's pregnancy lasts for approximately nine weeks.
- Towards the end of the cat's pregnancy, she will become restless in her search for a suitable den – usually somewhere warm, quiet and private – where she can give birth. Some domestic cats have been known to give birth inside wardrobes or drawers.
- An average litter contains four kittens. Cats are capable of bearing up to three litters a year. The reproductive potential of one pair of cats and their offspring is massive. In seven years one pair of cats and their offspring could, between them, produce a total of over 150,000 kittens.
- Kittens weigh about 4oz (113g) at birth.
- There is usually a delay of about half and hour between each kitten being born. Before the next kitten is born, the mother will break the birth sac of the newborn and lick the newborn's nose and mouth to stimulate it into taking its first breath. Usually, the mother will eat the umbilical cord, the placenta and the remains of the birth sac. The mother will then lick the newborn kitten's fur dry. This whole exhausting process is repeated with each newborn kitten. The entire birthing process usually takes about two hours. Very occasionally, one or two kittens of the litter are left to die. This is usually because the mother is just too exhausted to carry on, or because the kittens have some sort of defect.
- Domestic kittens are weaned at around four to seven weeks old.
- Young cats reach full independence at around six months.

- Grooming is an essential part of a cat's life, and a cat will spend much time licking its fur. However, a cat doesn't just groom itself to keep its fur clean of dirt. A cat will also groom itself in order to reinforce its own odour after being handled and to stimulate its skin secretions, which help to keep the fur waterproof. Cats also lick their coats in order to cool themselves during hot weather. Saliva has a cooling effect when it evaporates. Cats have to do this because their bodies lack sweat glands.
- Feral cats are descendants of cats that were once domesticated.
- The average life expectancy of a domestic cat is 9–15 years. Some cats can live beyond 20 years and, in exceptional cases, beyond 30 years.
- Road accidents are one of the most common causes of death for domestic cats.
- Cats are territorial animals and will mark their patch by scent-marking prominent places. To do this they either use special scent glands underneath their chins or they spray urine.
- Domestic cats only bury their faeces when they feel it might otherwise betray the whereabouts of their home. At other times, the remains are left uncovered as a territorial scent mark.
- It is not true that cats only purr when they are contented. Cats purr when they are feeling any intense emotion – whether it is pleasure or pain. In particular, cats purr when they are injured and in pain. Scientists in America have discovered that the frequency at which a cat purrs helps its bones and organs to mend and stimulates the skeletal system, preventing bones from weakening. Cats purr at a frequency of 25 to 50 hertz – the best frequency for bone growth and fracture healing and for the repair of tendons. Purring is also good for healing muscle and ligament injuries, for strengthening and toning muscles, for repairing any type of joint injury, for wound healing, for the reduction of swelling and infection, for pain relief and for the relief of chronic pulmonary disease. Cats get fewer diseases than dogs and heal better and more quickly, and it is believed that purring plays a part in this.
- When running at full speed, a domestic cat can reach 31mph (49.88km/h).
- The Turkish van cat likes water and enjoys going for a swim.
- Some white cats are genetically prone to deafness. This is especially true of white cats which have blue eyes.
- On average, a cat has 12 long whiskers (called vibrissae) around each side of its mouth, making it 24 altogether. These long whiskers are extremely sensitive and are thought to detect subtle air currents and the movement of prey in the dark. A cat's whiskers also act as a width gauge, so that a cat can judge whether it can fit through various spaces. The whiskers on the face of a cat form a unique pattern which gives each cat a 'fingerprint' from which it can be positively identified.
- Cats are believed to hiss when they are threatened because the hissing noise sounds very much like the hissing of a snake. This helps to scare enemies away.

When threatened, a cat may also arch its back. It does this to make itself appear larger and scarier to its attacker than it actually is.

- Cats have a righting reflex to help them land on their feet when they fall. As a cat starts to fall, it twists round in the air so that it will eventually land on all four feet with its legs stretched out and its back arched to reduce the impact. While the cat's body is twisting around in the air, its tail stiffens and serves as a counterbalancing device to help keep the cat stable. All this takes place in a fraction of a second – as an instinctive reflex. Cats have sometimes been known to land unharmed after falling from great heights. However, cats who fall from high places are, nevertheless, often injured or killed.

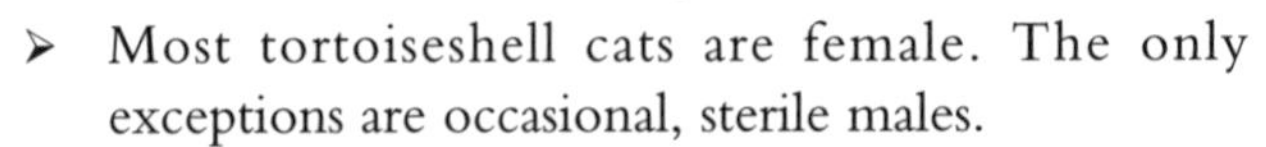

- Most tortoiseshell cats are female. The only exceptions are occasional, sterile males.
- When adult domestic cats knead with their front paws they are exhibiting an instinctive infantile reaction known a 'milk treading' – a movement designed to stimulate lactation.
- Siamese cats sometimes have a genetic fault which produces double vision. When a cat tries to correct this, the result is the characteristic Siamese squint.
- The Ancient Egyptians revered cats and happily shared their homes with them. They regarded domestic cats as the living embodiments of the cat goddess known as Bastet. The penalty for killing a cat in Ancient Egypt was death.
- Just over half of all cats become excited when exposed to a plant called catnip.
- Cats who are kept indoors will usually scratch furniture or carpets. This is because, for a cat, sharpening its claws is instinctive behaviour. Cats who are allowed to roam outdoors usually find a tree or a fence post on which to sharpen their claws. When a cat sharpens its claws it is getting rid of the old claw sheaths to reveal the new claws underneath. Cats also scratch to deposit scent from the glands underneath their paws. And cats scratch in order to strengthen the retraction mechanism of their claws.
- According to Hebrew folklore, cats came into existence after Noah prayed to God to help him to keep the number of rats down on his ark. Noah was apparently frightened that the rats were going to eat all the food. God answered Noah's prayer by making a lion on the ark produce a gigantic sneeze. And with that gigantic sneeze, out popped a small cat.
- When a cat greets its owner, it often rubs its body against him or her. Not only is the cat greeting its human owner but it is also marking its owner with its scent

from various scent glands on its body. At the same time, the cat is rubbing its own body with its owner's scent.

- Cats look upon their owners as mother cats and, therefore, usually love receiving affection from them.
- Cats may meow, hiss, purr, growl, mew, caterwaul and use many gestures (fur-raising, facial expressions and posture) to get across what they feel to other cats and to humans. One expert, Mildred Moelk, claimed in 1944 that cats produce 16 different, meaningful sounds – a mixture of vowels, consonants and diphthongs. Cats can change the meaning of their meow by altering tone, pitch, rhythm, pronunciation and volume.
- The stripy and blotchy markings on cats' coats are there as camouflage. They help to break up the cat's outline in just the same way as camouflage clothing worn by soldiers. The camouflage helps provide cats with protection from predators and helps them to hunt more effectively.

A cat living in the wild would, on average, eat ten mice a day. This is perhaps why cats prefer regular, small (mouse-sized) meals.

'No matter how much cats fight, there always seem to be plenty of kittens.'
ABRAHAM LINCOLN (1809–1865)

The Uninvited Cat

Nothing prepared me for what I could see
This wonderful spread laid out before me
There are cakes and pies and sandwiches galore
Why so much? Who is it for?

I take a nibble of the apple slice
And then some salmon which tastes very nice
I have a sniff at the vintage champagne
But go to the salmon again and again

I spy some pâte in a silver dish
Which looks rather splendid and smells of fish
I lick my lips at the clotted cream
And steal a few mouthfuls before I'm seen

I am now really full and so must retire
Into the living room next to the fire
I hope my owners don't suspect it was me
That came uninvited for afternoon tea.

Donna Antoinette Coleman

Talking Of Cats

There are a number of sayings which revolve around cats. Here are some of the best-known, together with their meanings (and in some cases their origins):

1. The cat's pyjamas (also the cat's whiskers): An excellent person or thing
2. A cat may look at a king: Spoken by an inferior, this suggests: 'I have as much right to look at you as you have to look at me. We are both equal.' Or: 'However grand you may think you are, you can't stop me looking at you.'
3. A wild-cat strike: An unofficial strike called by a number of individuals acting on their own initiative and without the trade union's approval.
4. Like a cat on a hot tin roof: Very agitated or nervous.

5. LIKE A CAT ON HOT BRICKS: Very agitated or nervous.
6. NOT TO HAVE A CAT IN HELL'S CHANCE: To have no chance at all.
7. TO PUT THE CAT AMONG THE PIGEONS: To do something likely to cause trouble or controversy.
8. TO WANT TO WAIT AND SEE WHICH WAY THE CAT JUMPS: To prefer to wait and see which direction events take before committing oneself.
9. A CAT'S PAW: A person used by another to perform a dangerous or unpleasant task.
10. TO RAIN CATS AND DOGS: To rain very heavily. The expression may have originated in days when street drainage was so bad that a heavy downpour was quite capable of drowning cats and dogs that were caught in it.
11. TO LET THE CAT OUT OF THE BAG: To carelessly reveal a secret.
12. TO BELL THE CAT: To attack a common enemy at great personal risk to oneself for the sake of others. The phrase is taken from Piers Plowman's fable of mice who wanted to hang a bell around the neck of a cat.

TWENTY FIVE FAMOUS AUTHORS WHO LOVED CATS

1. Honoré de Balzac
2. Emily Bronte
3. Lord Byron
4. Raymond Chandler
5. Jean Cocteau
6. Colette
7. Charles Dickens
8. Alexander Dumas
9. Anatole France
10. Thomas Hardy
11. Ernest Hemingway
12. Victor Hugo
13. Aldous Huxley
14. Henry James
15. Jerome K. Jerome
16. Samuel Johnson
17. Rudyard Kipling
18. Guy de Maupassant
19. Dorothy L. Sayers
20. Sir Walter Scott
21. William Makepeace Thackeray
22. Mark Twain
23. Horace Walpole
24. H.G. Wells
25. Emile Zola

Feral Cats

- ✧ Scientists claim that wild cats (aka feral cats) may spend as much as 12 out of every 24 hours hunting for food.
- ✧ A group of feral or wild cats is called a 'dout of cats' or 'a destruction of cats'.
- ✧ Feral male cats invariably live solitary lives but feral females often live in small groups, particularly when living on a farm or in some other specific group of buildings. Feral females often live with feral females (mothers and daughters) from other litters in a sort of female commune. In social circumstances such as this, feral females will happily care for the kittens of another – even suckling another queen's kittens.

How Old Is Your Cat In Human Terms?

Cats tend to have shorter lives than people – and to age more rapidly. The following table shows (roughly) how old a cat is in human terms.

- The cat who is 1-year-old is 15-years-old in human years.
- The cat who is 2-years-old is 25-years-old in human years.
- The cat who is 4-years-old is 40-years-old in human years.
- The cat who is 7-years-old is 50-years-old in human years.
- The cat who is 10-years-old is 60-years-old in human years.
- The cat who is 15-years-old is 75-years-old in human years.
- The cat who is 20-years-old is 105-years-old in human years.
- The cat who is 30-years-old is 120-years-old in human years.

The Ten Most Popular Sayings Involving Cats

(The date in brackets refers to the estimated origin of the saying)

1. When the cat's away the mouse will play. (1470)
2. A cat may look at a king. (1546)
3. Be careful not to let the cat out of the bag. (1760)
4. That's put the cat among the pigeons. (1706)
5. Watch which way the cat jumps. (1825)
6. An old cat laps as much milk as a young one. (1605)
7. A baited cat may grow as fierce as a lion. (1620)
8. The cat would eat fish but would not wet her feet. (1225)
9. As the cat plays with the mouse. (1340)
10. A cat in gloves catches no mice. (1573)

Ten Popular Names For Cats

1. Blackie
2. Fluffy
3. Ginger
4. Marmalade
5. Smokey
6. Sooty
7. Tiger
8. Tigger
9. Timmy
10. Tom

Cat-Loving Stars

1. Fred Astaire
2. Tallulah Bankhead
3. Brigitte Bardot
4. Warren Beatty
5. Doris Day
6. Robert De Niro
7. Charles Laughton
8. Edward G. Robinson
9. Elizabeth Taylor
10. Franco Zeffirelli

Cat Language

You can tell a good deal about what a cat is thinking from the way it holds its tail. For example:

- A tail held up straight means that the tail's owner is really pleased to see you.
- If a tail curves gently down and then up again at the tip it means that the cat is feeling relaxed.
- When a tail is slightly raised and softly curved it suggests that the cat is interested in something.
- If a female cat's tail is slanted to one side this is a 'come on' to tomcats. It means 'let's make love'.
- When a tail is lowered and fluffed out it denotes a pretty unhappy pussycat.
- A cat who holds its tail fairly upright, but with a twitching tip is feeling irritated.
- When a cat holds its tail straight up and fully bristled it is feeling rather aggressive. Watch out!
- If a cat's tail is swishing from side to side it suggests that the tail's owner is about to attack.
- When a cat's tail is still but has a rapidly twitching tip, it is a sign that the cat is about to attack.

Ten Artists and Composers Who Loved Cats

1. Borodin
2. Chopin
3. Debussy
4. Manet
5. Matisse
6. Picasso
7. Ravel
8. Stravinsky
9. Tchaikovsky
10. Warhol

Twelve Fast Animals

The cheetah is the fastest land animal (it can reach speeds in excess of 60mph (96.56km/h). But a number of animals can travel between 20 and in excess of 40mph – albeit often only for short distances. Here are just some of them:

1. Camel
2. Domestic cat
3. Gazelle
4. Giraffe
5. Grizzly bear
6. Kangaroo
7. Racehorse
8. Warthog
9. White rhinoceros
10. White-tailed deer
11. Wild boar
12. Zebra

'Nowadays we don't think much of a man's love for an animal; we mock people who are attached to cats. But if we stop loving animals, aren't we bound to stop loving humans too?'
Aleksandr Solzhenitsyn

Animals Have Feelings

Monkeys have a well-developed sense of grievance. Sarah Brosnan and Frans de Waal of Emory University in Atlanta, Georgia, studied the behaviour of female brown capuchin monkeys and spent two years teaching them to exchange tokens for food. So, for example, monkeys were allowed to exchange small pieces of rock for slices of cucumber. This worked well some of the time. However, when one monkey was handed a grape in return for a token, her neighbour was reluctant to hand over her token for a mere piece of cucumber. (In the world of the capuchin monkey a grape is infinitely more attractive than a piece of cucumber. It is the Choo sandal compared to the utility slipper.) Monkeys who were short-changed became sulky and sullen and even tossed their tokens away in disgust. In some circumstances, monkeys even forfeited food that they could see – and would normally have happily accepted – solely because they felt aggrieved. Monkeys, like humans, operate in social circles. When one monkey feels cheated, the system breaks down. Righteous indignation is not something exclusively found among humans.

It isn't just monkeys who have feelings. Observers at Bristol University discovered that cows have feelings; they bear grudges, form friendships, enjoy intellectual challenges, experience happiness, worry about the future and feel pain and fear.

Actually, of course, the scientists really need not have bothered. Anyone who has lived in the country will know that cows, like other animals, suffer agonies of despair when forcibly separated from their calves.

And yet the meat industry is allowed to separate cows from their families and friends, cram them into overcrowded lorries, transport them for hour after hour in unbearable conditions (so bad that even economy class airline passengers would protest) and then cruelly and thoughtlessly slaughter them in primitive conditions.

It makes you think, doesn't it?

Cows form friendships

Ten Fish Which Are Named After Animals

1. Buffalofish
2. Catfish
3. Dogfish
4. Elephantfish
5. Goatfish
6. Horsefish
7. Parrotfish
8. Sheepfish
9. Squirrelfish
10. Zebrafish

Cattle

- Domestic cattle are ruminant animals that belong to the family Bovidae. The Bovidae family also includes: gazelles, antelopes, goats and sheep.
- Domestic cattle can be found throughout much of the world.
- A 'heifer' usually refers to a female who has not yet calved or has only borne one calf. Young castrated males are usually referred to as 'steers'. An ox is a mature castrated male. 'Bulls' are mature males who have not been castrated. A calf is a very young male or female.
- Strictly speaking, in animal husbandry, the word 'cow' specifically refers to mature females of domesticated cattle that have given birth to offspring. However, the word 'cow' is often applied broadly to mean any domestic bovine animal.
- Domestic cattle are raised primarily for their milk and meat. Cattle are also used for their hides and, in some parts of the world, for pulling carts.
- Depending on the breed, bulls weigh 1,000-4,000lb (453.59-1,814kg). And cows weigh 800-2,400lb (363.87-1,088kg).
- British Friesian cows, known for their distinctive black and white colouring, are the foremost dairy breed in Britain. Friesians may also be reddish/brown and white in colour.
- The Holstein cow that originated in northern Holland and Friesland is the most popular dairy breed in the world. The Holstein, also known for its distinctive black and white colouring, is a relative of the British Friesian.
- Cattle are herbivores and naturally feed on grasses and plants.
- When cattle eat grass, they twist the grass around their tongues and then cut it with their bottom teeth. Cattle do not have upper front teeth.
- Cattle spend up to eight hours a day chewing the cud. Cud is a mixture of bile and half-digested food, which the cow continues to chew before sending it back down into its stomach for more digestion.

- Popular belief states that cattle have four stomachs; this is wrong. Cattle actually have a four-chambered stomach. These four chambers are each called: the rumen, the reticulum, the amasum and the abomasum. The digestion process in domestic cattle can take as long as 100 hours.
- Cattle should never be fed mouldy hay, straw or silage. If inhaled, the mould spores can cause serious respiratory diseases.
- Cattle have an amazing sense of smell and can detect smells approximately 5-6 miles (8-9.65km) away.
- Like most animals, cattle experience powerful emotions such as love, fear and pain.
- If allowed to survive naturally, cattle can live up to 25 years.
- The average age of a cow when she gives birth to her first calf is two-years-old.
- A cow's pregnancy lasts for approximately nine months.
- Cows give birth to one or two calves at a time. One is more usual.
- After giving birth, cows will usually eat the afterbirth. This can be risky, as there have been cases of cows choking to death when doing this.
- Cows develop strong bonds with their offspring and vice versa. When a calf is separated from its mother, both animals suffer enormous distress. It has been known for cows to escape from where they are being held and to walk miles to reach calves who have been sold at auction.
- Because their knees do not bend properly, cattle cannot walk down a flight of stairs. However, it is possible to lead cattle up a flight of stairs.
- It is not unknown for one cow to 'babysit' another's offspring, even if the two cows are unrelated.
- If a baby calf makes friends with another calf shortly after birth then it is usually a lifelong friendship.
- It is not unusual to see female cows mounting other females in a field. This is to let the bull know that they are ready to mate.
- Cows communicate to one another by mooing and by using a variety of physical movements.
- The cow used to be sacred in Egypt, to the god Isis.
- Cattle drink approximately 30 gallons (136 litres) of water a day.

- Just like a human's fingerprints, the markings on a cow's body are unique.
- Before she can produce milk, a cow must have her first calf. In her lifetime, a cow gives around 200,000 glasses of milk.
- Ninety per cent of the world's milk supply is provided by dairy cows.
- Farmers can milk up to 100 cows per hour using milking machines. Before milking machines were invented, farmers (or, more likely, milkmaids) could only milk five or six cows per hour.
- Research show that cows produce more milk when listening to classical music.
- Public health statistics show that there is a lower incidence of heart disease among those who drink Guernsey cows' milk than among those who drink milk taken from other cows.
- Jersey cattle are native to the Channel Islands and are thought to have descended from French cattle. Jersey cattle are usually fawn coloured and tend to be much smaller in build than other breeds of domestic cattle, with a small cow weighing approximately 860lb (390kg). Research in Denmark has shown that Jersey cattle suffer from fewer diseases than other cattle breeds. True Jersey cattle have black noses surrounded by pale coloured muzzles.
- Both male and female cattle may have horns. Some are naturally born without horns (a hornless animal is known as a 'poll') but most cattle have their horn nubs removed when they are calves.
- Cattle have 32 teeth.
- You should never turn your back on a bull.
- Cattle are social animals and often form hierarchical herds, with one member leading the herd. Cattle also develop friendships, and often form cliques with other 'cows'.
- Cattle are reputed to hold grudges against any human who has hurt them or any member of their family. There is good anecdotal evidence to support this.
- Research has shown that cattle have regional accents. A cow living in one region in a country will have a slightly different moo to cows living in another region in the same country.

Talking Of Cows

There are a number of sayings which revolve around cows. Here are some of the best-known, together with their meanings (and in some cases their origins):

1. Until the cows come home

For a long time (approaching if not quite reaching indefinitely).

The Plight Of The Cow

If I were as fluffy as a Persian cat
Or as interesting as the vampire bat
If I were as sweet as a little mouse
Or had a pretty shell for a house
If I were as cheeky as a monkey
Or had the character of the donkey
If I were as striking as a tiger
Or could spin a web just like the spider
If I were as tall as the tallest giraffe
Or had the ability to make people laugh
If I were as awesome as the grizzly bear
Or had the spirit of the mad March hare
If I were as tuneful as a nightingale
Or had the size of the big, blue whale
If I were beautiful, wild and free
Then perhaps, just perhaps, you wouldn't eat me.

Donna Antoinette Coleman

2. A milch cow
A universal provider. An easy touch. The word 'milch' is Anglo-Saxon and means 'milk giving'.

3. The sacred cow
An idea, custom or institution which is thought to be beyond criticism.

4. Malley's cow
An Australian expression referring to someone who has gone away leaving no indication where he may be found. In Australian folklore, Malley was a man who lost a cow he was supposed to be looking after.

Amazing Animal Stories (Part 1)

- There is a statue of a small Akita dog named Hachiko standing prominently in the forecourt of Japan's busiest railway station. Every morning, Hachiko would accompany his master to his train to work and arrive again at the end of the day to greet his master from his return journey. Sadly, Hachiko's master did not make the return journey one evening because he had suffered a fatal heart attack while at work. But Hachiko still waited patiently for his master to return. Hachiko returned at the same time the following day and every day since in the hope that his master would step off the train to greet him. Hachiko soon became well-known to the majority of the commuters, they would often stop to lavish affection on the small dog and give him treats. For an incredible nine years, Hachiko waited every evening in hope of his master's return. When Hachiko died, the Japanese erected a statue of him in his honour to commemorate his love and devotion to his master.

- When one of the members of the Bratcher family knocked down their pet dog, Brownie, they were absolutely heartbroken. They decided to bury the dead dog near their home. The next day, to the family's astonishment, they came back from their outing to find Brownie sitting on their doorstep covered in soil. The dog hadn't died at all. Brownie had been knocked unconscious. When he came round, he simply dug himself out of his grave and went back home.
- In Healdsburg, California, a parrot escaped and landed on a branch high up in a tree. However, when firemen came to the rescue, the bird wasn't very grateful. The parrot kept taunting the firemen by saying: 'I can talk, can you fly?'
- A Friesian cow called Daisy was sold for auction in Okehampton in Devon. Daisy was so upset about being parted from her baby calf that she escaped from her enclosure and ran the six miles (9.7km) back home to be with her calf. Daisy's new owner was so affected by Daisy's maternal loyalty to her calf, that he bought the calf as well.
- In the late 1960s, the Eire Government evacuated the entire population from the small island off the West Coast of Ireland. The only living creature to remain on the island was a donkey that was later named Islander. Islander lived off grass and seaweed, and stayed all by himself on the island for an incredible 18 years until he was eventually taken to an animal sanctuary in Devon.
- A family living in the poorest part of Naples consisted of two women and their ten children. The family lived in very poor conditions and had to share one room. Despite the family's extreme poverty and unbelievably cramped living space, they still managed to make room for a stray dog they had found who they named Rocky. With his loving personality and his eager willingness to play games with the children, Rocky soon became part of the family. The family's generosity in taking Rocky and finding the money to feed him was soon to be rewarded, but under tragic circumstances. One spring afternoon, two of the ten children who were aged three and six, were left on their own with Rocky in the building while their mother had to pop out for a few minutes. Shortly after the children's mother left, a fire broke out. Rocky fought through the flames, grabbed one of the girls by her dress and dragged her out onto the street. Realising that the other girl was still in the building, Rocky braved the flames again – and out

came the little girl. But this time Rocky did not come with the girl. Sadly, Rocky was found dead inside the room with his fur alight. Rocky had died of smoke inhalation, and the family buried him nearby. When word had spread about Rocky's heroism, many of the locals visited the dog's grave to pay their respects.

- In 1989, teenager Adam Maguire was surfing off the north coast of Sydney when a 12ft (3.66m) shark suddenly attacked him. The shark sank his teeth into the teenager's side. Once sharks have tasted blood they want more. Adam Maguire's friends could only watch in horror as they saw that their pal was about to be eaten. Just as the shark was about to move in for the kill, a school of dolphins miraculously showed up. The dolphins isolated the shark and then chased it away. Thanks to them, Adam Maguire survived.
- A golden Labrador called Sally loved her 79-year-old blind master so much that she willingly sacrificed her life for him. Bill Chamberlain was about to be hit by an oncoming car when his guide dog Sally stepped in and pushed him out of the way so that he would not get run over. It was Sally who died.
- A Labrador called Toffee was on a fishing trip in the West Indies with his master when he saw a dolphin playing in the water nearby. Toffee was so excited that he jumped into the water to greet the dolphin. When the two came face to face they started to play together in the water, with Toffee chasing the dolphin and the dolphin then chasing Toffee. Toffee and the dolphin played together every day after their first meeting.
- Staff working in the personnel department at Chester Zoo were perplexed when their telephones started ringing for no reason and they suddenly started to get a lot of crossed lines. The troublemaker turned out to be a 19ft (5.79m) tall giraffe called George who loved the mild electric shocks the telephone wires above his enclosure gave him when he licked them. The telephone wires had to be taken down and moved to an area where George couldn't get at them.
- Farmers living in South Wales couldn't understand how their sheep were escaping over cattle grids without getting their feet or legs trapped. Farm sheep were constantly escaping and joining stray, wild ponies on nearby moorland. Eventually the farmers lay in wait to see how the sheep were escaping. To their amazement, the sheep were simply lying down and rolling over the cattle grids. No one but the sheep had thought of that.
- A dog called Spot used to accompany the local road sweeper about his work in north Chingford. When the road sweeper retired, Spot tried to make friends with the sweeper's replacement but for some reason, the new pairing didn't work out. Spot was miserable doing nothing all day and was desperate to find a working companion. Eventually, to Spot's delight, he made friends with the local postman. And both were happy to have each other's company.
- The Watters brothers – both farmers – came up with the bright idea of using

pigs to round-up their sheep on their farm in Llandewi in Wales. The pigs were so successful at rounding-up the sheep that the brothers decided to train the pigs' offspring too. We haven't heard of any sheeppig trials being organised yet but it's only a matter of time.

- The people of Sao Paolo, Brazil were so disillusioned with food shortages, politics and the high cost of living that they decided to elect a rhinoceros to their municipal council. The rhinoceros won by a landslide victory of 50,000 votes.

'The dog taken by fever seeks rest in a quiet corner but is found eating herbs when his stomach is upset. Nobody taught him what herbs to eat, but he will instinctively seek those that make him vomit or improve his condition in some other way.'

HENRY SIGERIST

Cheetahs

- Cheetahs belong to the family Felidae. They can be found in Africa and via the Middle East all the way to southern Asia. The cheetah is critically endangered everywhere except in Africa. The cheetah's habitat includes savanna and arid forest.
- There are five subspecies of cheetah: the central African cheetah, the East African cheetah, the West African cheetah, the southern African cheetah and the Asiatic cheetah.
- The cheetah has a slender body, a flexible spine, long legs, a small head, rounded ears, a distinctive sandy-yellow coat with lots of small black spots, a black 'stripe' running from the corner of each eye to its mouth, and a long tail.
- The cheetah uses its 32in (85.34cm) long tail – which is decorated with black spots and black rings – as a balancing aid.
- Excluding its tail, the cheetah can grow to 4ft 6in (1.37m) long. Adult cheetahs can weigh 140lb (63.50kg) or more. Male cheetahs are around ten per cent heavier than females.
- The cheetah is the world's fastest land animal. Some animal experts claim that cheetahs can attain speeds of 70mph (112.65km/h). They can certainly achieve speeds in excess of 60mph (96.56km/h).
- The cheetah can accelerate from 0–45mph (0–72km/h) in just over two seconds.
- Although regarded as the world's fastest land animal, the cheetah does not have a lot of stamina and, therefore, can only pursue its prey for short periods at a time (less than a minute) before it overheats.
- Many people find it difficult to tell cheetahs and leopards apart because they both have black coloured spots on their coats. The most obvious difference between the two mammals is the cheetah's black stripe running from the corner of each eye to its jaw. The leopard does not have these black stripes.
- Cheetahs are not capable of roaring like the other big cats. Some of the cheetah's vocalisations include: yelps, hisses, growls, and yips.
- Occasionally, cheetahs will go for up to ten days without drinking any water.
- Unlike other members of the cat family, the adult cheetah's blunt claws are only partly retractable. This is to give it added traction when in pursuit of its prey.
- Cheetahs hunt during the day, whereas other big cats do their hunting during the evening. Cheetahs sometimes hunt in pairs or in small family groups.
- Unlike other big cats, cheetahs like to eat their meat fresh, leaving the remains for other animals and birds to feed on.
- The cheetah stalks its prey (for several hours if it has to) before charging at it from about 100ft (30.48m) away.

- Once the cheetah has caught up with its prey, it trips the animal by catching one of its front legs, pounces and strangles the prey with a powerful jaw-crushing bite to the throat.
- Cheetahs are carnivores. In the wild, the cheetah's diet includes: impalas, gazelles, wildebeest calves, hares and bustards.
- Cheetahs eat, on average, about 4lb (1.81kg) of meat a day.
- Cheetahs have very good eyesight and are able to spot prey from as far as three miles (4.83km) away.
- When the cheetah eats its kill, it is always on the alert for scavengers such as hyenas and vultures. Many a cheetah has lost its prey to animals such as these, as well as to predators such as lions. If there is cover available, the cheetah usually likes to eat its prey there, away from any animal that is likely to spot it.
- When in heat, females spray various landmarks with their urine to attract males. Males follow the trail and respond to the receptive female's scent by 'yelping'. It is usually the dominant male in the group who gets to mate the female.
- The cheetah's pregnancy may last up to 95 days.
- The average size of a cheetah's litter is four cubs.
- At birth, cubs are about 12in (30.48cm) long. They weigh 8-11oz (226-311g).
- To protect the cubs from predators, the female cheetah will move them to a new hiding place every couple of days.
- Cubs' main predators are lions.
- Infant mortality rates among cubs are high. On average, only one in three cubs reaches maturity. But on the Serengeti Plains of Tanzania, where a high percentage of cubs fall prey to lions, the average survival rate to adulthood is about 1 in 20.
- Shortly after birth, young cubs grow manes of pale coloured hair – called mantles. These stretch from their heads, along their necks and backs and to the bases of their tails. There are several possible explanations for why cubs have mantles. One of the theories is that cubs' mantles are there to deter predators because the mantles mimic the hair of one or two ferocious wild animals. Another more credible theory is that cubs' mantles help to camouflage these vulnerable animals.
- Cheetah cubs are usually fully weaned by the time they are three-months-old.
- Cubs tend to stay with their mothers for around 18 months after they are born.
- After the young cheetahs have left their mother, the offspring usually stay together for several more months to increase their chances of survival. When the time is right, the young female siblings leave the group one by one to lead solitary lives. Male siblings usually stay together permanently.
- The average lifespan of cheetahs living in the wild is 10-12 years.
- The main threats to the cheetah's survival are persecution by man and loss of habitat.

Animals Are Sentient Creatures

A surprising number of apparently intelligent individuals (including, of course, a variety of vivisectors, hunters and butchers) excuse the cruel way they treat animals by claiming that animals don't have feelings.

This is nonsense.

The truth, as anyone who is capable of reading and observing will know, is that animals are sentient and exhibit many of those qualities which speciesists like to think of as being the preserve of the human race.

One of the absurdities of the argument about hunting which has raged for recent years has been the sight of apparently intelligent people arguing about whether or not animals which are hunted suffer physical pain and/or mental anguish when they are being pursued. How can there possibly be any doubt about this? Those who do express doubt about this are telling us a great deal about their own innate lack of understanding and compassion, and their inability to learn from simple observation. If observation is not enough, there is more than enough scientific evidence to show that birds, mammals, fish, reptiles and crustaceans all have nervous systems and all suffer pain. Indeed, as anyone who has ever watched them miss their footing or knock a vase from a shelf will confirm, cats even suffer from embarrassment.

The animal abusers claim that animals cannot reason. But it is clear that it is the animal abusers who find reason a difficult concept. Hunters (and their supporters) frequently claim that the animals they hunt (foxes, deer and so on) are not 'sentient' creatures and are, therefore, undeserving of our sympathy. In truth, it is easier to argue that a hunter who chases a fox, digs it out when it goes to ground and then stands by and watches a pack of dogs tearing it apart is not a sentient creature.

The facts are abundantly clear: animals are sentient creatures. As J. Howard Moore put it: 'The human species constitutes but one branch in the gigantic arbour of life.'

Darwin showed that fear produces similar responses in both humans and animals. The eyes and mouth open, the heart beats rapidly, teeth chatter, muscles tremble, hairs stand on end and so on. Parrots, like human beings, turn away and cover their eyes when confronted with a sight which overwhelms them. Young elephants who have seen their families killed by poachers wake up screaming in the night. Elephants who are suddenly separated from their social group may die suddenly of 'broken heart syndrome'. Apes may fall down and faint when suddenly coming across a snake. If a man shouts at a dog, the dog will often cower and back away in fear.

The fact is that many animals are brighter than many people. We do not abuse babies simply because they cannot speak two languages or finish *The Times* crossword while having breakfast. Why, then, do our rules of behaviour allow us to assume that we have the authority to abuse animals?

Animals have passionate relationships with one another, they exhibit clear signs of love, they develop social lives which are every bit as complex as our own. Animals frequently make friends across the species barriers. There is much evidence showing that animals have helped animals belonging to a different species.

Why do we have to be the only species to abuse all other creatures? Is our contempt for, and cruelty to, other creatures really to be regarded as a sign of our wisdom, superiority and civilisation? What arrogance we show in the way we treat animals. Where is our humility and sense of respect?

Those who torture and kill animals have to claim that animals have no feelings – otherwise they would be admitting that by the barbaric treatment of sensitive animals they themselves have acted cruelly.

But how they can continue to do this when there is so much scientific evidence to prove that they are utterly wrong? Gorillas, for example, are known to laugh when they are tickled and to cry when they grieve. They can make tools. They think about their past and plan for their future.

Vivisectors tear animals away from their partners, their friends and their relatives with no regard for their feelings – or for the feelings of the animals they have left behind. They claim that this doesn't matter because animals aren't sentient creatures.

But experimenters have deliberately planned and carried out many experiments designed to make animals feel depressed. Does not the ability of the experimental scientists to 'make' animals feel depressed provide proof that animals are sentient creatures?

No one with any intelligence or sensitivity of their own can possibly doubt that animals are capable of suffering. Those who treat animals without respect degrade us all and diminish our worth as a species.

The Biggest And Most Powerful Mammals

1. Bison
2. Blue whale*
3. Bull
4. Camel
5. Elephant
6. Giraffe
7. Gorilla
8. Hippopotamus
9. Horse
10. Rhinoceros

* *(weighs up to 122 tons (124 tonnes) and is the largest of all animals)*

With the exception of the blue whale (which does eat krill – tiny shrimp-like creatures), all these animals are vegetarian.

CHIMPANZEES

- Along with orang-utans and gorillas, chimpanzees are great apes. They belong to the family Hominidae. Chimpanzees can be found in western and central parts of Africa, mainly in forests and woodland savanna.
- Chimpanzees are the most intelligent of the three great apes and are humans' closest relatives.
- There are two species of chimpanzee: the bonobo (also known as the pygmy chimpanzee) and the common chimpanzee. Bonobos can only be found in the forest areas of Zaire in central Africa. The bonobo was once considered a subspecies of the common chimpanzee.
- The common chimpanzee weighs approximately 130lb (58.96kg) or more. Female chimpanzees of both species are about 10-20 per cent lighter than male chimpanzees. Bonobos are more slender in build than common chimpanzees. Despite the bonobo's other name – the pygmy chimpanzee – there is no noticeable difference in size between the two species of chimpanzee. However, the bonobo can easily be distinguished from the common chimpanzee by its less protruding, completely black face and its neat, central hair parting on its crown.
- Chimpanzees have legs longer than their arms and walk along the ground on all fours. They walk on the knuckles of their hands and the flat soles of their feet. Chimpanzees have an opposable big toe on each foot, which means that they can use their feet rather like their hands – for gripping and investigating things. The bonobo has webbing between its second and third toes which the common chimpanzee and the other apes do not have. Both species of chimpanzee are able to walk upright when they choose to do so.
- Chimpanzees are highly social mammals and live in flexible groups known as communities that can consist of anywhere between 15 and over 100 members. Unlike female chimpanzees, males usually stay in their natal communities for life.
- The chimpanzee's diet includes: ants, termites, flowers, seeds, leaves, shoots, bark, pith, nuts, fruits, berries, honey and birds' eggs. Chimpanzees also eat bush pigs, small antelopes, monkeys and, occasionally, birds. Chimpanzees tend to hunt alone. Sometimes, a mother may go hunting with several of her offspring. Occasionally, chimpanzees will hunt in groups. When they do this they may divide the spoils according to the amount of work each chimp did.
- Bonobos do less hunting than common chimpanzees.
- Chimpanzees have very large appetites. It is not unheard of for a chimpanzee to eat as many as 50 bananas in one sitting.
- Chimpanzees can live 45 years or more.
- Chimpanzees can use and make tools. For example, they often prepare sticks which they use for digging out termites. Chimpanzees have been reported to pass down their learnt skills to subsequent generations.
- A male chimpanzee was once observed giving first aid to a distressed female chimpanzee who had sought his help. He was carefully removing grit from her eye.

- At night, the chimpanzee makes itself a nest by intertwining branches in the trees to build a stable but comfortable mattress. The chimpanzee usually builds a new nest for itself every night. Baby chimpanzees usually sleep in the nest with their mothers.
- Chimpanzees living in the wild tend to have their first babies at around the ages of 12-13 years.
- The female chimpanzee develops a large pink swelling on her hindquarters when she is ready to mate. This swelling will then alert the males in the group to the female's sexual condition. The female will probably mate with some or with all of the males in the group. Sometimes one of the males in the group will manage to persuade the female to go off with him for several weeks – away from the rest of the males in the group.
- When on heat, female common chimpanzees mate up to six times a day.
- A chimpanzee's pregnancy lasts approximately eight months.
- Chimpanzees usually give birth to one baby at a time.
- A newborn baby chimpanzee weighs approximately 3lb (1.36kg).
- A few days after birth, a baby chimpanzee will cling to its mother's underside as a means of transport. At around six-months-old, the baby chimp will cling onto its mother's back as a means of getting around. The young chimpanzee will travel around on its mother's back for several years or more.
- It can take approximately four years before the young chimpanzee is fully weaned.
- During her lifetime, the female chimpanzee may give birth to four or five young.
- Females give birth about every five years or more.
- To reduce tension or to strengthen bonds, female bonobos will frequently rub their genitals with other bonobos.
- When kissing, bonobos like to use their tongues, and they sometimes mate in the standard human 'missionary' position.
- When threatened by a passing predator on the ground, chimpanzees usually climb up into the trees for safety. Sometimes, chimpanzees will make lots of noises and break branches from trees and throw them to the ground in an attempt to scare predators away.
- Chimpanzee males are known to roam around in gangs looking for other neighbouring communities. Common chimpanzees can be vicious when they fight; using sticks and stones as weapons. When a fight does break out, fatalities can occur.
- Chimpanzees groom one another to remove parasites and to keep their fur clean. Grooming helps to strengthen relationships between chimpanzees.
- Chimpanzees have 32 teeth.
- Chimpanzees have extremely expressive faces and have a variety of facial expressions which they use to communicate to one another. For example, when

a chimpanzee wants to play, it will usually open its mouth with its lips covering its teeth in a non-threatening way to show that it only wants to play and not fight.

- Bonobos often resolve conflicts by engaging in sexual activities with each other.
- By the time chimpanzees have reached old age, they have often lost the hair from their heads.
- Chimpanzees' shrieks can be heard about 0.62 miles (1km) away.
- Chimpanzees are capable of conversing in sign language.
- Chimpanzees are an endangered species. Destruction of habitat is the chimpanzee's main threat.

Animals Have Powerful Memories

Many animals have excellent memories. Chimpanzees, for example, have much better memories than human beings. Young chimpanzees outperformed university students in memory tests devised by Japanese scientists. The tasks involved remembering the location of numbers on a screen and correctly recalling the sequence. Researchers at Kyoto University tested 12 students and three chimps who had been taught the numbers one to nine. The numbers were shown on a computer screen and were obscured with white squares after each participant touched the first number. The aim was to touch all the squares in ascending order. The chimps finished this task faster than the humans with exactly the same accuracy. When the test was repeated at faster speed the best chimp scored 80% while the humans managed only 40% accuracy. When the best chimp was matched against a human memory champion, the chimp managed a 90% score compared to the human champion's 33%. (The human memory champion could memorise the order of a shuffled deck of cards in 30 seconds.) The findings were published in the journal *Current Biology* in December 2007. Scientists concluded that humans may have underestimated the intelligence of our closest living relatives. Other tests have shown that chimpanzees perform much better than humans on tests measuring both spatial memory and facial recognition.

Also, not so long ago, a chimpanzee called Ayumu beat the British memory champion, Ben Pridmore, at a computer game.

Chimpanzees aren't the only animals to have good memories. Many creatures – even seemingly simple ones – have memories which humans might envy. Here are just a few more examples:

- Ants retrace their steps after long journeys and can recognise friends after months of separation.
- When a limpet has finished roaming, it will return to the exact spot on the same rock where it had been settled previously.

- Birds fly back year after year to the same nesting spots – to within the inch.
- Fish, too, return to the same stretch of water to hatch their young.
- Horses used in delivery routes frequently know exactly where and when to stop – and for how long.
- An elephant which was recaptured after fifteen years of freedom in the jungle, remembered all the commands he had been taught before his years of freedom.
- A lion recognised its keeper after seven years of separation.
- One observant city dweller who regularly fed the pigeons on his windowsill noticed that even after long absences (sometimes lasting several months), pigeons would tap at his window and peer expectantly into his apartment the moment the shutters were raised and a light switched on. The pigeons never bothered to do this at the windows where they had not been fed.

Wild Animals In Captivity

When animals are born in zoos, the keepers usually offer this evidence that the animals must be happy. Animals may be happy in zoos but the results of procreation cannot be offered as evidence. Would the zookeepers also claim that the fact that babies were born in concentration camps is evidence that concentration camp inmates were happy?

Captive animals suffer a lot of physical and mental ill health. Gorillas in captivity are more likely to die of heart disease than gorillas in the wild. Many have eating disorders and are infertile. Captive elephants and giraffes develop arthritis and foot problems (disorders which are far less common among animals in the wild). It has been alleged that three quarters of the black rhinoceroses in captivity are killed by a blood disease that doesn't seem to affect black rhinoceroses living in the wild.

Captive animals show stereotypical movements such as pacing, rocking or weaving. They develop all sorts of unusual habits: rubbing themselves against the bars of their cage or walking backwards and forwards in unsuccessful attempts to soothe their frustrations.

Sometimes, captive animals will become angry. For example, elephants are the most peaceful of vegetarians but in zoos they occasionally become homicidal.

Stress is a major factor in the development of disease among animals, and there is clear evidence that animals in any sort of captivity suffer a great deal of stress.

Scientists at Stanford University captured healthy wild African green monkeys and cruelly caged them separately in order to measure the effects of stress on their immune systems. The monkeys rapidly fell ill. Even though they were given all the nutrients they needed, they contracted infectious diseases. Some of them died. Other studies have shown exactly the same thing. Animals which normally live in the wild do not adapt well when kept in captivity. Their immune systems collapse when they are separated from their families and friends and shut up in cages. Even if wild animals are caught when still young, they will often die within weeks or months if they are locked in a cage. Creatures as varied as gorillas and white sharks all tend to fall ill and die if locked up. An animal's immune system is inextricably linked to its surroundings and to its exposure to stress. (All this means, of course, that when vivisectors lock animals up in cages in order to conduct experiments, they are altering the outcome of their experiments before they even start.)

Under normal circumstances, an animal will use its own internal mechanical and physiological mechanisms to protect itself from illness. It will rest when it needs to rest. It will groom itself to keep itself clean. It will change its diet when appropriate. And when it is ill it will seek out plants or other substances with which to medicate itself.

All of this proves yet again the scientific pointlessness of doing experiments on laboratory animals. When they are captive, animals do not behave normally.

There are, of course, other reasons for the poor health animals suffer in captivity.

Animals in captivity simply don't have access to the normal variety of foods they might find in the wild (some of which they would undoubtedly use as medicaments). They don't have the same natural grooming opportunities, the same opportunity for exercise, the same variety of companions and the same soils. Because they are in cages or restricted areas, they are unable to move away from pathogen hot spots and they may be unable to develop proper social relationships with other animals of the same species. (For animals in laboratories these problems are exaggerated, of course.)

Elephants are the most peaceful of vegetarians but in zoos they occasionally become homicidal

Cleanliness

Animals like to keep themselves clean. For example, chimpanzees have a horror of being soiled with excrement. After defecating, they wipe themselves with handfuls of leaves. They routinely clean themselves if their bodies are contaminated with urine, blood or mud. They do this because they recognise that these contaminants are potential sources of infection. A male chimpanzee will even clean his penis after copulation.

External contaminants are treated with the same concern. After a young chimpanzee had stamped on a human being's head, the chimpanzee sniffed her foot, picked up some leaves and cleaned it thoroughly.

Ten Famous Animal Movies

1. Lassie Come Home
2. Bambi
3. Dumbo
4. 101 Dalmatians
5. Free Willy
6. Finding Nemo
7. Jungle Book
8. The Lion King
9. Babe
10. The Fox and the Hound

How To Survive An Encounter With A Crocodile

Here are our suggestions offered with absolutely no guarantees:

1. If a crocodile tries to attack you, it is recommended that you run (obviously, away from the crocodile) as fast as you can. A crocodile will only run a short distance before it gives up, and even then it doesn't run very fast. Although the crocodile doesn't run very fast on land, it can, however, lunge from the water at an amazing speed. Whatever you do, don't go into the water. Crocodiles are excellent swimmers and will almost certainly out-swim you.
2. If the worst has happened and the crocodile grabs you, try poking its eyes. Crocodiles are known to release victims from their jaws immediately if the victim

pokes its eyes. If that fails, try screaming at the top of your voice. Hopefully, this will make the animal retreat, as crocodiles don't like their prey to fight back.

3. Don't waste vital time and energy in trying to prise the crocodile's jaws open because you won't be able to do this. A crocodile's grip is extremely strong. Conversely, the muscles that the crocodile uses to open its jaws are not very strong – an elastic band over the crocodile's jaws is enough to keep them shut.
4. If all of the above fail, you could try playing dead. A crocodile stops shaking its prey if it believes it to be dead. The crocodile usually catches and kills its prey, and stores it to eat later. With any luck you might be able to make your escape before it comes back to devour you for its supper.
5. Good luck!

'There are two things for which animals are to be envied: they know nothing of future evils, or of what people say about them.'
VOLTAIRE (1694-1778)

RED DEER

- Red deer belong to the family Cervidae, and are native to northern Africa, Asia and Europe.
- Throughout the world, the red deer is the most widespread of deer species.
- There are thought to be around 40 species of deer.
- There are believed to be more than 250,000 red deer in Scotland.
- Red deer mainly occupy woodland.
- The female red deer is usually called a hind. The male deer is called a stag. The baby deer is called a fawn or a calf.
- The red deer has an elongated body, an angular shaped head, slender legs, a short tail and large ears.
- Red deer can weigh 551lb (249.92kg) or more.
- Red deer can grow to 6½ft (198.12cm) or more in length and stand 3ft 4in-4ft (103.63-121.92cm) high at the shoulder.
- The red deer is Britain's largest native land mammal.
- The red deer's coat is a reddish brown colour during the warmer months. Its coat changes to a brown or grey colour during the colder months. Red deer have a buff-coloured rump patch and tail. Just before the mating period, hormonal

changes occur in stags, which bring about the development of a shaggy mane and a thickening of the neck.

- Deer are ruminants, which mean that they chew the cud.
- Female red deer do not have antlers. Only stags have antlers.
- Stags grow new antlers every year. The old ones are discarded (or cast). It takes approximately three months before a stag's antlers are fully-grown. The older the stag gets, the more impressive its antlers usually become (although, after 11 years of age, a deer will be past its prime and its antlers will be less impressive).
- A deer's antlers are made of bone.
- The deer's new antlers are covered in a layer of furry 'skin' known as velvet. This layer of skin peels off when the antlers are fully-grown to reveal bare antlers. The deer will assist in removing the velvet by vigorously brushing its antlers against trees or shrubs. Velvet contains blood vessels which supply the bone underneath with food and oxygen.
- A deer's antlers can grow to around 28in (71.12cm) or, occasionally, even more.
- The individual pieces of bone on a deer's antlers are called points, prongs or tines.

- There are usually no more than 10-12 tines on a stag's antlers. However, occasionally, a stag can have as many as 14 tines; this is referred to as an imperial.
- Some stags do not grow any antlers at all. These stags are referred to as hummels. It is thought that a setback during their early significant years of development is responsible for the non-existent antlers.
- The red deer is vegetarian. Its diet includes: grasses, sedges, heather, rushes, seedlings, tree foliage and bark.
- A group of deer is called a herd.
- Hinds and stags tend to live in separate groups: stags usually live in unrelated groups, and hinds usually live in matriarchal groups. The only time the different sexes get together is during the mating season.
- The courting and mating period for deer (which is usually in the autumn) is called the rutting season or 'the rut'. This is the time when stags emit plenty of bellowing roars to try to attract a harem of females. This is also the time of year when stags are more likely to fight each other to chase away any rivalry. Stags use their antlers when they fight. However, stags try to avoid fights if they can, they usually like to stave off any competition by giving displays of their strength. This may involve lots of bellowing roars and thrashing of antlers against trees. If the emission of loud, deep roaring has not been successful then the next stage of the contest is usually a tense, parallel walk, where both stags walk up and down and side by side. And then, if the dispute still hasn't been settled by one of the stags backing down, a fight usually ensues. Often the outperforming contest will have stopped long before the fighting stage.
- It is not unknown for stags to get their antlers interlocked during the fighting stage, and to find that they are unable to free themselves from each other. When this happens, the stags usually die.
- If one stag or both stags have cast their antlers, any disputes are usually settled by 'boxing matches'.
- Stags aren't the only ones that fight. Hinds will fight to establish hierarchy within their groups.
- A stag's sexual attraction to females is usually increased if the stag has large antlers. Females see large antlers as denoting good genes because it signifies that the stag has found enough food and nutrients to promote good growth.
- A successful stag can attract as many as 20 or more hinds (females) in his harem. In open country, it can be much more than 20 hinds.
- The female deer's pregnancy may last up to 240 days.
- The female red deer normally gives birth to one young.
- Shortly after birth, the mother will usually hide its baby in long vegetation to keep it safe from any predators while she goes off to feed.
- The mother familiarises herself with her calf's scent from its pre-orbital glands

(scent gland in front of each eye) soon after birth. The mother can smell the scent from the pre-orbital glands from quite a distance away. If the calf should feel threatened, it will close its pre-orbital glands. The mother then senses the disruption in the scent. This alerts her to come to her calf's aid.

- A fifth of all calves die in their first month of life.
- Foxes and golden eagles are the newborn red deer's main predators. To minimise the risk of scent-smelling predators, the mother will eat its baby's faeces and lap up its baby's urine.
- The baby deer or fawn is reddish brown in colour and has numerous white spots on its coat. The fawn loses its spots during its first moult in the summer.
- The milk that male baby deer receive from their mothers is higher in protein than the milk given to female offspring. Male offspring also receive more milk from their mothers.
- Deer can live for more than 20 years in captivity.

Strange But True (Part 2)

☞ When exiting a cave, bats always turn left.

☞ It's physically impossible for pigs to look up at the sky.

☞ A giraffe's heart is 2ft (0.611m) long.

☞ Alligators cannot move backwards.

☞ An ostrich's eye is bigger than its brain.

☞ A single poison arrow frog can kill as many as 2,200 people.

☞ The largest animal is the blue whale, which can grow to 100ft (30.48m) long.

☞ The moth does not eat clothing but its larvae do. However, not all species of moth produce larvae that eat clothing – the percentage that do is actually quite small.

The Names Of Santa's Reindeer

1. Blitzen
2. Comet
3. Cupid
4. Dancer
5. Dasher
6. Donner
7. Prancer
8. Rudolph
9. Vixen

- The North African ostrich is the largest living bird in the world.
- In just one night, a mole can dig a tunnel as long as 300ft (91.44m).
- A crocodile is unable to stick out its tongue.

- Monkeys cannot recognise themselves in the mirror, but chimpanzees can.
- Every year, over 10,000 birds die because they have accidentally flown into windows.
- A hummingbird weighs less than a penny.
- Flutterby was the butterfly's original name.
- Bats possess the highest frequency hearing.
- In New Zealand, there are more sheep than people.
- A cat cannot move its jaw sideways.
- The lovely koala bear is considered to be the world's fussiest eater.
- When a sand tiger shark is pregnant, her growing babies will fight one another in the womb until only one of them is left to be born.
- The bar-tailed godwit bird gets rid of its liver, kidneys and most of its intestine so that it can eat extra food before embarking on its long journey from its breeding ground in Alaska to New Zealand. Once it reaches its destination, it starts rebuilding its organs.
- A slug's sticky trail does not have any breaks in it, whereas a snail's sticky trail does.
- The electric eel can generate 600 volts of electricity.
- Gerbils can suffer from depression if it loses its partner.
- Male seahorses give birth.
- When erect, the average humpback whale's penis is 10ft (3.048m) long.

☞ The colour of a yak's milk isn't white – it's pink!

☞ When frightened (and it doesn't happen very often) sharks have been known to swim round and round in a figure of eight.

☞ If an octopus becomes really hungry, it will eat its own arms.

☞ It is not unusual for male sea lions to have more than 100 wives.

☞ The leech has 32 brains.

☞ A llama will softly blow on you if it wants to greet you.

☞ There has never been an incident of a non-rabid wolf ever attacking a human being.

☞ Once upon a time, there were more sea lions in the world than humans.

☞ A camel's milk never curdles.

☞ Jellyfish are made up of more than 95 per cent water.

☞ Every day, more than 100 whales are killed by fishermen.

☞ Jaguars are frightened of dogs.

☞ Rats can kill themselves by over-exercising.

☞ It has been known for elephants to remain standing after they have died.

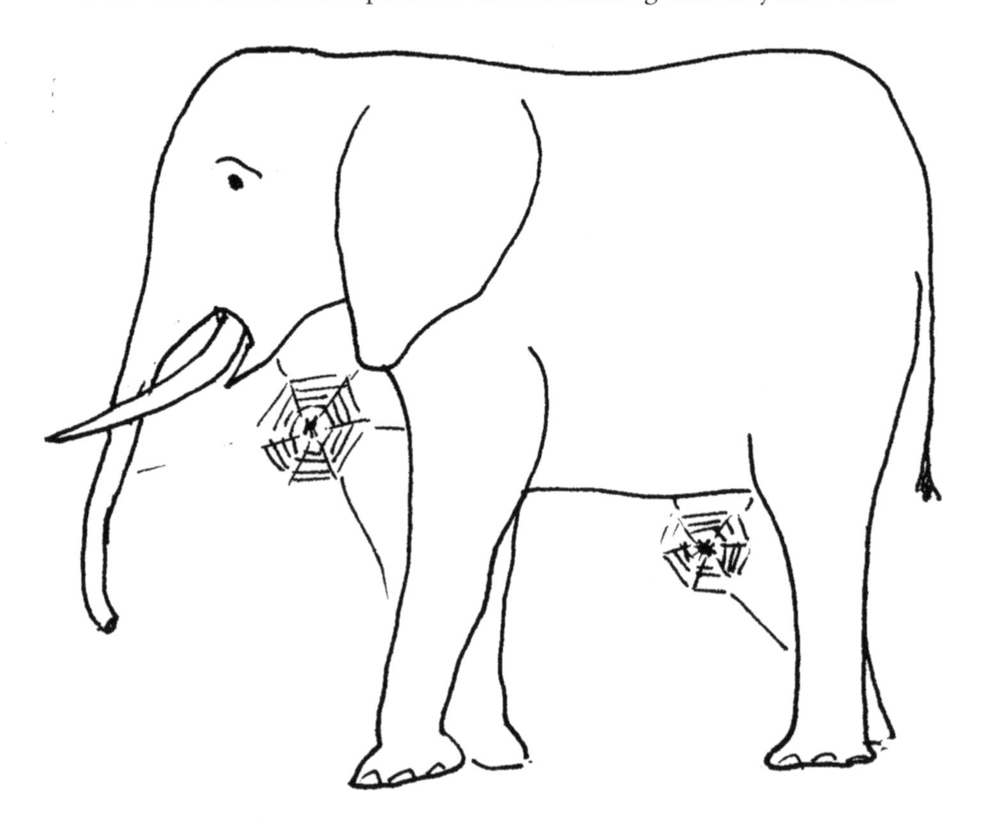

Dogs (Domestic)

- Along with foxes, wolves and wild dogs, domestic dogs belong to the family, Canidae. The scientific name for all domestic dogs is Canis lupus familiaris.
- All of today's domestic dogs are descended from the grey wolf. Domestic dogs have kept many of the wolf's characteristics, but selective breeding has meant that dogs occur in all colours, shapes and sizes. The DNA of dogs and wolves is almost identical.
- Recent research suggests that the ancestors of modern domestic dogs may have been domesticated as far back as 100,000 years ago.
- For thousands of years, humans have selectively bred dogs for various purposes such as guarding, herding, hunting, and, in recent times, for specialised tasks or for the sake of appearance. Hundreds of breeds of dog are recognised by kennel clubs all over the world. Different countries have different systems for categorising dog breeds. In Britain, the Kennel Club divides dogs into the following groups: working, pastoral, gundogs, hounds, terriers, utility and toys.
- The largest dog is the Irish wolfhound, which reaches 34in (86.36cm) in height and weighs upwards of 120lb (54.43kg). The smallest dog is the Chihuahua, which weighs up to 6lb (2.72kg).
- The Cardigan Welsh corgi is believed to be Britain's oldest pure-bred dog. Its ancestors can be traced back as far as 1200 BC.
- The average lifespan of a dog is approximately 12 years. However, it is not unknown for dogs to live 20 years or more.
- Small dogs tend to have longer lifespans than large dogs. For example, Great Danes don't usually live beyond the age of nine years, whereas Yorkshire terriers can live for 16 years or more.
- The world's fastest dog is the greyhound. The greyhound's maximum recorded speed is 41.72mph (67.14 km/h).
- Dogs are traditionally classified as carnivores but, like humans, they can live very well on an omnivorous diet consisting on a mixture of plant and animal foodstuffs. Dogs can, if required, live on a vegetarian diet.
- A dog weighing approximately 10lb (4.53kg) needs, on average, 8oz (226g) of food a day.
- A female dog (called a bitch) usually comes into season (or heat) twice a year. Bitches normally come into their first season when they are around nine months old although, it is not uncommon for bitches to experience their first season as early as six months of age.
- A bitch will allow a male dog (called a 'dog') to mate with her from about 12 days after having come into season. If the dog attempts to mate with the bitch before she is in full oestrus then his attempts will usually be rebuffed.

- A bitch's pregnancy normally lasts for 63 days.
- The number of pups in a litter depends on the breed of dog. For example, large breeds such as the golden retriever may have seven or more pups in a litter, whereas toy breeds such as the Cavalier King Charles spaniel tend to have much smaller litters. In addition, some experts believe that the day of conception decides the number of pups in a litter.
- Puppies are born with their eyes closed, and will start to open their eyes at around ten-days-old.
- Puppies usually sleep up to 14 hours a day.
- A dog's mother is called a dam. A dog's father is called a sire.
- Dogs have three eyelids. The third eyelid is in the inner corner of the eye hidden between the main upper and lower lids. This eyelid moves across the eye to clean away any debris – rather like a windscreen wiper on a car.
- The chow chow's tongue is bluish-black in colour.
- The African wolf dog called the basenji does not bark.
- The Labrador retriever, originally employed to help fishermen land their nets and still a good swimmer, is the most popular dog among private owners. The German shepherd is the second most popular.
- The German shepherd (or Alsatian) is thought to be the most direct descendant of the wolf.
- It is a myth that dogs can only see in black and white. Dogs see colour very well. Dogs do, however, suffer from colour blindness but only with the colours red and green. So when a guide dog has stopped at a set of traffic lights and waits until it is safe to guide his or her master across the road, the guide dog is not judging by the colour of the traffic lights but by the flow of the traffic.
- Dogs have 42 teeth.
- Dogs are capable of hearing sounds that aren't within people's hearing range, and have a remarkable degree of ear mobility which enables them to identify the location of sounds.
- Dogs do not have many sweat glands, which is why they pant in order to keep cool. When dogs pant, they normally have their tongues out of their mouths. The air evaporates the saliva on their tongues, thus cooling the air that enters their bodies. Although dogs pant to keep cool, they are unable to protect themselves from very warm temperatures and can easily suffer from heatstroke which can kill them. For this reason, dogs should never be left inside closed cars during warm weather. Dogs should always be carefully monitored during the warmer months and be given plenty of water to drink.
- The Aztecs used to sacrifice dogs at funerals in the belief that they would guide their dead masters to a better world.

- Dogs are very sensitive to 'atmospheres' and can sense human moods. Dog owners often say that when they are upset or depressed their dog tries to comfort them in some way.
- In the late 19th century, the Dobermann pinscher was developed by a German tax collector and a keen dog-pound keeper called Herr Dobermann who wanted a guard dog to protect him on his tax collecting rounds.
- Dalmatian puppies do not have spots when they are born.
- Bitches can be so altruistic that they will often allow the young of other animals to suckle them.
- Dogs that appear to be howling at the moon are following their distant ancestral instincts by calling the pack together.
- Dogs are social animals and can be extremely loyal and affectionate.
- Sense of smell is the dog's most acute sense. Just by sniffing the scent marks another dog leaves behind, a dog is able to discern the age, sex, social status, mood and sexual receptivity of that dog.
- A dog's nose is wet so that it can effortlessly accumulate scent particles.
- Unlike cats, dogs' claws are non-retractable. Dogs walk on their toes rather than the soles of their feet.
- Chocolate is toxic to dogs and can kill them. Some of the other foods that are poisonous to dogs include: Macadamia nuts, grapes, raisins and onions. Poultry bones are dangerous to dogs as they may splinter and cause choking.
- Dogs' ancestors used to live in packs and always had a pack leader whom they respected. That is why the trained domesticated dog is usually obedient to its master. The dog perceives its master to be the pack leader. If a number of dogs live together then there is usually a canine pack leader who the other dogs respect, but the human master still maintains his or her position as substitute pack leader.

Ten Popular Names For Dogs

1. Alfie
2. Ben
3. Buster
4. Fido
5. Holly
6. Lady
7. Lassie
8. Lucky
9. Rosie
10. Sam

Talking Of Dogs

There are a number of sayings which revolve around dogs. Here are some of the best-known, together with their meanings (and in some cases their origins):

Hangdog look

In medieval Europe, it was customary to take animals to court and to try them for their crimes. Among the animals successfully prosecuted and condemned to death in this way were rats, pigs, dogs and even a plague of insects that had ruined crops. For example, in 1595, a dog was hung in the town of Leyden after it had bitten a child's finger. And so the phrase a 'hangdog look', means a guilty, shame-faced, expression.

Hangdog

A hair of the dog (that bit you)

An alcoholic drink taken as a cure for a hangover. It has, for thousands of years, been believed that 'like cures like'. It used to be thought that the best cure for a dog bite was to apply to the wound some hair taken from the dog that had done the biting.

To be like a dog with a bone

To be persistent and determined.

Love me, love my dog
This proverb originated in the 11th century with St Bernard of Clairvaux. At the time, dogs were despised as dangerous animals who carried disease. In saying: 'love me, love my dog', St Bernard of Clairvaux was saying that people would have to accept him with all his faults.

A dog and pony show
An elaborate and ostentatious event.

Not a dog's chance
To have no chance at all.

To put on the dog
To behave in a pretentious or ostentatious way.

A dog in the manger
A spoilsport – a person who ruins the enjoyment of others, even if he gains nothing by doing so. The saying comes from an old fable about a dog who made his bed in the hay-manger so as to stop the ox from eating the hay, even though the dog did not want to eat the hay himself.

Dog eat dog
To be ruthless and competitive.

A dog's age
A long time.

A dog's dinner (or breakfast)
A mess.

A dog's life
An unhappy, oppressed existence.

To go to the dogs
To deteriorate badly.

Don't keep a dog and bark yourself
Don't do your servants' work.

Four Dogs Who Think They Are Bigger Than They Are

1. Pekinese
2. Jack Russell
3. Pomeranian
4. Yorkshire Terrier

The Legend Of Lassie

- The original Lassie, who starred in the classic 1943 movie, *Lassie Come Home* was a male collie called Pal.
- Pal was taken by his owner to the highly prestigious Weatherwax Kennels (which taught dogs obedience and trained dogs for movies) to be coached out of his bad habit of chasing cars.
- Pal's owner was allegedly unable to pay the bill, and let the Weatherwax family keep Pal in lieu of his debt.
- Pal wasn't a typical show collie. He was smaller than a standard collie and had a narrow white blaze on the ridge of his nose, which was considered undesirable at the time.
- Frank Weatherwax, who trained Pal, took Pal to MGM – when they were making preparations for *Lassie Come Home* – to show them the skills that this highly intelligent dog had learnt. Although impressed with Pal's performance, the same thing couldn't be said for his appearance, especially as Pal's coat wasn't looking at its best. Consequently, MGM turned Pal down for the starring role.
- MGM had bought an expensive show collie to play Lassie, and hired Pal to be the stand-in for the famous river scene in the movie.
- Pal had done such a spectacular job of crossing the hazardous river rapids – MGM hired him for the starring role. And, thus, Lassie was born.
- Pal died at the age of nineteen – a very good age for a dog.
- Eric Knight wrote the novel *Lassie Come Home*. Lassie was based on Eric Knight's own collie called Toots.
- Rumour has it that the Weatherwax family was never able to cure Pal out of his bad habit of chasing cars.

Five Of The Laziest Animals

1. Hippopatmus: spends most of the day wallowing in mud or bathing in water.

2. Sloth: sleeps in the trees for 15 hours a day. Visits the ground just once a week (to defecate).

3. Koala bear: spends up to 20 hours a day sleeping.

4. Domestic cat: the phrase 'cat nap' came from the cat's ability to sleep almost instantly. And wake up almost instantly too.

5. Giant tortoise: spends most of the day lazing in the sun.

Fifteen Of Our Favourite Scientific Names For Animals

1. Banded mongoose – Mungos mungo
2. Black rat – Rattus rattus
3. Eurasian beaver – Castor fiber
4. Fat dormouse – Glis glis
5. Grizzly bear – Ursus arctos horribilis
6. Guinea baboon – Papio papio
7. Indian rhinoceros – Rhinocerus unicornis
8. Llama – Lama glama
9. Mountain hare – Lepus timidus
10. Norway lemming – Lemmus lemmus
11. Red kangaroo – Marcropus rufus
12. Vampire bat – Desmodus rotundus
13. Western lowland Gorilla – Gorilla gorilla gorilla
14. Wild boar – Sus scrofa
15. Wolverine – Gulo gulo

'Nobody knows at what stage of evolution brains began to provide the wherewithal for subjective mental life. We assume that other people have conscious experiences – thoughts, feelings and sensations. We are prepared to allow that apes, cats and dogs, possibly even pigs, sheep and birds, enjoy a private, subjective mental life, maybe even fish and reptiles, but it is hard (and not entirely enjoyable) envisaging the consciousness of dung beetles, and almost unimaginable that slugs, worms and bacteria have feelings. How, when and where consciousness started we simply do not know. But one thing is certain: whatever its origins, a capacity for conscious representation of the external world evidently had survival value for organisms so blessed. It enabled registration, in a relatively unambiguous form, of the end products of extensive preconscious cerebral activity. It provided a means for the establishment of priorities and plans for action, and it enabled those 'feelings' which signal the necessity for adaptive behaviour.'

Professor Norman F. Dixon

Dolphins (Bottlenose)

- The bottlenose dolphin belongs to the family Delphinidae, and can be found in seas worldwide except in polar waters. There are 32 species of dolphin.
- The bottlenose dolphin is the most widespread of all dolphins.
- There are thought to be two species of bottlenose dolphin: Tursiops truncatus and Tursiops aduncus.
- The dolphin has a magnificent torpedo-shaped body, a dorsal fin on its back, a pectoral fin on either side of its body, a tail that moves up and down (unlike a fish's tail which moves from side to side), a nostril/blowhole on the top of its head for breathing in air, a rounded forehead called a melon, an ear opening on each side of its head, and a short beak-like snout often with a white patch on the tip of its lower jaw. The bottlenose dolphin usually has a dark-grey back with a pale belly. The dolphin has a layer of blubber underneath its skin to help protect it from the cold and to be used as a source of energy when there is a shortage of food. The bottlenose dolphin is the largest of the beaked dolphins. It can weigh 1,323lb (600.10kg) or more and can grow more than 13ft (3.96m) in length.
- The bottlenose dolphin acquired its name because observers likened the shape of its snout to an old-fashioned glass bottle.
- The bottlenose dolphin has lungs – not gills, which means that it is unable to breathe underwater. When swimming underwater, the dolphin frequently comes to the surface of the water for air. Before taking in air through its nostril/blowhole which is situated on the top of its head, the dolphin blows out some stale, moist air (not water as most people believe) through its blowhole. The dolphin's blowhole is kept shut under water by some remarkably strong muscles.
- The dolphin's skin secretes an oily substance, which is thought to help the dolphin to swim more smoothly.
- Over one third of the dolphin's body is made up of muscle.
- The bottlenose dolphin's diet mainly consists of fish, krill and cephalopods.
- When hunting, the dolphin uses echolocation to detect its prey. The dolphin emits sound waves which produce an 'echo' if they hit any objects up to 328ft (100m) away. With echolocation, the dolphin is able to pick up the size of its prey, its body structure and even how fast it is travelling. The dolphin also uses echolocation for navigation. Trained dolphins can use their navigational sonar to detect underwater mines.
- Dolphins are unable to chew their food.
- It is believed that dolphins have no sense of smell.
- The dolphin's courtship often involves a lively game of chase. Courting pairs of dolphins gently caress one another before having sex.
- The bottlenose dolphin's pregnancy may last 12-14 months.
- The dolphin usually gives birth to one young.

- A baby dolphin is called a calf.
- Baby dolphins are born tail first, and are approximately one third of the length of its mother when born.
- It is usual for female dolphins to act as midwives and assist one another during the birthing process. For example, as soon as the calf has been born, one or more females will help guide it to the water's surface to take its first breath. The 'midwives' will also protect mother and baby from any nearby predators.
- The mother's milk is extremely rich and contains a lot of fat; this is to help the young calf to gain weight quickly.
- A dolphin mother will go for a whole month without sleep so that she can look after her newborn baby efficiently. Going for a whole month without sleep enables the mother to keep her vulnerable calf safe from predators and to help keep her calf warm until it develops enough blubber to keep out the cold.
- The calf is dependent upon its mother's milk for up to 18-20 months after birth.
- It is not uncommon for baby dolphins to be born with whiskers on their snouts. However, these whiskers fall out within months of birth.
- Female dolphins with young calves often form groups called 'bands' with other female dolphins (usually relatives) who have young calves. The females in the band take turns babysitting the young calves when any of the mothers has to go hunting. Young calves are at risk of being killed by predators such as whales and sharks, which means that they can never be left on their own.
- The female dolphin has a calf every two to four years.
- Dolphins can reach speeds of up to 25mph (40.23km/h).
- A dolphin's eyes can move independently from each other.
- More male than female bottlenose dolphins die before reaching adulthood. No one really knows why this is.
- When dolphins want to rest, one half of their brain is used for breathing control and steering in the water, while the other half of the brain goes into a relaxed state. Amazingly, dolphins rest each side of their brain alternatively for several hours at a time. Doing this enables dolphins to have about eight hours of sleep a day.
- Some dolphins have two pointless hind-leg bones underneath their skin. These vestigial bones reinforce the scientific theory that dolphins used to be land animals.
- Dolphins have large brains relative to their body size, and are considered to be extremely intelligent. They are also very inquisitive, friendly, acrobatic and playful animals.
- Dolphins like to leap playfully out of the water and plunge back in with a splash. This is known as 'breaching'. When dolphins swim by leaping out and diving back into the water, this is known as 'porpoising'.
- Dolphins also 'spy-hop' where they raise their heads vertically out of the water.

It is thought that the reason why dolphins spy-hop is because they are surveying their surroundings for potential prey.

- Dolphins have been known to help humans in distress at sea.

- Dolphins love to caress and touch one another with their flippers.
- Dolphins can dive to depths of more than 1,640ft (500m) and stay underwater for up to 15 minutes.
- Dolphins are social animals who are usually found in schools (or pods) comprising 3-15 members. Schools sometimes group together to form herds of hundreds of dolphins.
- Male dolphins may live 30 years or more, and female dolphins may live 50 years or more.
- The dolphin's voice consists of a variety of cries, clicks and whistles. Dolphins communicate with one another by making whistling sounds of different pitches. Researchers have identified almost 200 unique whistle noises including, for example, a sound used by dolphins who have been separated from their pods. Biologist Dr Liz Hawkins from the Whale Research Centre at Southern Cross University, New South Wales, Australia, who recorded 1,647 whistles from 51 different groups of dolphins living off the New South Wales coast said: 'This communication is highly complex and it is contextual, so it could be termed a language.' Dolphins who live in Cardigan Bay, Wales have been found to make different sounds to dolphins who live in other areas. It seems that the Welsh dolphins have a 'Welsh' accent. (Accents are apparently not uncommon among animals. Other researchers have shown that cows moo in regional accents.)
- Most dolphins have their own unique identification whistle which is known as a 'signature whistle'. This signature whistle is often used to communicate to

other members in a group who are out of visual range. Dolphins are capable of mimicking the signature whistles of other dolphins.

- Dolphins are members of the whale family.
- In addition to natural predators, water pollution and nets used for tuna fishing are a threat to dolphins. However, most fishermen hunting for tuna now use dolphin-friendly nets. If you eat tuna, you should see a dolphin seal of approval on the tin. If not, then you should boycott that particular brand of tuna fish. In some parts of the world, dolphins are deliberately killed by fishermen as they are seen as serious competitors for food.

How Animals Treat Themselves When They Are Ill

Animals know that there are four main ways to deal with a threatening situation:

a) they can escape from the problem

b) they can remove the problem

c) they can wait for the problem to go away

d) they can search for a solution

These basic responses apply to threats from illness just as much as they apply to threats from predators.

An animal's body, like a human body, can protect, defend and repair itself when under threat. In-built mechanisms enable the animal to exist comfortably under quite extraordinarily extreme external conditions. The body's internal mechanisms (some of which are mechanical but most of which are physiological) work readily, speedily and automatically to protect the body from external threats.

Animals recognise the power of 'bodypower'. They know that sometimes not taking medicine is the best way to get well. They understand that fasting, resting, staying warm, allowing vomiting and diarrhoea to do their work, may be the best way.

If, however, these systems do not or cannot function and do not deal with the problem then the animal's instincts and behavioural habits will take over.

So, to give a simple example, if the weather is too hot for the internal temperature control mechanisms to defend the animal's integrity and protect it from damage, then the animal will find some shade or will swim in a pool.

However, if physiological mechanisms and instincts all fail, and the animal falls ill then the creature will treat itself using medicaments taken from its surroundings.

Animals don't rely on outside doctors, they generally self medicate. They use their experience to avoid illness and prevent themselves from illness. When they fall ill they treat themselves. Animals may learn from one another – and if an animal needs help another will often provide it – but there are no specialist animals working as doctors.

The aim of self-medication is, of course, to re-establish a feeling of well-being. To do that, the patient (whether human or animal) needs to have an understanding of his or her own body. He or she needs to know his or her strengths and weaknesses; he or she needs to know what is normal and what is not.

Animals will often seek out and consume something they don't normally eat and that has no nutritional benefit. If their health then improves within a reasonable time, it is fair to assume that there is a link.

Naturally, the animal needs to know where to find the medicaments it may need. And this is where animals excel. Indeed, thanks to instinct and intuition, animals are so good at finding and using natural remedies that many of man's most effective medicinal solutions were identified by observing animals.

In modern orthodox medicine, doctors working in the West tend to treat disease by attacking the pathogen alleged to be responsible. Modern, western medicine turns the patient into a battlefield – with the result that, in many instances, the treatment does more harm than good. The modern doctor tends to ignore the fact that, for example, infections often take hold during stressful conditions, and to forget (if they ever knew) that strengthening the human organism is invariably just as important as attacking the disorder. Attacking only the infection or disability means treating only the symptoms rather than the cause.

In contrast, traditional Chinese medicine takes a more holistic approach, assuming that the pathogen is not the direct cause of the disease, but merely a symptom of an imbalance, a disruption of physiological or psychological homoestatis.

Animals tend to understand that when a disease strikes it is often because their organism has in some way been weakened (by, for example, drought, famine or overcrowding) and that if they are to get wholly well again, they must tackle internal – as well as external – causes of disease. The animal approach is a holistic one; treating the whole organism – and attacking any infection – in whatever ways will best produce a positive outcome.

It is, of course, only animals living in the wild who are able to treat themselves. Animals on farms, although being far more likely to fall ill than animals in the wild, are denied the opportunity to treat themselves by changing their circumstances. Despite the fact that there is a considerable amount of evidence showing that animals such as cows and sheep are quite capable of diagnosing and treating themselves, farm animals have very limited access to the varieties of natural plants available in the wild.

We have listed examples of some of the ways that animals treat themselves when they are ill. We could learn a great deal by watching how animals deal with disease – particularly infectious disease. Humans have always learned a great deal about medicine and health care by observing animals. We could learn much more.

Many plants with medicinal properties are named after the animals that use them as medicines. Folk medicine or rural medicine is often based upon the observations people have made while watching animals. And the names we give to plants are often a result. So we have catnip, pigweed, hare's lettuce and horny-goat weed. In

Five Animals Who Used To Be Television Stars

1. Black Beauty
2. Champion the Wonder Horse
3. Flipper (the dolphin)
4. Gentle Ben (the bear)
5. Lassie

The Average Number Of Young Born To Some Animals

Anteater	1
Beaver	3-4
Chipmunk	4-5
Dingo	1-10
Gerbil	1-12
Hamster	6-10
Hare	1-10
Lemur	1
Leopard	1-6
Meerkat	2-5
Mole	3-4
Weasel	1-7
Blue Whale	1
Wolverine	1-6
Yak	1

Longevity In Some Animals

- Shrew – 12-30 months.
- Aardvark – 10 years in captivity.
- African wild dog – 10 years.
- Caribou – 4½ years.
- Common warthog – 12-15 years.
- Coyote – up to 14½ years.
- Dormouse – up to 6 years.
- European mole – up to 4 years.
- Jackal – 4-8 years.
- Mink – 12 years in captivity.
- Mongoose – 10 years.
- Platypus – 10 years or more.
- Walrus – 40 years or more.
- Wild boar – 15-20 years.
- Wolverine – 17 years.
- North American beaver – 10-15 years.
- Anteater – up to 26 years in captivity.
- Kangaroo rat – up to 9 years in captivity.

North America, the Navajo and Blackfeet Indians observed wild bears digging up roots of ligusticum plants and using them with obvious benefits to their health. So they called the plant 'bear medicine'. In Canada, the Chippewa Indians give the same name, for the same reason, to apocynum. In Europe, herbalists watched sick dogs eating agropyron repens grass that they called it 'dog grass'. Modern farming methods, which result in animals being confined to small fields or even smaller sheds, mean that we can no longer learn in the same way. (They also mean that animals, deprived of the opportunity to go out and find healing medicines, can't heal themselves either.)

We can learn from watching how animals boost their immune systems and change their behaviour to preserve their health. Most important, perhaps, is the fact that from animals we can learn that successful good health depends on avoidance and prevention. Treatment should be used only as a last resort.

☑ Ranchers in Utah used to turn out sick cattle with diarrhoea to fend for themselves. Initially this was done simply to get rid of the ailing animal and to prevent the spread of any disease. The ranchers were, however, surprised when after a few days their cattle repeatedly returned – quite well. An observant rancher followed sick animals and saw that they travelled to clay banks and fed on the clay until they got better. The clay absorbed the toxins and viruses causing the diarrhoea. Sadly, cattle on most farms are given little or no opportunity to self medicate. And in many countries the medicinal benefits of clay are completely ignored. It is estimated that in Britain, around 170,000 calves a year die of diarrhoea caused by bacterial infections. But in the UK, foods and medicines are dealt with by different Government departments. Clay isn't accepted as either and so can't be given. This is sad. We live in a world of potential toxins. Animals throughout the world use clay to deal with poisoning – clay detoxifies by binding onto the harmful substances. Indeed, humans could probably benefit too. Clay pills might save many lives. However, there isn't much profit to be made out of selling clay and so no one is fighting for the right to do so.

☑ A worker from the World Wildlife Fund followed a pregnant African elephant for more than a year. During that time the elephant ate a predictable diet, roaming about three miles (4.82km) a day. At the end of her pregnancy, the elephant walked more than 15 miles (24.14km) in a single day and headed for a tree of the boraginacea family. Once she had arrived at the tree, she ate it. All of it. She ate the leaves, she ate the branches and she ate the trunk. Four days later, she gave birth to a healthy calf. Kenyan women brew a tea from the leaves of this tree to induce labour.

☑ Sheep can diagnose and treat their own ailments. In a cruel experiment at Utah State university, scientists fed lambs food that would make them ill. Some of the lambs were then given food containing medicine which would help them get better quickly. Others were left to get better naturally. When, five months later, the lambs were poisoned again, only the ones which had been given the food containing medicine knew which foods they needed to eat to get better.

- ☑ In the Han Dynasty, a general called Ma-Wu and his army retreated to a poor part of China to lick their wounds. Many soldiers and horses died. Those left were ill, excreting blood in urine. One groom noticed his three horses were healthy. Wisely, he watched to see what they ate. He noticed that they were eating a good deal of a small plantain plant. He boiled some of the plant and ate it. The blood quickly disappeared from his urine. He then gave the same plant to the other men and horses. They were all cured. The plant is now known to contain ingredients which make it anti-inflammatory and anti-microbial.

- ☑ In the 17th century, English doctors regarded watching animals as a reputable way of learning about medicines. Queen Anne's personal physician went to the marshes of Essex, where he knew the locals put their sheep when they suffered from a disorder known as 'the rott'. He watched what they ate and by doing so discovered herbs with which he could help human patients with consumption.

Bears rub themselves on trees which have resin in their bark

- Native American Indians learnt so much from watching how bears treated themselves when they were ill that advanced healers were known as Bear Medicine Men.
- When cod and shark find themselves in polluted waters they will swim away as quickly as they can.
- Atlantic salmon will not swim up rivers which are polluted with copper or zinc mine wastes
- Chinese herdsmen have seen elderly deer (just the older ones) nibbling at the bark and roots of the fleece flower. When the bark and roots were analysed, scientists found that they contained ingredients likely to help reduce hypertension, cholesterol levels, coronary heart disease and other disorders common in old age.
- A herbalist in Tanzania rescued an orphaned porcupine. When the animal became ill with diarrhoea and bloating, the porcupine went into the forest and dug up and ate a plant which turned out to be useful for treating internal parasites in humans.
- A Creole herbalist in Venezuela watched deer chewing the seed cases of a plant. He subsequently found it helped his human patients
- In the Middle Ages, English doctors noticed that when an animal licked its wounds the injury would heal more quickly. The doctors decided that animals' tongues must have some marvellous healing property, and so they got into the habit of cutting the tongues out of puppies and using them as wound dressings. This didn't work terribly well and eventually (some centuries later) the doctors realised that it was the saliva not the tongue which contained both an antiseptic and agents which encouraged wound closure.
- Domestic cats and dogs chew grass. There are two reasons for this. First, grass is an emetic (causing regurgitation or vomiting) and a purgative scour (getting rid of worms living further down the intestine). Animals choose different types of grasses for different functions. The animals eat grass in order to make themselves sick if they have eaten something which is making them ill (or which, they suspect, may make them ill).
- Elephants, who are herbivores, need a lot of sodium but there isn't much present in plants. Without the sodium they become ill. So the elephants need to find their sodium elsewhere. In Kenya, there is a series of caves high up on the side of an inactive volcano called Mount Elgon. These caves have been created by generations of elephants. Over the last two million years, the elephants have eaten five million litres of rock. Inside the caves, the elephants have to crawl on their knees to dig out lumps of sodium-rich rock. They also drink the mineral-rich waters which are rich in calcium and magnesium.
- Gorillas in Rwanda eat rock which they dig out of the slopes of Mount Visoke during the dry season. The rock the gorillas mine and eat contains a good deal of iron, aluminium and clay. The gorillas eat the rock as a medicine. The clay helps

stop diarrhoea (a common problem among gorillas because much of their plant based diet in the dry season causes diarrhoea and dangerous fluid loss). The aluminium has a useful antacid effect. The iron is useful because in the dry season the gorillas have to go higher to find vegetation and may develop altitude anaemia.

- Chimpanzees in Tanzania have been seen to eat earth from termite mounds. But they only do this when they are suffering diarrhoea and other gastrointestinal problems. The termite mound is rich in clay that helps prevent diarrhoea. Termite mound earth is also used by elephants, giraffes and rhinoceroses. (Clay-type products would be good for humans in these circumstances. However, they are only rarely prescribed.)

- Eating charcoal is an effective way to adsorb toxins. It is used in human medicine to treat drug overdoses and poisoning, and for wind and bloating. When wild animals find charcoal after forest fires or lightning strikes, they eat the burnt wood. Charcoal doesn't have much nutritional value. The only reason to eat it is for its toxin binding properties. Deer and ponies have been seen doing this in the New Forest in England. In Kenya, camels have been seen to eat charcoal. Monkeys have been seen to do it on the island of Zanzibar. Their diet includes trees which are high in toxins but the charcoal absorbs these toxins. The monkeys have been measured as consuming precisely the amount of charcoal recommended as an effective veterinary dose. (The heavier the monkey, the more charcoal it eats.)

- When rats are given the poison paraquat they will survive if they find clay to eat to adsorb the poison. The rats have to eat the clay for several weeks in order to make sure it carries all the poison out of their bodies. They know this.

- Civets, colobus monkeys, elephants, bison, pigs, tigers, camels, bears, wild dogs, rhinoceroses, Indian mole rats and jackals are all known to eat plants for their medicinal properties. Toxic plant compounds are sometimes used to control internal parasites.

- Indian wild bison feed on the bark of horrahena antidysentaria – which is also used to treat dysentery in humans. This plant contains a drug which is active against amoebic dysentery protozoa.

- Chimpanzees have been observed to eat at least 26 different plant species that are prescribed in traditional human medicine for the treatment of internal parasites. They have been observed to increase their intake of drug-rich plants when necessary.

- Animals sometimes take plants not for their drug action but for mechanical aid. So, for example, chimpanzees in Africa have been seen swallowing the leaves of 19 different types of plant from many different plant groups. Scientists could find no reason for this – none of the plants had any compound which had any effect on parasites. The only thing the leaves had in common was their rough texture and indigestibility. It turned out that the animals were folding up the leaves and then swallowing them. The parasitic worms in the chimpanzees' intestines were being captured by the tiny barbs on the leaves. Folding the leaves increased the chances of the worms being trapped and then excreted.

- Most wild animals have a low sugar diet and have few problems with tooth decay, but chimpanzees eat a good deal of sugary fruit and suffer from both tooth decay and gum disease. To cope with these two problems they chew on the antibacterial bark of trees. They also inspect and clean one another's teeth. One chimpanzee was seen to pry out the bad teeth of another animal by using a wooden lever she had made.
- Stags who are injured in the Neydharting area of Austria will drag themselves miles to immerse themselves and their wounds in the black, muddy waters of the moors. The waters and mud have been found to contain over 300 bioactive herbs, many antimicrobials, vitamins and hormones.
- A capuchin monkey who was badly wounded took a stick, chewed the end to make a brush and then used the brush to apply sugary syrup to the wound area (she had been given the syrup as food). Strong sugar is a good ointment for wounds. Like honey, it has an antibacterial effect. The monkey did this without seeing other monkeys do it.
- If a capuchin monkey has an itch, it will scratch itself with a fuzzy seedpod until the scratchy hairs are worn off. It will then discard the useless seedpod and get another.
- Californian ground squirrels will deliberately taunt rattlesnakes so that they are bitten. Ground squirrels are resistant to the venom, but the snake venom stimulates the animals' immune systems and helps slow the spread of cancer and other serious disorders.
- If adult male baboons become wounded (through fighting or hunting), they keep their wounds clean by licking and grooming. Their wounds will also be carefully groomed by female baboons.
- Many other animals routinely treat their own wounds. Wounded elk, moose, bears and caribou roll in clay. Bears and deer rub themselves on trees which have resin in their bark. Wounded cattle and deer roll in sphagnum moss. Deer living near the sea will walk out into the salty water. Many animals dip wounded areas into cold water to stop bleeding and ease pain. Elephants will cover and pack a wound with mud. In many cases, herbalists have found that the substances (tree bark, mud, etc) contain antiseptics which will protect the wound and help ensure that it heals.
- Animals have even been known to make plaster casts. A Pyrenean mountain goat has been seen to make itself a plaster using clay, lichen and grass. An injured woodcock took clay from the edge of a stream and smeared it on his leg near the knee then he pulled roots of grass and put them into the clay. He then added more clay. In the end, he had created a very effective clay cast designed

to hold his broken leg together. Other natural historians have observed that snipe who have had a leg broken by a gun shot will bind the leg with leaves and feathers using mud or clay to hold the cast together.

- ☑ If chimpanzees who are wounded can reach the area, they will lick their wounds. If they cannot reach they will lick their fingers and dab at the wounds. They also dab leaves on a wound, lick the leaves and dab them on the wound again. Infant chimpanzees will lick the wounds of their mothers. The saliva of all mammals is an excellent disinfectant for their own wounds. Domestic dogs lick their wounds (which then stay free from infection even though they also lick their anuses). Dog saliva contains antimicrobials capable of killing bacteria such as staphylococcus, escherichia coli and streptococcus. Rat saliva contains substances which help speed up the closure of wounds. Human saliva contains healing substances too, and we could speed up wound healing by licking our own wounds. Our saliva contains mucins and fibronectins which inactivate microbes by binding them, lactoferrins which kill iron-dependent bacteria by taking their iron, peroxidases which poison bacteria, histatin which is a strong antifungal agent and a type of antibody that is active against viruses such as influenza and polio.
- ☑ Fever is a defence mechanism designed to help the body combat infection; a high fever will often kill bacteria. Some animals will take advantage of this phenomenon and deliberately make their temperature rise. So-called cold-blooded animals (e.g. crabs, toads and tortoises) which actively moderate their own temperature will take action to bring on a fever to kill an infection. Lizards who are ill will find somewhere warmer to lie. Fish will move to warmer waters. Ants will bask in the sun if they are ill. Honeybees will vibrate their wing muscles enough to raise the temperature of their hives to prevent larvae being infected if there is a fungus in the hive. Hedgehogs will sunbathe if they are ill (this helps to push their body temperature higher, and the sunlight acts as an antimicrobial agent).
- ☑ Fasting can help an infected animal get better quicker. Sick animals will, like human beings, go off their food. Bacteria need iron, and the body reduces the availability of iron during an infection by not eating.
- ☑ Some animals will deliberately eat plants which boost their immune systems.
- ☑ Bees are very good at fighting infection. They collect resins produced by trees to protect their buds and make propolis from the resin. They coat the inside of their hive with this, making an environment so sterile it would be the envy of any operating team. The propolis contains hundreds of flavonoids, phenolics and aromatic compounds. If an invading animal gets into the hive and dies, the bees will embalm it by covering it with propolis – to protect against infection. Honey, made as food for winter, is packed with potent antimicrobials to stop it going off. Today, doctors are again using honey on human patients. They use it to stimulate the immune system and to treat wounds.

- ☑ Capuchin monkeys rub natural substances into their fur to repel pests. So, for example, they use the stems of clematis (which kill bacteria and deaden pain).
- ☑ White-nosed coatis, rub resin from the trattinnickia tree into their coats. The menthol-like smelling resin repels fleas, lice, ticks and mosquitoes.
- ☑ Black, brown and Kodiak bears make up a herbal paste out of osha roots. They use this as a topical anaesthetic and antibacterial.
- ☑ Cats don't just roll in catnip for fun. They also do it because it helps repel pests. The plant's ingredients are insecticidal.
- ☑ The European hedgehog is vulnerable to fleas and ticks and cannot groom itself for obvious reasons. So it anoints itself with mint, oil, and fermenting fruit.

Why Farm Animals Are So Unhealthy

Farm animals are more likely to fall ill than animals in the wild for several reasons.

First, stocking densities tend to be so high that parasites, for example, spread easily and quickly and become endemic.

Second, animals kept on farms are unlikely to have proper opportunities to exercise. Many, who live indoors, are even denied the health giving properties of sunshine and fresh air. Farm animals may be exempt from the worst excesses of drought and starvation but their lifestyles are far from healthy. Inevitably, the circumstances in which animals are kept result in psychological problems too.

Third, animals are unlikely to be able to enjoy the sort of range of foodstuffs that would be available to them in the wild. The diet farmers give to captive animals bears no relationship to the diet they normally live on. For example, farmers often give animal waste to vegetarian animals. In the USA, chicken excrement is fed directly to cattle ('to give them protein'), and the French Government has admitted illegally feeding human sewage to French cattle. Farmers in Britain routinely fed their cattle the ground-up brains and spinal cords of other cattle. (It was this that caused the disastrous outbreak of mad cow disease). Farmers ignored the fact that herbivorous ruminants don't eat meat and never engage in cannibalism.

The inescapable fact is that farm animals are bred for profit and, in general, the health of the animals is only of concern if it restricts the farmer's ability to add the animals to the food chain and, therefore, interferes with profitability. Farmers may, indeed, be tempted to hide and cover up illness if this threatens to restrict their ability to add the animal to the food chain. An animal which needs special drugs may be excluded from the food chain on safety grounds – even though healthy animals are routinely given a wide variety of 'acceptable' prescription drugs. For example, far more antibiotics are given to healthy animals than to sick human beings. Antibiotics produce muscle growth in animals, and more muscle means more meat which means more profit.)

In wild or semi-wild conditions, chickens live in forests in small groups. They scratch around on the forest floor eating worms, insects and bits of fresh plant. They use the dust and the sun to keep their feathers bright, and they bathe when it rains. At night they roost in trees (their claws are adapted for hanging onto branches even while asleep) so that they are safe from predators.

This is a healthy lifestyle for a chicken.

However, this isn't how chickens are kept on most modern farms. Chicken farmers have selectively bred chickens to grow faster and faster. They have doubled the maturing speed at which a chicken matures in just two decades. Muscle is laid down before the bird's heart and circulation can cope, and the result is that the birds are constantly ill. Their bones aren't capable of supporting their excess weight, and so they get broken bones. They die of thirst and starvation because they cannot reach the automated food and water delivery systems which supply their cages. Eighty per cent of broiler chickens suffer broken bones, and 17,000 birds die every day in the United Kingdom because of heart failure. Farmers regard these deaths as an acceptable cost of doing business. The food the chickens are fed is selected according to the cheapest possible formulation, and contains just the basic ingredients. (One popular ingredient is ground-up dead chicken. They have to do something with all those dead birds.) The chickens are routinely given antibiotics to try to keep them healthy (despite the fact that farmers know that this habit is a major cause of the development of antibiotic-resistant organisms), and they are kept in the half dark so that they stay quiet. They suffer from exceptionally high temperatures (especially when the weather is warm), they stand in their own excrement (which is acidic, and so it blisters their feet) and the air they breathe in is full of fumes, bacteria and dust. It is hardly surprising that half of the broiler flocks in the United Kingdom are colonised with campylobacter which can cause neurological problems, arthritis, headache, backache, fever, nausea, pain and diarrhoea in the people who eat them.

The chickens, like other farm animals, are given no freedom and no chance at all to self medicate.

Donkeys

- The donkey belongs to the horse family Equidae, and is descended from the African wild ass.
- Donkeys originally came from Asia and Africa.
- At the shoulder, the average donkey stands about 40in (101.6cm) high.
- Like horses, donkeys are measured in hands. They are measured from the withers (the highest part of its back, at the base of the neck) to the ground. A miniature donkey is considered to be under 9 hands when adult.
- The donkey's coat varies in colour from white to black to any shade of grey or brown. Some donkeys are skewbald (they have a coat with irregular patches of

white and another colour, not black) or piebald (they have a coat with irregular patches of two colours, typically black and white), and there are even donkeys who have a pink hue to their coats.

- Baby donkeys are called foals. A female donkey foal is called a filly, and a male donkey foal is called a colt. A gelding is an adult male donkey that has been castrated. A male that is kept as a stud for breeding is called a stallion donkey. An adult female donkey is called a mare. The terms 'jack' for a male donkey and 'jenny' for a female donkey are now used less often. Other words used to refer to donkeys include: ass, burro, moke and cuddy.
- The donkey usually sleeps standing up.

- It was the Romans who first introduced the donkey to Britain around the ninth and tenth centuries.
- Donkeys' milk contains less fat than cows' milk. Donkeys' milk is reputed to have a similar effect to Viagra.
- Contrary to popular belief, donkeys are extremely intelligent animals. Their tendency to be stubborn is not born out of stupidity but is born out of intelligence. Unlike a horse, a donkey is much more cautious about being led into a situation which might put it in danger. And like humans, donkeys can be stubborn when it comes to doing something which they don't find enjoyable.
- The donkey has a persistent nature. Unlike the horse, the donkey doesn't usually give in.
- The average lifespan of a donkey is around 25-30 years. But some donkeys have been known to live as long as 60 years.
- The donkey has long ears with lots of hair inside them and a tail rather like a cow's with a tuft of hair at the end of it. The tail is used as a swish to get rid of annoying or disease-carrying insects.
- In Britain, there is a Victorian bylaw which states that donkeys must not stand in groups of more than ten, and that they must all face the same direction when standing.
- Just like sheep, donkeys hate the rain. It is cruel to keep a donkey in a field without some form of shelter.
- Once a donkey has bonded with a herd of sheep or goats, it will do its utmost to protect that herd from any nearby predators.
- China is believed to have the largest donkey population in the world.
- A donkey's pregnancy can last anywhere from 11 and 13 months.
- The donkey usually gives birth to one foal.
- After its waters have broken, the mare will usually give birth within half an hour.
- Donkeys, like many other animals, are not born with immunity. They acquire immunity from their first feed by drinking their mother's special milk called 'colostrum'.
- Most donkeys have a dark-coloured cross on their shoulders (a dark line from their mane right to their tail and a dark crosswise line on their shoulders). The traditional belief is that the cross on the donkey's shoulders appeared at the time when donkeys carried Jesus Christ into Jerusalem on what is now known as Palm Sunday.
- A donkey's bray (loud, harsh cry) is reputed to travel just over 1.86 miles (3km).
- Donkeys like routine.
- Donkeys' hooves grow throughout their lives, and a domestic donkey's hooves usually have to be trimmed every couple of months.
- Donkeys don't stop growing until they are approximately four years of age.

- In the late nineteenth century, there were believed to be around 100,000 working donkeys in London.
- Donkeys are hardy, surefooted animals and are capable of carrying heavy loads over extremely rough terrain.
- The donkey has a very patient, inquisitive, docile and friendly nature.
- Donkeys cannot vomit.
- Donkeys love to roll on the ground.
- Donkeys are known to have a calming effect on nervous horses.
- A mule is a cross between a male donkey and a female horse. Horse-donkey hybrids are nearly always sterile.
- Donkeys are browsers – not pure grazers. (A grazer eats grass and a browser eats leaves, twigs and all sorts of other foods).
- Yew trees are poisonous to donkeys and can kill them.
- Donkeys love eating brambles.
- Up until it is ten-years-old, a donkey can be aged correctly by its teeth.
- The donkey's original terrain was desert, and it is thought that the donkey's long ears helped to pick up the communication sounds of their distant neighbours in those surroundings.
- Just like horses, a donkey who is kept alone will be unhappy. Donkeys are social animals and, therefore, need friends.
- When alarmed, a donkey's instinct is to stand perfectly still.

Animals' Homing Instincts

Like birds, many animals have remarkable homing skills. Using the earth's magnetic field, the angle of the sun and its own biological clock, an animal which is taken from its home can find its way back over remarkably long distances. Cats in particular seem to have an astonishing ability to find their way home. (There is some evidence that human beings used to have this skill, have lost it, but can regain it if they try.) There are many well-authenticated stories of animals who have found their way home across vast distances. Here are a dozen:

1. After she was sent to Nebraska, a cat called Cookie travelled 550 miles (885.13km) to get back to her home in Chicago.
2. A cat called Howie travelled across 1,000 miles (1,609km) of wilderness and desert in the Australian outback to find his owner when she moved home. Howie's adventure included crossing several rivers.
3. When truck driver, Geoff Hancock, stopped at a cafe 1,800 miles (2,896km) away from his home, his fox terrier, called Whisky, jumped out of the vehicle. It was nine months before Whisky finally arrived safely home after travelling solo for 1,800 miles.

4. A cat called Tom crossed the USA, travelling 2,500 miles (4,023km) from Florida to California in order to find his owners in their new home. His journey took him just over two years.
5. Kuzya, a Russian cat, travelled 1,300 miles (2,092km) across Siberia to get back together with the people he lived with. Kuzya got lost when his family was travelling on holiday. After weeks of desperate searching, Kuzya's family eventually gave up and went home. But Kuzya turned up three months later in perfect health.
6. Ken Phillips and his teenage son lost their cat, Silky, in Australia. Over six months later, Silky arrived at the family home in Melbourne, Australia, after covering a distance of approximately 1,500 miles (2,414km).
7. While Barbara Paule was driving her truck in Ohio, her cat, Muddy Water White, jumped out of the truck and disappeared. Three years later, Muddy Water White turned up on Barbara's doorstep – 400 miles (643km) away from the spot where she vanished from the truck. Owing to the fact that poor Muddy was so dishevelled, it took his owner three days to recognise him.
8. After Murka the tortoiseshell cat had killed several pet canaries, her owner sent her 400 miles (643km) to live with his mother. A couple of days later, Murka disappeared from her new home. Murka eventually returned to her original home pregnant and reportedly hungry (presumably for canaries).
9. Cats usually travel from a new home back to an old home, but there are stories of cats finding their way from their old homes to their owners' new homes. For example, a cat named Tom once travelled over 2,500 miles (4,023km), from Florida to California, to find her owners in their new home.
10. A snake which was carried 100 miles (160.93km) away from home managed to find its way back.
11. An English setter called Bede got lost while holidaying in Cornwall with his owner Louis Heston. Amazingly, six months later, Bede turned up at his owner's home after travelling a distance of more than 300 miles (482km).
12. During World War I, a man called Jones-Brown enlisted in the army and, naturally, had to leave his dog Prince, an Irish terrier, behind with his family in Ireland. Prince became depressed and would not eat. When he was taken on a trip to England with the family, the dog disappeared. Mrs Jones-Brown wrote to her husband to tell him the sad news that his dog had gone. Her husband wrote back to tell her that Prince was with him. The dog had somehow managed to cross the English Channel and find his master.

'Animals are such agreeable friends – they ask no questions, they pass no criticisms.'

GEORGE ELLIOT (1819-1880)

ELEPHANTS

- ✶ Elephants belong to the family Elephantidae. It used to be thought that there were only two species of elephant but it in fact there are three species: the African savanna elephant, the African forest elephant and the Asian (or Indian) elephant. Elephants occupy habitats that range from savanna to dense jungle.
- ✶ The savanna elephant lives in sub-Saharan East and Central Africa. The forest elephant lives in Central and West Africa and the Asian elephant lives in South and South-East Asia. The savanna elephant is the largest living land animal in the world. The savanna elephant weighs approximately 7 tons (7.14 tonnes) and can grow to 16ft long (4.87m). The Asian elephant weighs approximately 5 tons (5.1 tonnes) and can grow to 11ft long (3.35m).
- ✶ There are quite a number of anatomical differences between African and Asian elephants but the most obvious is the ears. African elephants have larger ears than their Asian cousins.

- ✶ The elephant is the second tallest animal in the world. (The tallest is the giraffe). The savanna elephant can grow to 13ft tall (3.96m).
- ✶ The adult female elephant is called a cow. The adult male elephant is called a bull. The baby elephant is called a calf.
- ✶ An elephant's amazing feature is its long trunk, which is a union of its upper nose and lip. Elephants use their trunks for breathing, reaching for food, drinking, wrestling with rivals, lifting objects, communicating with one another and sniffing the air to detect any intruders. Elephants also use their trunks for bathing. Elephants regularly have dust baths, where they use their trunks to throw dust over their bodies in order to keep their skin free from parasites. The trunks of Asian elephants have fewer wrinkles than the trunks of African elephants. Asian elephants only have one lip at the tip of their trunks, whereas African elephants have two.

- ✶ An elephant's ivory tusks are exceptionally large incisors which continue to grow throughout the animal's lifetime. The record for the longest African elephant tusk is just over 11½ft (3.50m). Elephants use their tusks for: self-defence, digging, scraping bark off trees, and a rest for their trunks. Elephants usually have one tusk longer than the other, that's because the dominant tusk (the master tusk) usually gets worn down more quickly. Tusks are usually absent in female Asian elephants. Bull Asian elephants may also be tuskless; these elephants are known locally as 'muknas'.
- ✶ Elephants are herbivores, feeding mainly on plant matter. An average elephant weighing approximately 2 tons, needs to consume around 330lb (149.68kg) or more plant matter a day. African elephants spend around 20 hours a day feeding. The elephant's main diet consists of grasses, leaves, shoots, roots, bark, and fruit. Elephants in need of minerals, which may be lacking in their diets, will also eat mineral-rich soil (containing minerals such as sodium) or mineral-rich rocks. The elephant is unable to feed from the ground with its mouth; it uses its extremely dextrous trunk (which contains thousands of muscles and no bones) to tear up vegetation to put into its mouth.
- ✶ Elephants live in matriarchal family groups called herds; usually comprising several closely related females and their offspring. The eldest female, who is likely to be the grandmother or even the great-grandmother of the herd, is often the leader, and she is called the matriarch. The matriarch is very much respected by the rest of the herd. It is the matriarch who makes all of the decisions such as how far they will travel each day and how fast their walking pace should be. The matriarch has much knowledge, which she has learnt over the years as well as knowledge that has been passed on to her by her mother. For example, the matriarch usually knows where to find water in times of drought, and where to go to find food. Males leave the family herd (or are expelled) when they reach puberty. Males either live in small bachelor herds or wander on their own, and will join the matriarch herd only to mate. The bonds shared by males living in bachelor herds are nowhere near as strong as the bonds shared by females living in family herds. Unlike female herds, the males in bachelor herds are usually unrelated. A bachelor herd is normally dominated by the largest bull.
- ✶ When the herd is threatened and there is no time to run away, the females of the herd normally face outward and form a ring around the younger members of the herd to protect them.
- ✶ Asian bulls come into a phase called 'musth' when they are approximately 20-years-old. This is a time when the usually placid animals start displaying some rather aggressive behaviour in trying to compete with other bulls for a chance to mate with a female in oestrus. A bull will fight with another bull (for hours if he has to) for a chance to mate with a female. During musth, the bull dribbles pungent smelling urine and discharges a copious honey-like secretion from its temporal glands (a small opening situated on each side of the elephant's head between its eye and ear). African elephants usually do not come into 'musth'

until they are 25-29 years old. Their phase of musth is not so pronounced as the musth experienced by Asian elephants. Females in oestrus prefer to mate with big bulls in musth. Females are only in oestrus for approximately three to six days.

* The female is 10-15 years old when she is ready to breed. Mating is often preceded by affectionate play where the male and the female caress each other and entwine their trunks. Affectionate play may also involve a chase.
* An elephant's pregnancy can last up to a staggering 22 months. The elephant's average litter contains just one young.
* At birth, a calf can weigh as much as 265lb (120.20kg) and stand nearly 3ft (0.91m) high.
* One of the females in the group (usually an older, more experienced female) may act as a midwife and assist in the birth of the calf. She may, for example, help by removing the foetal sac of the newborn calf while the new mother recuperates.
* Baby calves can usually stand within half an hour of birth.
* The baby calf uses its mouth to suckle from the nipple of one of its mother's two mammary glands, which are situated between her front legs. Baby elephants have to learn how to feed and drink using their trunks. They do this by watching their mother and the other elephants in the group.
* For several months after birth, the baby calf will eat its mother's dung. Eating its mother's dung helps to establish essential micro-organisms in its gut, which it needs in order to digest its food.
* Female elephants (or cows) may produce a calf every three to four years. There may, however, be longer gaps between births.
* Elephants can swim, and if they have to cross deep rivers then they usually use their trunks as snorkels.

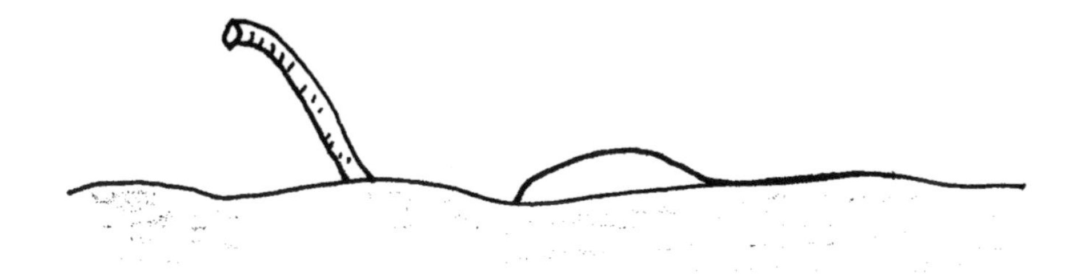

* The young females in the group will often act as babysitters for the new calf, which gives them valuable practice for when they have calves of their own.
* The elephant calf's main predators include crocodiles and lions.
* When an elephant loses a member of its herd, the screams of anguish are heartbreaking. Elephants grieve enormously over the death of loved-ones. Elephant mothers share extremely close bonds with their calves.

- ✶ Elephants can live 80 years or more in captivity. In the wild, the elephant's average lifespan is around 60 years.
- ✶ An elephant's heels are actually resting on huge pads of fatty and elastic connective tissue. This means that the elephant actually walks on its toes. An elephant's broad feet are designed so well that they spread the weight of the animal very efficiently – so efficiently, in fact, that it's possible for a 7 ton (7.11 tonne) elephant to barely leave any tracks on the ground.
- ✶ Elephants may sleep standing or lying on one side. The elephant sleeps, on average, a little more than two hours a night. The elephant cannot sleep for long periods on its side because the weight of its body could damage its internal organs. Older elephants tend to sleep standing up because of the difficulty they have getting up again when they have been lying down.
- ✶ Elephants dislike chilli. Farmers in parts of Africa burn chilli mixed with elephants' faeces to deter elephants from eating their crops.
- ✶ The elephant is an extremely intelligent animal. Its brain is four times larger than the human brain

✶ Elephants are extremely loving and affectionate animals and often use their trunks to caress one another.

✶ Elephants may 'trumpet' loudly through their trunks when they are about to attack, to scare off intruders, when calling to the rest of the group for help, as a warning call, when at play, or when excited or startled.

✶ Elephants emit sounds that are inaudible to the human ear. They use these infrasonic sounds to communicate with one another. For example, they use these sounds to let potential mates know that they are ready to breed, to warn other elephants of danger or to locate the group. Elephants make low frequency calls to communicate over long distances. It is believed that these inaudible sounds can be heard by other elephants at least 5 miles (8km) away – and possibly considerably further. As well as travelling through the air, these rumbles pass through the ground as seismic waves. To pick up the seismic waves, elephants will keep very still and learn forward, putting their weight on their front legs. All the elephants in a herd do this at the same time. Elephants' feet are so sensitive to subtle vibrations that they can distinguish the calls made by friends from those made by strangers even when the other elephants are several miles away.

✶ The adult elephant's audible vocal repertoire includes: rumbling, trumpeting, growling and roaring.

✶ The elephant has large ears to help cool down its body when it feels overheated. The temperature of the blood decreases as it passes through the blood vessels in the ears. Elephants also use their ears (which may be 6ft (1.83m) long) like parabolas to catch sounds. (Though, as already pointed out, elephants don't just rely on their ears as listening aids. They also use their feet as listening devices.) The elephant also cools itself down by spraying water over its body with its trunk. During times of extreme drought, elephants have been known to put their trunks down their throats to get to their pharyngeal pouch (which can hold about 0.88 gallons (4 litres) of water to be used in emergencies) to suck out water so that they can spray their bodies with it to keep cool. Elephants also wallow themselves in mud to keep cool. The mud also helps to protect their skin from the sun's rays. For extra protection, especially against biting insects, elephants may then spray their mud-coated bodies with dust.

✶ Elephants use their acute sense of smell to detect any nearby threats by raising their trunks into the breeze.

✶ When an elephant makes a full-scale charge at its enemy (which doesn't happen very often as elephants prefer to scare off their enemies by using various threats of display such as head-shaking), it usually stretches out its enormous ears in an attempt to make its already large frame appear even larger. (In the same way that a cat's hairs stand on end when it is facing a potential enemy.) The spreading of the ears is usually followed by ear flapping, the raising of the trunk and loud trumpeting whilst charging full speed at its enemy. The flapping action of the ears helps to cool the elephant down because stressful situations tend to make the animal feel uncomfortably hot.

* When charging, elephants are reputed to reach speeds of up to 25mph (40.23km/h).
* The minimum amount of fluid elephants need to drink is approximately 17.6 gallons (80 litres) a day. To drink, elephants draw the water up through their trunks and, with the aid of gravity, pour the water into their mouths.
* Elephants have an unusual interest in elephant carcasses and bones. They are especially fascinated by the skulls of dead elephants. They will spend many hours examining and sniffing them. Elephants are not interested in the carcasses of other animals.
* Elephants often greet one another with their trunks. And, if for some reason they have been separated and are then reunited, they will show that they are overjoyed at seeing one another again. When the group is reunited, there is much rumbling and excited trumpeting.
* Elephants are not afraid of mice (that is a myth) but they are afraid of honeybees.
* Elephants have long memories.
* Herds of elephants are safer when there is an older elephant in a herd because of the older elephant's knowledge and memories.
* Trained elephants can understand 115 different vocal commands.
* The elephant is considered to be an endangered species. Demand for ivory has caused a decline in numbers over the last 150 years. During the 1980s, thousands of elephants were killed every year in order to supply the world ivory trade. Competition between humans for land space has also put these magnificent creatures in danger.

'When the kunkis (tame elephants) are sick, the mahouts take them to the forest where the elephants pick the herbs or plants they need. Somehow they're able to prescribe their own medicine.'
DINESH CHOUDHURY

ANIMALS HAVE POWERFUL IMAGINATIONS

There is plenty of evidence to show that many creatures other than human beings have powerful imaginations.

1. Cats, dogs and horses and many other creatures dream.
2. Parrots talk in their sleep.
3. Horses frequently stampede because they are frightened by objects (such as large rocks or posts) which are no threat to them. This must show a sense of imagination because the horse, like a child, has created a terror out of nothing.
4. Spiders will hold down the edges of their webs with stones to steady them during gales which have not yet started. Does this show an ability to predict the weather or imagination?
5. We may underestimate animals more often than we think.

How Animals Protect Themselves From Insects

Insect bites aren't just irritating; they can spread disease and kill. Biting insects spread malaria, bubonic plague, sleeping sickness, dengue, filariasis, yellow fever and many more diseases. Just six blood-sucking ticks can kill a gazelle. Malaria, estimated to have killed half the people who have ever lived, is spread by mosquitoes. A horse can lose up to a pint (0.57 litres) of blood a day to blood sucking flies.

Recognising this danger, animals do many things to protect themselves:

- North American caribou avoid insects by huddling together on small patches of ice.
- Wild horses move to windy hills where the grazing is poor because flies find it difficult to land on them in those conditions.
- Elephants, rhinoceroses and buffalo are all susceptible to blood suckers (despite their thick hides), so they roll in thick mud for protection. Some elephants carry palm leaves in their trunks to flick away flies. Elephants in Nepal have been seen to strip off excess leaves and twigs in order to make a fly swatter with the right length and flexibility.
- Tigers lie in water with just their heads above the surface.
- Chimpanzees use leafy twigs to swat flies.
- A horse being bothered by flies will gallop around, roll in the mud, shake its head and flick its tail to get rid of flies.
- Animals hang around forest fires because there are no flies.
- Camels in the desert (where there are no trees or fence posts for rubbing against) will rub against one another.
- Elephants can twitch their skin so powerfully that insects are trapped and killed in their skin folds.
- Herons peck at mosquitoes at the rate of 3,000 an hour.
- Primates groom one another, picking out parasites and sometimes eating the insects they've found.
- The female wood mouse will sometimes only allow a male to have sex with her after he has groomed her and got rid of her ticks.
- Mated penguins groom one another and have fewer ticks than solitary birds.
- When impalas groom one another for ticks they take turns: 'You remove my ticks, I'll remove yours.'
- Some animals help creatures of another species. So, for example, black caracara birds clean the ticks from bare-skinned tapirs.

Foxes (Red)

- Just like wolves and dogs, foxes belong to the family, Canidae. The red fox is the most widespread of fox species.
- There are two species of red fox: 'Vulpes vulpes' (which is found in northern Africa, temperate Asia and throughout Europe) and Vulpes fulva (which is found in North America). The red fox can also be found in Australia where it was originally introduced to be hunted for sport. (Foxes are often bred for hunting in countries where fox hunting is legal – rather destroying the argument that foxes are hunted because they are a threat to farm livestock and, therefore, need to be exterminated.)
- The male fox is called a dog. The female fox is called a vixen. The baby fox is called a cub.
- A group of foxes is known as a skulk.
- The red fox is the largest of the fox species. The fennec fox (which can be found throughout the Sahara) is the smallest.
- The red fox can grow to 35in (88.9cm) in length (not including its tail). On average, the dog-fox weighs 15lb (6.8kg) and the vixen weighs 12lb (5.44kg).
- The red fox's coat, which it sheds annually, is usually red-brown in colour. The fox has a white or pale underside, a pointed muzzle and a large, bushy tail which may be white at the tip. Its tail can grow to nearly 20in (50.8cm) in length. The fox's triangular shaped ears and the lower part of its limbs are usually black.
- Red foxes have very short lifespans in the wild, very few live to see their fourth birthday. However, in captivity it is not unheard of for foxes to live up to 13 years.
- In some areas foxes are monogamous; in others they may live in small hierarchical family groups which may comprise a dominant adult female, a dominant adult male, their offspring that year and maybe several subordinate females from previous litters. These subordinate vixens may help with the rearing of cubs.
- Subordinate foxes usually greet dominant foxes in the group by submissively crouching low while wagging their tails and holding back their ears.
- It is usually the dominant female of the group that gets to breed, but the subordinate vixens of the group may help to rear the cubs. The female usually uses a den during breeding times. Dens may be under tree roots or in a rock crevice. However, vixens tend to favour ready-made dens such as badger setts or rabbit burrows.
- The collective name for a fox's den is an earth.
- Foxes' vocalisations include: barks, yaps, deep howls, whimpers and screams. Foxes are believed to have around 28 different calls of communication.
- Another form of communication that foxes use is scent, often leaving their droppings in conspicuous places.

- Although foxes are classified as carnivores, they do, in fact, have an omnivorous diet: feeding on food of both plant and animal origin.
- Foxes feed on small mammals, carrion, birds, birds' eggs, frogs, earthworms, snails, grasshoppers, beetles, fruit and grass. And, occasionally, food scavenged from dustbins. Foxes living along coastal areas tend to feed on crabs and fish. When other foods are scarce, the common earthworm makes up over 60 per cent of the fox's diet.
- Foxes have an acute sense of hearing. It is believed that foxes are able to hear the squeak of a mouse from as far as 300ft (91.44m) away.
- When catching prey, the fox may use its 'characteristic leap' where it leaps about 3ft (0.91m) into the air above its prey and then dives front paws first, pinning down its prey.
- Most foxes hunt alone.
- In order to protect itself from going hungry during times of food scarcity, or to protect its food from other rivals, the fox hoards surplus food by burying it. The fox will then rely on its excellent memory at a later date to unearth its caches. Foxes have been unfairly accused of being sadists who kill for pleasure by killing more chickens than they can eat when they've stumbled upon a chicken coop. Dead chickens are left behind in a coop only because the fox has been disturbed.
- During the mating season, the vixen will emit what has been described as 'eerie screams' to attract a potential mate. Mating usually takes place around middle to late winter. And cubs are often born around springtime (pregnancy lasts for approximately 53 days). A typical litter contains four to eight fox cubs. However, foxes can give birth to as many as 12 cubs in one litter. Foxes breed once a year.
- Fox cubs are born in the den with their eyes closed, which they open when they are about 10-14 days old. Newborn fox cubs weigh around 4oz (113g), and their coats are dark brown in colour.
- Fox cubs remain in the den for approximately four weeks with their mother staying close beside them for much of the time, while the dog-fox plays a large part in supplying the food.
- Both the female and the male fox are loving and loyal to their cubs. If the mother should die for any reason, the male fox will do its best to bring up its cubs, provided, of course, that the cubs are no longer wholly dependent on their mother's milk.
- The fox cubs are fully weaned at around eight to ten weeks.
- Some of the predators which threaten young foxes include: dogs, badgers, eagles and other foxes.
- Before the ages of three to four months, fox cubs will often have vicious fights with one another to establish their position of dominance in the group.
- Foxes have a tendency to leave their cubs for long periods. So people out walking who come across what appear to be abandoned fox cubs, should leave them alone. Fox cubs who are cared for by humans do not usually flourish. (And if

the mother really has died then the father or other family members will look after the orphaned cubs.)

- Foxes do not have to be killed in order to regulate their population. If too many fox cubs are born, some will die because of the competition for food.
- Cars and lorries are the biggest killers of foxes. For example, around 20,000 foxes a year are killed on Britain's roads.
- Foxes do not hibernate, which means that they can be seen all year round.
- Foxes are predominantly nocturnal animals but they have frequently been sighted during the daytime, especially in areas where they do not feel persecuted.
- Foxes are territorial and will often mark the boundaries of their territory with their scent. A fox's territory may be as large as 8 sq. miles (20.7 sq. km).
- Foxes very rarely attack or kill cats.
- Contrary to popular belief, foxes kill very few lambs. So few, in fact, that the British Ministry of Agriculture does not list the fox as a significant cause of yearly lamb mortality.
- Humans who enjoy hunting sometimes claim that the fact that an injured fox will continue to run (even though it may, for example, have a broken leg) proves that foxes enjoy being hunted. This, of course, is nonsense. The fox continues to run in order to stay alive. There are numerous recorded accounts of human beings continuing to run away from danger, despite having broken legs, because not running away would expose them to real danger.

Amazing Animal Stories (Part 2)

- Approximately 80 whales had beached themselves on New Zealand's Tokerau Beach one September day in 1983. Locals tried to keep the whales alive by splashing water over them to help keep their skins moist. When the tide finally came in, the whales started to float in the right direction but soon became disorientated and beached themselves again. There seemed to be no hope for the whales, until a school of dolphins came to their rescue. The dolphins successfully led the whales into the safety of the sea.
- In the 1980s, 81-year-old Norman Stephenson from Bradford left his home to go for a walk along the steep Pennine hillside. Around the time of Mr Stephenson's departure, a Samoyed bitch called Laska – for some unknown reason – also made her way to the Pennine hillside after escaping from her owners' house when workmen had left the front door open. Very soon, a storm started to build up and it began to rain heavily. Mr Stephenson slipped on the wet earth and fell down into a ditch. Shortly after Mr Stephenson's accident, Laska found him and used her body to protect the man from the foul weather. Laska did this for an amazing 16 hours. It was hikers who stumbled across the

pair the next day and raised the alarm. Thanks to Laska, Mr Stephenson lived to tell the incredible tale. And as for Laska, she was just happy to be reunited with her distraught but very relieved owners.

- Nipper, the five-year-old collie, bravely rescued his animal friends when fire broke out at his owners' farm in Sussex. Nipper boldly made his way back and forth through the smoke to shepherd his furry friends who consisted of lambs and calves – to safety. As a consequence of Nipper's valour, he received blisters to his paws and singed fur.
- When brother and sister, Sean and Erin Callahan, were out playing near their home in Texas with their four-year-old poodle, Leo, they came across a rattlesnake. The rattlesnake was about to attack when Leo the poodle quickly arranged his position so that he stood between Sean and the snake. As a result of Leo's heroism, the children managed to escape. Amazingly, Leo survived despite being bitten six times on the head by the rattlesnake.
- A Labrador called Bruce saved a four-year-old Welsh boy from sinking into the mud and drowning. When the four-year-old boy sank above his waist into the riverside mud, Bruce used his quick wit by lying on his side and clasping the boy's shoulder between his teeth to prevent him from sinking any further into the mud. Thankfully, the boy's mother spotted their dilemma and called for help.
- While out bathing in Lake Sommersville in Texas, Pricilla the pig spotted a young boy in trouble. Pricilla quickly swam towards the boy and used her snout to try to keep his head above the water. As soon as the boy clutched onto her collar, Priscilla brought the boy safely to shore.
- Ray and his fiancée were out on a nature trail walk with their dog, Woodie, when Ray decided to climb up a nearby cliff to take some photographs of the scenery. When Ray was out of view, Woodie kept pulling frantically on his lead, which was most unusual for him. Once Woodie managed to break free, he ran up the cliff and disappeared from sight too. Ray's fiancée followed their trail to find out where the pair had gone. Once she had reached the top of the cliff, to her horror, she saw her fiancé lying unconscious in a stream at the bottom of the cliff with Woodie by his side. Woodie had obviously jumped off the cliff to save his owner as he was now nudging Ray's head to try to keep it above the water to prevent him from drowning. Despite their injuries, both Ray and Woodie survived.
- Carletta the cow saved her owner Bruno Cipriano from being gored to death by a boar at his farm in Tuscany. Carletta charged at the boar and used her horns to head-butt it until the boar ran away.
- Emma the Cow was so distraught that her calf had been taken away from her and sent to the abattoir that she made it her mission to find her baby. Just before milking time, Emma escaped from the field where she was kept (by forcing her way through the gate) and ran the 4¼ mile (6.84km) trek to find her calf. Amazingly, Emma managed to track down the abattoir where her calf was about

to be slaughtered, and made such a fuss when she got there that even the workers admitted to being afraid. Suddenly, one of the calves in line to be slaughtered had obviously recognised its mother's cries and ran frantically towards her. Emma was so happy to be reunited with her calf that she couldn't stop licking and nuzzling her baby with such adoring affection. Touched by what had happened, the abattoir workers decided to spare the calf from such a dreadful end. When Emma's owner was contacted and told about the incident, he took pity on the mother and calf and decided to keep them both. Sadly, the little calf was so traumatised by its experiences at the abattoir that its body went into shock and it died shortly afterwards.

- When Elisabeth Bienz moved home, she left her cat Moudi behind with her parents. Moudi the cat disappeared soon after Elisabeth left home. However, every time Elisabeth visited her parents' home, Moudi would suddenly appear from nowhere – looking well-fed and well-looked after. Elisabeth's parents had no idea where Moudi disappeared to the rest of the time, or how she knew that Elisabeth was at home.
- Margaret and Richard Edwards became owners of a sick lamb which some farming friends had given to them. They bottle-fed and nursed the sick lamb to health, and every night the little lamb used to sit indoors with Margaret. For some reason, the lamb had formed a particular attachment to Richard. The attachment was so strong that the little lamb used to know when his owner was going to turn up. He would sit by the front door ten minutes beforehand waiting with anticipation for Richard to arrive. Even if Richard arrived home unexpectedly or in a different car, the lamb would still know when his owner was about to arrive.
- In 1988, Molly Parfett's husband died in hospital after suffering from a massive stroke. Shortly after the funeral, she noticed that their dog, Joe, would disappear for hours at a time. Where he disappeared to was a complete mystery to Molly. However, the mystery of Joe's disappearance was soon solved when it transpired that Joe was found sitting by his master's grave. Molly could not understand how Joe knew about her husband's death and more astonishingly, how he knew where Molly's husband was buried.
- There is a monument near Derwent Dam in Derbyshire with the following inscription: 'In Commemoration of the devotion of Tip the sheepdog who stayed by the body of her dead master, Mr Joseph Tagg, on the Howden Moor for fifteen weeks from 12th December 1953 to 27th March 1954.'
- When Marian went away to college, she had to leave her cat Carlo, whom she had lived with for seven years, behind with her family. It wasn't very often that Marian used to ring home but when she did, Carlo would run excitedly to the phone before Marian's mum even had time to pick up the receiver. Carlo wouldn't run to the telephone when anybody else called, only when Marian called.
- Farmer Alfred Gruenemeyer, who lived near Coburg in central Germany, treated

his animals more like pets than livestock. And so when, at the age of 67, Mr Gruenemeyer died – his animals were devastated. A young bull called Barnaby was so distressed that he left his field, walked for a mile, leapt the cemetery wall, found the farmer's grave and started a vigil which lasted for several days. Attempts to chase the young bull away failed when they found out just how unnerving an angry bull can be. It wasn't until several days later that the bull calmed down enough to be led back to his pasture. Mr Gruenemeyer was said by neighbours to have allowed his animals to roam in and out of his house. 'He talked to them like Dr Dolittle,' said one. `Mind you, his house smelled a bit.'

- ✶ Henry Walker lost hope of ever finding his pet falcon again after the bird flew away. However, he decided to telephone the police in the vague hope that his falcon might be found. Bizarrely, Henry Walker dialled the wrong number and ended up speaking to a family living nearby who told him that his pet falcon was perched upon their garden fence. Henry Walker rushed round to where the family lived and managed to bring his pet falcon safely home.
- ✶ For some unknown reason, Spot the crossbred sheepdog decided to hop onto a coach in Cardiff. Once he had made himself seated, he refused to budge. When the London-bound National Express coach arrived at the Victoria Coach Station in London, Spot decided to get off. Half an hour later, just as the coach was about to leave the station to return to Cardiff, Spot hopped back on and occupied the same seat. Altogether, Spot's whole journey covered 310 miles (498.89km).

GIRAFFES

- ♦ The giraffe and the okapi are the only two species that make up the family Giraffidae.
- ♦ Giraffes are found in open woodland and dry savanna throughout much of Africa south of the Sahara Desert.
- ♦ Giraffes are the tallest of all mammals. Male giraffes can grow to 18ft or more (5.49m). Female giraffes are slightly smaller, growing to approximately 16ft (4.88m) in height. The giraffe's height allows it to keep an eye open for predators and to eat leaves from the highest branches of the acacia trees.
- ♦ The giraffe has an exceptionally long neck; an intricate pattern of variably sized brownish coloured patches on its coat; a mane; a downward sloping back; long legs; a long, tufted tail and two to five (depending on species) bony, skin-covered horns on its head. The giraffe's two main horns, which are crowned with tufts of hair, are situated on its head above its large eyes. Any additional horns the giraffe may have are simply bony growths.
- ♦ Surprisingly, giraffes have just seven vertebrae in their necks – the same number as humans. The giraffe's vertebrae are very elongated, and it is this which give it an exceptionally long neck.

- There are generally believed to be nine subspecies of giraffe. Of all the subspecies, the reticulated giraffe has the most distinctive markings on its body – its chestnut-coloured patches are separated by a latticework of thin white lines.
- The markings on a giraffe are just like fingerprints: each giraffe has its own unique markings.
- The female giraffe is called a cow. The male giraffe is called a bull. The baby giraffe is called a calf. The giraffe is a ruminant animal which means that it 'chews the cud' (partly digested food is returned from the stomach for further chewing).
- The giraffe's closest relative is the okapi. The okapi is around 7ft (2.13m) tall (or less), has a white face, a purple-brown coat and zebra-like stripes on its rump and upper limbs. The okapi was officially discovered in 1901 and is reputed to be one of the world's shyest animals.
- The giraffe's vocal cords are thought to be immature and ineffective but it is a myth that giraffes are mute. The giraffe's occasional (and they are occasional) vocalisations include: hisses, snorts, whistles and grunts. Giraffe calves will make bleating noises when they are in distress.
- The giraffe's extraordinarily dextrous tongue is blue-black in colour and is around 18in (45.72cm) long. The giraffe sometimes uses its tongue to clean out its ears.
- The giraffe needs to splay its front legs widely (or splay its legs slightly while bending its knees) in order to bow down to drink. Bending down to drink water can make the giraffe vulnerable to attacks from crocodiles or other predators. Very wisely, one or two other giraffes may act as sentries while the others are drinking. Fortunately, the giraffe doesn't have to drink often because 70 per cent of its fluid intake comes from its diet. This means that giraffes can, if necessary, go for long periods without drinking water.
- In order to pump blood up its long neck, the giraffe has very high blood pressure (approximately twice that found in the cow, for example). A unique circulatory system means that the blood pressure in the brain is maintained at a much lower level than in the rest of the body. A unique pressure regulating mechanism involving a network of capillaries means that the blood flow to its brain is carefully regulated to ensure that the giraffe's blood pressure doesn't rise too high when it bends down to drink. Without this adaptation the giraffe would suffer from burst blood vessels in its brain every time it bent its neck to drink.
- Giraffes are herbivores and live primarily on acacia leaves. Acacia trees have evolved to defend themselves against giraffes. The trees have developed sharp thorns to discourage browsing, and the trees release a chemical that makes the leaves toxic and taste rather unpleasant. Giraffes are aware of this and are able to sense which leaves are the least toxic to eat.
- Giraffes may spend up to 20 hours a day feeding.
- Giraffes are shy, peaceful animals.

Giraffe calves usually attend 'nursery group' where mothers will leave their calves in the care of several adults.

- Giraffes look very graceful when they walk. This is because both left legs, then both right legs, move forward together. This rolling gait is called 'pacing'. Apart from giraffes, only camels and cats walk this way.
- When escaping from predators, giraffes can gallop at speeds of 30mph (48.28 km/h) or more.
- It is the larger, dominant males (bulls) that get to mate the females.
- Before mating, a bull giraffe will taste the urine of a cow giraffe to check that she is at her most fertile. The bull makes the cow urinate by hitting his head against her rear.
- A giraffe's pregnancy lasts approximately 15 months.
- Females have a special calving area, somewhere quiet, when giving birth. They will use their calving area every time they calf.
- A giraffe's litter usually contains one calf: twins are rare.
- In its lifetime, the female giraffe can produce up to ten young.
- Giraffes give birth standing up. And while the calf is being born, the mother is keeping a constant lookout for any nearby predators.
- The baby calf can be over 6ft (1.83m) tall when it is born.
- Calves are usually up and about within an hour of birth. It is important that the calf is able to get onto its feet as soon as possible because of possible attacks from predators.
- Sadly, 50 per cent of calves don't reach six-months-old as most are killed by predators.
- The giraffe's main predator is the lion. Other predators include: leopards, hyenas and African wild dogs. Baby calves are especially vulnerable to predators but adult giraffes can usually fend them off and are capable of killing a lion with just one kick from their cloven hooves.
- If a baby giraffe is threatened, the mother will often stand over the calf to protect it and use her feet as weapons.
- By the time the calf is a year old, it will have just about doubled its height.
- Giraffes tend to live in loose herds where they come and go of their own free will. Giraffe herds usually consist of females and youngsters. Bulls tend to live alone, although there are a few bachelor herds.
- Sub-adult males often engage in friendly 'necking' contests to establish dominance. During these contests they intertwine their necks, wrestle and swing their heads at each other until one of them submits. Not only do these sparring contests help to establish hierarchy within the group but it also helps the young males to hone their fighting skills for when they are older.
- Very occasionally, bulls will fight one another aggressively for a chance to mate with females in oestrus. Mature bulls are capable of delivering such heavy blows with their heads that one blow can knock their opponent to the ground. It is often the more mature, dominant male who has mating rights.

- Male giraffes' skulls tend to become stronger and heavier through bone deposition as they get older. As a result, older bulls are able to fight off younger rival males by delivering them heavier blows.
- In the wild, giraffes can live 20 years or more.
- Giraffes survive on very little sleep. In the wild they may have no more than 20-30 minutes of deep sleep a day. Sleep may be taken in very short spells. The risk of predators makes it impossible for giraffes to sleep for long. Giraffes can have 'half-sleep', either standing up or lying down with their necks erect. Giraffes usually have their deep sleep at night. When going to sleep, they usually lie down and curl their necks back to rest their heads on their rumps.

Strange But True (Part 3)

- A pregnant kangaroo and wallaby can keep their embryo in suspended animation if conditions aren't right – e.g. a shortage of food or bad weather or a lot of sickness about. The mother automatically suspends the embryo's development.
- A blue whale who is nursing, produces up to 94 gallons (428 litres) of milk a day. Her baby feeds up to 50 times a day and grows 250lb (113.39kg) a day.
- Ostriches urinate on their legs to keep cool when the weather is hot.
- The female blanket octopus is 40,000 times heavier than the male. The male is just as big as the pupil in the female's eye.
- Sheep can remember the faces of 50 sheep and ten humans for up to two years.
- Cats have better memories than dogs.
- Dolphins can swim over 20mph (32.18km/h) by leaping out of the water to conserve energy. (It's easier to fly through the air than to swim through the water)
- The leatherback turtle can dive as deep as 3,281ft (1000m).
- A gecko can go up a window at 3.5ft (1.07m) per second. It can hang from a wall by one toe.
- Pregnant elephants in East Africa eat a small tree called a boraginaceae. They will walk miles to find such a tree.
- Sloths move so slowly that fungus grows on their feet.
- An ant can lift over 50 times its own weight.
- The housefly tastes things with its feet – which are ten million times more sensitive than the human tongue.
- Ducks on the outer edge of a sleeping group sleep with one eye open and half their brain asleep.

- There is a breed of spider mite which exists entirely of females. There are no males.
- Female spotted hyenas are bigger than the males and control them completely. It is the females who decide who mates with whom.
- Hummingbirds can fly backwards.
- The male species of Darwin's frog swallows the eggs the female has laid. The eggs grow in his throat before hopping out of his mouth when fully formed.
- The female pigeon can't lay eggs if on her own. There must be other pigeons around for her ovaries to function. If there aren't any others around then the sight of her own reflection will do.
- A female baboon's bottom gets bigger the more babies she has.
- People who love penguins are called sphenisciphiles.

- Herring communicate by breaking wind. They fart-chat to tell one another where they are.
- Lesbian relationships have been observed among such domestic animals as horses, cows, rabbits, hamsters, mice, guinea pigs, sheep, pigs and goats, and among such wild animals as lions, monkeys and porcupines.
- The giant African snail can grow to 1ft (0.3m) long.
- Horns and antlers are quite different. Horns grow from the skull and are permanent. Antlers grow from a 'bud' and are shed every spring after the breeding season has passed and fighting for females is no longer necessary.

- ☞ Myxomatosis, which is spread by biting insects such as fleas and mosquitoes, first hit the rabbit population in the 1950s and killed more than 100 million rabbits.
- ☞ Henry I of Saxony brought in a law which fined people sixty bushels of corn for murdering a cat.
- ☞ Cockroaches are resistant to radiation.
- ☞ An American farmer had all his cows fitted with specially designed bras. He believed that the support given by the bras to the udders dramatically increased the cows' milk production.
- ☞ The crocodile may be the world's largest reptile, but its brain is just slightly larger than a man's thumb.
- ☞ The saying: 'It is easier for a camel to pass through the eye of a needle than for a rich man to enter heaven', is actually a mistranslation from the Greek. The scribe responsible confused the word 'kamelos' meaning camel with the word 'kamilos' meaning rope. So the phrase should read: 'It is easier for a rope to pass through the eye of a needle than for a rich man to enter heaven', which, though more prosaic, has the benefit of being understandable.
- ☞ Mosquitoes prefer biting blondes to brunettes.
- ☞ Cats sometimes give their offspring live prey to play with in order to help develop their hunting skills.
- ☞ There is no such thing as a panther. The animals most people regard as panthers are either leopards (in Africa or Asia) or jaguars (in South America) or pumas (in North America). (The puma is also known as a cougar or a mountain lion.) The black panther is a puma, leopard or a jaguar that exhibits an excessive amount of dark pigment (melanin) in its skin and fur.
- ☞ Mongooses were brought over to Hawaii to help kill the rats. But things didn't quite work out, as mongooses do their hunting during the daytime and rats usually go out during the night-time.
- ☞ An ostrich's egg is so strong that a human can stand on one without breaking it. (Although, we certainly don't recommend that you try this).
- ☞ There is a lizard that is officially known as the 'Jesus Christ Lizard' because of its extraordinary ability to walk on water.
- ☞ Moose possess really poor eyesight and have been known to mate with cars as a result.
- ☞ Rats have been seen swimming three miles (4.8km) from land. (Though there is no evidence that they got back safely.)
- ☞ Vultures play a vital role in cleaning up carcasses which would otherwise rot and spread disease.

Animals Commonly Used By Vivisectors

1. Kittens
2. Cats
3. Puppies
4. Dogs
5. Guinea pigs
6. Chimpanzees
7. Monkeys
8. Baboons
9. Rabbits
10. Hamsters

Pets Most Commonly Stolen By Or On Behalf Of Vivisectors

1. Dogs
2. Cats
3. Kittens
4. Puppies
5. Rabbits

'Whosoever tortures animals has no soul, and the good spirit of the God is not in him. Even should he look deep inside himself, one can never trust him.'
JOHANN WOLFGANG VON GOETHE (1749-1832)

Ten Famous People Who Were Vehemently Opposed To Experiments On Animals

1. Henry David Thoreau
2. Abraham Lincoln
3. Albert Schweitzer
4. Albert Einstein
5. Charles Darwin
6. C. S. Lewis
7. Robert Browning
8. Mark Twain
9. George Bernard Shaw
10. Mahatma Gandhi

GOATS (DOMESTIC)

- Goats belong to the family Bovidae (the same family as cows and sheep), and were first domesticated around 10,000 years ago. The goat was one of the first animals to be domesticated by humans.
- Domestic goats are believed to be descended from the pasang, which is thought to be native to Asia.
- Goats can be found on every continent throughout the world except Antarctica.
- Feral goats are descended from domestic goats who escaped into the wild. The main anatomical difference between feral and domestic goats is that feral goats are shorter and stockier in build than their domestic cousins. If left wild, domestic goats rapidly become feral.
- There are thought to be over 200 identifiable breeds of goat in the world.
- The female goat is referred to as a nanny or a doe. The male goat is referred to as a buck or a billy. The castrated male goat is called a wether. The baby goat is called a kid.
- On average, an adult domestic goat weighs 99lb (44.9kg) and is 2ft 1in (0.64m) tall. Goats have beards, cloven feet (each foot is divided into two digits), a short tail and hollow horns. Females as well as males grow beards, although not all females grow beards. Many goats are born with horns but may have their horns removed (called disbudding) shortly after birth. Some species of goat are purposely bred not to have horns. Male goats have larger horns than female goats.
- Goats come in a wide variety of colours: white, black, brown, pied, etc. The valais blackneck goat, for example, has an unusual colouration in which the front half (shoulders, head, neck, chest and front legs) of the goat's coat is dark in colour and the other half is white in colour.
- Goats are hardy animals, and are adaptable to almost any habitat. Goats can thrive on areas of rough land where sheep and cattle are unable to survive.
- Goats are herbivores, feeding on vegetation.
- Goats are ruminants, which means that they 'chew the cud' (regurgitating their food and chewing it again).
- The goat's natural diet includes: grass, brambles, shrubs, bark and foliage from certain types of trees.
- Goats are browsers rather than grazers (which means that they don't live primarily on grass but feed on leaves, twigs, etc.)
- Contrary to their reputation, goats are fastidious eaters. When domesticated, they prefer to eat food from clean dishes and will often refuse to eat food that is of poor quality or is spoiled. The misconception that goats will eat anything no doubt originates from the fact that goats have a tendency to chew on most things without actually swallowing them. Goats are also fastidious about what

they drink and, therefore, usually prefer fresh, clean water. It is not unknown for goats to drink up to 4 gallons (18.18 litres) of water a day.

- Yew, foxglove and rhododendron are just a few of the plants that are poisonous to goats. Yew and foxglove are especially poisonous to goats if ingested – and can kill them.
- Goats do not have any top front teeth.
- A group of goats is called a herd or a trip.
- Goats are very social, intelligent, active and inquisitive animals.
- In Britain, about 75 per cent of goats' milk is used to produce cheese.
- The human stomach digests goats' milk far easier than it digests cows' milk. Added to this, goats' milk contains more proteins and minerals than cows' milk, and it contains less fat.
- The Saanen goat is considered to be one of the most popular species of dairy goat. This is due to its ability to produce large quantities of milk, yielding up to 1,500 litres (or more) of milk in one year.
- Amazingly, it has been known for the occasional healthy, fertile male goat to produce milk. If milked, the goat will even develop an udder.
- A male goat (buck or billy) is around four-months-old when he begins to reach sexual maturity.
- When a female goat has come into season (oestrus), she will stand by a receptive male goat and wag her tail in a sideways motion.
- A goat's pregnancy lasts for about five months.
- A goat's average litter is either two or three kids.
- The female goat has one udder with two teats, which means that only two kids can suckle at any one time. Unfortunately, if more than two kids are born then the other offspring will have to wait its turn to feed.
- It is believed that goats were the first to discover coffee beans in Ethiopia in 850 AD. A goat herder called Kaldi noticed that his goats used to become unusually active whenever they ate the red berries from the shrub coffea. So the goat herder picked a handful of berries and gave them to the local monks after explaining what had happened to his goats. The monks decided to test the berries for themselves by putting the berries in some boiling water and then drinking the brew. After drinking the brew, the monks noticed that they felt more alert. So they decided to carry on using the brew themselves and supply it to the local villagers to keep them awake for Midnight Mass.
- Goats are herd animals and, in the wild, tend to live in hierarchical herds consisting of anything from 5 to 20 individuals.
- The average lifespan of a goat is approximately 15 years.
- Most goats are usually kept for their milk production, but some breeds such as the angora and the cashmere are kept for their fleeces.

- Female goats live longer than male goats. And, if the female goat is allowed to retire early from breeding, then she is likely to live an additional five years or more.
- Goats have 'rectangular' pupils.
- It is not advisable to keep horned goats with goats that are not horned. Horned goats have a tendency to be aggressive towards non-horned goats.
- Anglo-Nubian goats have large 'Roman' noses and big floppy ears.
- Not all goats have a pungent odour. Male goats who have not been castrated have a tendency to be smelly, especially during the mating (or rutting) season. The unpleasant smell of the fertile male goat is exacerbated by the fact that he has an urge to urinate on himself. The fertile buck's pungent odour excites female goats.
- It is the angora goat that produces mohair (angora wool comes from angora rabbits). The angora's coat has fibres up to 7.9in (20cm) long. In addition to the manufacture of fluffy sweaters and many other products, mohair is used for the manufacture of judges' wigs.
- With the exception of the dog, the goat is the most widespread of all domesticated animals. There are an estimated three to four billion domesticated goats on the planet.
- It was probably goats which made the Sahara desert into a desert – by stripping all the vegetation. Land in the Middle East and Greece was impoverished by goats. It is no exaggeration to say that as a result of eating all the vegetation, goats have changed the climate of the Mediterranean and southern Europe and are a cause of permanent changes in our weather. The damage done by goats has also led to much fighting as men have struggled to protect their remaining areas of fertile land.

Gorillas

- Along with orang-utans and chimpanzees, gorillas are great apes belonging to the family, Hominidae. The gorilla is a native of equatorial Africa and can mainly be found in forests and swampy glades.
- There are two species of gorilla: the western gorilla (of which there are two subspecies: the western lowland gorilla and the cross river gorilla) and the eastern gorilla (of which there are three subspecies: the eastern lowland gorilla, the mountain gorilla and a third unnamed variety).
- The gorilla has a massive body covered in dark hair which turns grey when it is older; a large head (in adult males there is a tall, bony crest on top of the skull); small ears; large nostrils (nostrils differing in size between the species); prominent

brow ridges; long arms; large hands; large feet with an opposable big toe on each foot; short, stocky legs and a protruding abdomen.

- The gorilla is the largest of living primates. An adult gorilla can weigh as much as 600lb (272.15kg).
- The gorilla is the second closest relative to human beings in the animal kingdom. (The chimpanzee is the first.)
- Mature adult male gorillas (typically over 12 years of age) are often referred to as silverbacks because of the broad saddle-shaped area of conspicuous silver-white fur on their backs. Immature male gorillas that haven't yet developed silver backs are often referred to as 'blackbacks'. When standing on its hind legs, an adult silverback gorilla is over 6½ft (1.98m) tall. Male gorillas are almost twice as large as female gorillas.
- The gorilla usually walks on all fours – walking on the soles of its feet and using the backs of its knuckles to take the weight of its forequarters.
- When gorillas were first brought to European zoos, it was assumed from their size that meat must be an essential part of their diet. But they are vegetarian, eating a wide range of plants, seeds and fruits supplemented by the odd, more or less, accidental slug or caterpillar. The gorilla's diet includes: shoots, stems, leaves, roots, thistles, nettles, celery, fungi, soft bark, fruits and, very occasionally, grubs, ants, termites and insect larvae. Owing to their vast size and to the lack of protein in much of their diet, gorillas have to spend a great deal of their day eating. Gorillas will sometimes eat their own faeces because this enables them to get the best out of their low protein diet.
- Gorillas tend to feed in the morning with a break for a few hours around midday spent resting, and then feed again in the afternoon.

Mixed Parents

Names given to the young of mixed parentage animals:

Carideer	caribou and reindeer
Dzo	yak and domestic cow
Geep	goat and sheep
Hinny	stallion and she-ass
Liger	male lion and female tiger
Mule	male ass and mare (female horse)
Tigon	male tiger and female lion
Yakalo	yak and buffalo
Zebroid	zebra and horse
Zedonk	zebra and donkey
Zobo	zebu and yak
Zum	yak and cow

- Gorillas are fussy eaters, carefully selecting and preparing every mouthful of food before they eat.
- Gorillas use 'napkins' after eating messy fruits. They use giant leaves to wipe their faces and hands clean. They discard their 'napkins' after use.
- Gorillas tend to live in stable family groups. Western gorillas usually form small groups of five to ten members. Eastern gorillas tend to form larger groups of 15-20 – sometimes creating groups with more than 30 members. There is usually one mature silverback male – often the oldest and the strongest – acting as guardian and leader of the group (or harem), which usually consists of adult females and their young. Around the time of puberty, many young male gorillas will leave their family groups (of their own accord) and travel on their own, or with other males, eventually going on to form their own family groups or harems. A high percentage of female gorillas will also leave their natal group – usually at puberty – to join other nearby groups. Adult females in a harem or group are often unrelated.
- Gorillas are extremely intelligent animals and are capable of learning hundreds of words in sign language.
- The gorilla's vocal sounds include: snorts, coughs, grunts, hoots, hiccups and belches.
- The western lowland gorilla can be identified by the reddish tinged hairs on its scalp.
- Every gorilla has a unique pattern of skin folds above its nostrils.
- The traditional and iconic display of chest beating followed by growls and hoots, a rearing up on the hind legs and the ripping up and throwing of vegetation is used to intimidate any male rivals, to defend the group or to establish dominance within the group. The chest beating display is also used to attract females from other groups. Contrary to popular belief, the gorilla does not clench its fists to beat its chest – it cups its hands.
- When nervous, gorillas tend to yawn. The gorilla does this so that it can show off its sharp teeth to any aggressor as a warning.
- Just like some humans, gorillas have been seen with their tongues sticking out at the sides of their mouths when in deep concentration.
- Before going to sleep at night, the gorilla prepares a nest made out of branches and leaves. Because of their massive weight, adult male gorillas usually build their nests on the ground or close to the ground, while the lighter females and young may take to the trees. The females usually build their nests in the forks of trees, and will share their nests with their babies. Gorillas make a new nest for themselves every night, which helps to cut down on the number of parasites. Gorillas in western Africa don't usually build nests.
- The female gorilla is around 10-years-old before she begins to breed. Gorillas breed at any time of the year.
- The female gorilla's pregnancy lasts for approximately eight and a half months.
- Females usually give birth approximately every four years.

Noisiest animals

1. Blue whale
Loudest animal in the world. Its deep rumbling sounds are louder than those made when a jet aeroplane takes off.
2. Howler monkey
The loudest land animal. Its whoop can be heard more than 1½ miles (2.5km) away.
3. Kittiwake
A type of seagull named after its call.
4. Cicada
Loudest insect. It sings to attract females and calls out if in danger.
5. Barn owl
Its shrill night-time screeches are pretty scary.

- The female gorilla gives birth to one young. On the rare occasion when twins are born, it is usual for just one of the two to survive. This is because the mother is unable to give equal care to two offspring.
- Baby gorillas weigh approximately 4-5lb (1.8-2.26kg) at birth.
- Unlike orang-utans, which show no cradling preference, gorillas usually cradle their young on their left side.
- It is believed that one in three young gorillas dies without reaching its third birthday.
- The mother gorilla carries her baby around with her on her back for the first few months of its life. The infant is usually two and a half to three years old when it is finally weaned.
- Like a number of mammals in the animal kingdom, male gorillas have been known to kill another male's offspring in order to bring the mother into oestrus much earlier.
- Young gorillas have been seen playing children's playground games such as tag and follow-the-leader.
- Gorillas groom one another to help keep one another's fur clean. They pick out parasites and dirt. This also helps strengthen bonds. However, it is rare for adult females who are unrelated to other females in a silverback's harem to groom one another. Females' attachments are to their offspring and to the adult silverbacks in their groups.
- The movie King Kong (based on the novel by Edgar Wallace) portrayed the gorilla as a fierce and dangerous creature. The reality is that gorillas are shy, gentle, peaceful animals and will only attack humans if they or any member of their group feels threatened.

- Gorillas live for approximately 50 years in captivity.
- Due to loss of habitat and to being hunted, the gorilla has become an endangered species. The mountain gorilla is the most endangered of the subspecies.
- Gorillas become extremely attached to one another. Wild baby gorillas who have lost their mothers often lose their appetites, stop playing and become deeply depressed.
- Gorillas, like other great apes and, indeed, monkeys, hate direct human eye contact as they signify it as challenging behaviour. What torture it must be for gorillas in zoos to have lots of inquisitive tourists staring at them every day.

'A sick animal retires to a secluded place and fasts until its body is restored to normal. During the fast, it partakes only of water and the medicinal herbs which inherited intelligence teaches it instinctively to seek. I have watched...self healing so often.'

JULIETTE DE BAIRACLI

FEEDING THE BIRDS

People in urban communities have been feeding the birds for as long as there have been cities, birds and a little food to spare. Providing birds with a few spare crumbs on a cold, winter's day is a traditional part of civilised life in cities and towns. It is, perhaps, a way of rewarding birds for their presence in what might otherwise be a sterile place; it is a way of offering a little encouragement to welcome visitors. It is, for all of us, a way of reminding us of our humanity. And it is a way for even the lonely to remind themselves that they are not alone.

But modern politicians disapprove of birds in cities and towns. They object because of the guano which is deposited on buildings, limousines and expensive overcoats. However, even to heartless politicians this doesn't seem a sufficiently strong reason to keep birds out of towns, and so they claim (without burdening their argument with evidence) that birds are dangerous to human health. It's an easy argument to propose and one which, if repeated often enough, becomes convincing. To the millions who still believe that our representatives genuinely have our best interests at heart, and always tell the truth, it probably seems believable.

There is, of course, little or no evidence that the birds in our towns and cities are any threat to human life. Indeed, on the contrary, it isn't difficult to argue that the unfettered joy they bring can do anything but good.

However, birds do undeniably make a mess on buildings, statues and the heads of important people rushing about with delicate dignities to protect.

And so the authorities in many towns and cities are now taking draconian steps to rid the streets and buildings of birds. Vast amounts of public money are spent on hiring bird exterminators to spread poison and to otherwise spread the word that it isn't just for humans that cities are an unpleasant place to live.

Naturally, the authorities also make bird-feeding illegal. Public squares where it used to be possible to buy bird seed, are now patrolled by patrols of officially employed anti-jollity patrols empowered to arrest, fine and, in the end, imprison anyone who dares to throw a few crumbs to a sparrow.

We firmly believe that feeding birds is every bit as good for the people who do the feeding as it is for the birds themselves.

And so, with that thought in mind, here are six things to say if you are threatened with arrest for feeding the birds:

1. 'My little girl's budgie escaped last Wednesday. She is distraught. The budgie will die if I don't catch it soon. I saw it over there and was trying to attract it to me so that I could catch it and take it home.'
2. 'We should be aiding the survival of birds because the flapping of their wings helps to cool down the earth thus decreasing global warming.'
3. 'I was having a snack. I'm afraid I always was a very messy eater, and I inadvertently spilt some crumbs on the ground. I was about to pick them up but the birds were too quick for me.'

4. 'I'm over-feeding the birds so that they won't be able to fly away and, therefore, will be easier for the authorities to catch. Do you think I might apply for a local authority grant to help me with this work?'

5. 'Klryk pehklw knfhe qhelk? Ple nxveow lejs wjdhp hekshp hekh hk whjelq xhwlho wncbew kdgh w wdpan!' (Try to say this with as much dignity as you can muster.)
6. 'To your untrained eye these birds may all look like common sparrows and pigeons but that one over there – the one struggling with that piece of pie crust – is, I believe, one of the few remaining specimens of a particularly rare breed of bird. The snag is that it's sometimes difficult to dissuade the sparrows and pigeons from helping themselves to the food we are trying to get to the rare bird. Now would you please help me by distributing the rest of this food so that the endangered bird can eat and stay alive?'

How To Survive An Encounter With A Grizzly Bear

Brown bears hardly ever attack humans. They will only do so if they are startled or if they're approached when they're with their cubs or a carcass. But if you should be unfortunate enough to encounter an aggressive bear, here are our suggestions (no promises, no guarantees!):

1. Do not make eye contact with the bear. Back away very slowly. Talk calmly to the bear if you can. Doing this may be all that is needed for the bear to lose interest and leave you alone. If the worst happens and the bear charges at you, do not shout or scream no matter how much you want to. Screaming and yelling might cause the bear to act far more aggressively towards you. Bears sometimes make 'bluff charges', where they will charge and stop a certain distance away from you.
2. If you are attacked by a grizzly bear, the best form of defence you can use may be to play dead (although, if it's a black bear, this is one of the worst things you can do). Roll up into a small ball and try not to make a sound. Bringing your knees up to your chest helps to protect your vital organs. When rolled up into a ball, interlock your fingers behind your neck. If you suspect that the bear has lost interest in you, do not move until you're certain that it is nowhere near.
3. Never run away from a bear. A bear will almost certainly outrun you – they can run at speeds of 30mph (48.28km/h) or more. However, if you are not far away from safety and believe that you can make it in time then do seek refuge.
4. Water and trees do not make good refuges. Bears are first-rate swimmers and they can climb trees. More mature bears have difficulty climbing trees so will probably shake you out of a tree. But if there is no other place to hide, then climbing a tree to escape from a mature bear might be your only option.
5. With any potentially dangerous animal, the best line of defence is avoidance. Use your common sense. Avoid areas where you are likely to encounter bears.

Never surprise a bear. When walking where bears are expected to be, use whistles, clap or sing loudly so that bears know you're coming. Find out where bears usually feed and avoid those areas. Always ask a park ranger if there are any bears in the area, and if you should see one then do notify him or her so that other walkers can be warned. If you should see cubs, never approach them no matter how cute they look – the mummy bear is usually not far away.

Never surprise a bear

6. If you're camping in bear territory, you should never leave food in your tent. Leaving food in your tent is almost certain to attract bears as they have a very good sense of smell. It is recommended that you leave food and anything that contains food odours such as empty food packets or containers, a good distance away from the tent. And when you are walking anywhere with food, make sure that you put the food inside good quality sealed containers so that bears cannot pick up on the smell. Bears have such a keen sense of smell that they can smell a wrap of chewing gum hidden away in a car's glove compartment.
7. Bears are usually only aggressive towards humans when defending their cubs or a carcass or if they are startled. However, anyone who's daft enough to go camping in 'bear territory' really does so at their own peril!
8. Good luck!

Hedgehogs (Western European)

- ⇨ Hedgehogs belong to the family, Erinaceidae. The western European (or common) hedgehog can be found in western and northern Europe.
- ⇨ The male hedgehog is called a boar. The female hedgehog is called a sow.
- ⇨ Fully-grown hedgehogs are about 9-11in (23-27cm) in length and weigh approximately 2.2-4.4lb (1-2 kg). Females are slightly smaller than male hedgehogs.
- ⇨ The hedgehog has a pointed whiskered snout, black eyes, round ears and a rotund body. Its front feet are larger than its hind feet and it has a short tail. The hedgehog has five toes on each foot. The hedgehog's face and underparts are covered in coarse fur and there are short, sharp spines (about 1in long) all over its back and sides.
- ⇨ There are approximately 5,000 spines on the average adult European hedgehog. These white and brown striped spines are actually modified hairs. They are amazingly strong.
- ⇨ Hedgehogs are found in numerous places including hedgerows, fields, parks, gardens and on the edges of woodlands.
- ⇨ A hedgehog's main diet includes: insects, earthworms, slugs and snails. Hedgehogs will also eat frogs, birds' eggs, chicks, small mammals, carrion and fruit.
- ⇨ A hedgehog's home is called a nest. The nest is usually made up of dry grass, leaves and twigs.
- ⇨ During the breeding season, starting about April, hedgehogs involve themselves in a rather tedious courtship ritual. The male will circle the female, while the female snorts and hisses aggressively at the male. This strange ritual can go on for hours. At the end of it, copulation may not take place at all.
- ⇨ In order for the male hedgehog to mount the female safely, the female has to adopt a very special posture. She lays her spines flat (unfortunately for the male, some spines invariably remain upright), arches her back downwards by pressing her belly to the ground and keeps her snout pointing upwards.
- ⇨ A hedgehog's pregnancy usually lasts 30-35 days.
- ⇨ A hedgehog's litter normally contains four or five young.
- ⇨ Baby hedgehogs generally weigh no more than 0.9oz (25.5g) at birth.
- ⇨ Shortly after birth, the baby hedgehog's spines emerge from underneath its skin.
- ⇨ The young hedgehog is fully weaned at about six-weeks-old.
- ⇨ The female may bear two litters of young each year.
- ⇨ Sadly, over 50 per cent of hedgehogs do not survive their first winter.
- ⇨ When defending itself, the hedgehog will turn itself into a spiny ball by tucking its head and legs up in towards its belly; using its muscles and excess skin to draw its body closer together, and erecting its normally sleeked-back spines. If

it has to, the hedgehog will stay in this position for hours.

- ⇨ Hedgehogs are riddled with fleas. This is particularly true of town-dwelling hedgehogs. Some hedgehogs have been known to carry as many as 1,000 fleas. The fleas that hedgehogs carry are specific to them and do not live for long on people or pets. Amazingly, hedgehogs in New Zealand (where the European hedgehog was introduced by British settlers in the 19th century) do not have fleas.
- ⇨ Cows' milk can make hedgehogs very ill, as hedgehogs find milk difficult to digest. Hedgehogs usually enjoy dog or cat food, pieces of fruit and plenty of fresh, clean water to drink.
- ⇨ Hedgehogs hibernate during the cold winter months, and live on their fat reserves during hibernation. So the summer and early autumn are a crucial time. They must fatten up in order to survive the cold months ahead. In Europe, hedgehogs usually hibernate from October to April in a sheltered nest made of grass and leaves. Female hedgehogs tend to stay in hibernation for up to four weeks longer than male hedgehogs.
- ⇨ Nobody really knows why, but the hedgehog will cover itself with copious amounts of frothy saliva (this is known as self-anointing) if it comes into contact with certain types of strong odours. The hedgehog also exhibits this bizarre behaviour when coming into contact with foxes or other hedgehogs.
- ⇨ There has been a reduction in the number of hedgehogs in recent years. This is largely a result of hedgehogs being killed on the roads.
- ⇨ Some of the hedgehog's many vocalisations include: snuffling, snorting, squealing, hissing and grunting.
- ⇨ The maximum running speed of a hedgehog is thought to be 6mph (9.65km/h).
- ⇨ Some of the poisons used to kill garden pests such as slugs and snails can kill hedgehogs.
- ⇨ Hedgehogs are usually much loved by gardeners as they kill a lot of garden 'pests'.
- ⇨ When mowing grass, make sure that there are no hedgehogs around. It is not uncommon for hedgehogs to be killed by lawnmowers. Also, watch out for bonfires. Before lighting a bonfire, make sure that there are no hedgehogs inside. Bonfires make good hibernation spots for hedgehogs.
- ⇨ Hedgehogs can live seven years or more, but two to three years is more usual.
- ⇨ Hedgehogs can swim very well if it has to but only over short distances. However, many hedgehogs drown each year in garden ponds. This is because hedgehogs cannot climb out of ponds. If you have a pond then do make sure that it is 'hedgehog friendly' by making a slipway out of the pond which a hedgehog can use if necessary.
- ⇨ Hedgehogs are solitary animals.
- ⇨ The hedgehog's main predators are badgers and large owls.
- ⇨ Hedgehogs are largely nocturnal animals.

- ⇨ Hedgehogs have been known to travel two miles (3.38km) or more in search of food. Male hedgehogs usually wander a lot further than female hedgehogs.
- ⇨ Picnickers should be aware of discarding tins in the open. It is not uncommon for hedgehogs to get stuck inside a carelessly discarded tin can, and to die a horrible death as a result.

'The fox knows many things – the hedgehog knows one big thing'.
ARCHILOCHUS (GREEK POET C. 680–C. 640 BC)

STRANGE BUT TRUE (PART 4)

- ✶ A gorilla weighs two or three times as much as the average man, but the average length of a male gorilla's penis is just 1in (2.54cm). In contrast, the penis of a bull elephant can be 6ft (1.83m) long, and that of the blue whale up to 10ft (305m) in length.
- ✶ Two hunters tied a stick of gelignite to a rabbit for a 'laugh'. They then lit the fuse and released the rabbit. They stopped laughing when the rabbit doubled back and hopped under their car.
- ✶ Naked mole rats don't feel pain.
- ✶ Male apes and monkeys have a bone in their penis.
- ✶ Most dog bite victims are bitten either by their own dogs or by dogs with whom they have regular contact. And the bite most commonly occurs in the dog's own home. Male dogs bite more than female dogs. The types of dogs that bite most are: Staffordshire bull terriers, Jack Russell terriers and Alsatians.
- ✶ Some South Africans regard rat meat as a gastronomic treat. The rats they eat weigh up to 20lb (9kg).
- ✶ A bull's ejaculate contains seven billion sperm.
- ✶ Police sniffer dogs find it difficult to separate the trails of identical twins, compared to those of people unrelated to each other. (If we didn't douse ourselves with perfumes of one kind or another we would all probably be able to identify one another by smell).
- ✶ Contrary to popular belief, owls cannot turn their heads full circle.
- ✶ It is not unknown for vampire bats to risk their lives in order to share their food with starving roost-mates.
- ✶ A complete sex reversal can occur in some species of domestic fowl if the left ovary is destroyed by disease. The right ovary will then develop into a functional testis. There are instances recorded where a hen started off laying eggs and finished up as a cock – able to fertilise females.
- ✶ Lapdogs originally became popular because they attracted fleas away from their owners.

* In Australia, 28 per cent of people are bitten by redback spiders while putting on their shoes.
* Ostriches are able to roar like lions.
* Some lions respond excitedly to catnip in the same way that domestic cats do.
* 18. When the film *Babe* (about a talking piglet) was shown in Hong Kong, they changed the title to *The Happy Dumpling-To-Be Who Talks And Solves Agricultural Problems*.
* Dogs kill more people each year than sharks do.
  The only animal that has been taught to stand on its head is the elephant.
* The human race owes its life to cats. After all, it was cats who helped to eradicate the Black Plague in the fourteenth century.
* The Chinese don't have a Man in the Moon – they have a three-legged toad and a rabbit.
* There is a crab called the decorator crab which dresses up in bits of shell, seaweed and anything it can find on the ocean floor so that it is camouflaged from predators.
* Her Royal Highness Queen Elizabeth II owns all the swans in England.
* Woodlice are essentially aquatic insects and have gills. Woodlice are able to live on land by carrying a storage of water underneath their bodies. If woodlice dry out, they suffocate.
* There is a sea squirt living in the seas near Japan that eats its own brain. Once the sea squirt has reached maturity, it attaches itself to a rock and stays there forever. The sea squirt decides that it no longer needs its brain, and it eats it (the sea squirt then becomes a politician!)
* Tigers hate the smell of alcohol, and are more likely to attack if they can smell alcohol on your breath.
* Only female mosquitoes suck blood.
* The common poorwill is the only bird that is said to 'hibernate'.
* The death puffer fish is a delicacy in Japan. The flesh of the fish is edible but its blood and some of its organs are toxic to humans. If the fish is not prepared properly then anybody who eats it will die. There have been quite a few incidents of Japanese people having died as a consequence of eating a death puffer fish (or 'fugu' as it's called over there) that hasn't been properly prepared. Unbelievably, there are plenty of kamikaze diners who are willing to die to prove their 'manhood'.
* Of any bird, crows have the biggest brains relative to body size, which is why they are so clever.
* Pygmy shrews need so much energy that they have to eat their own weight in food on a daily basis.
* Chocolate and avocados are poisonous to parrots.
* The smell of vultures' vomit is so bad that dogs have been known to die after coming into contact with it.

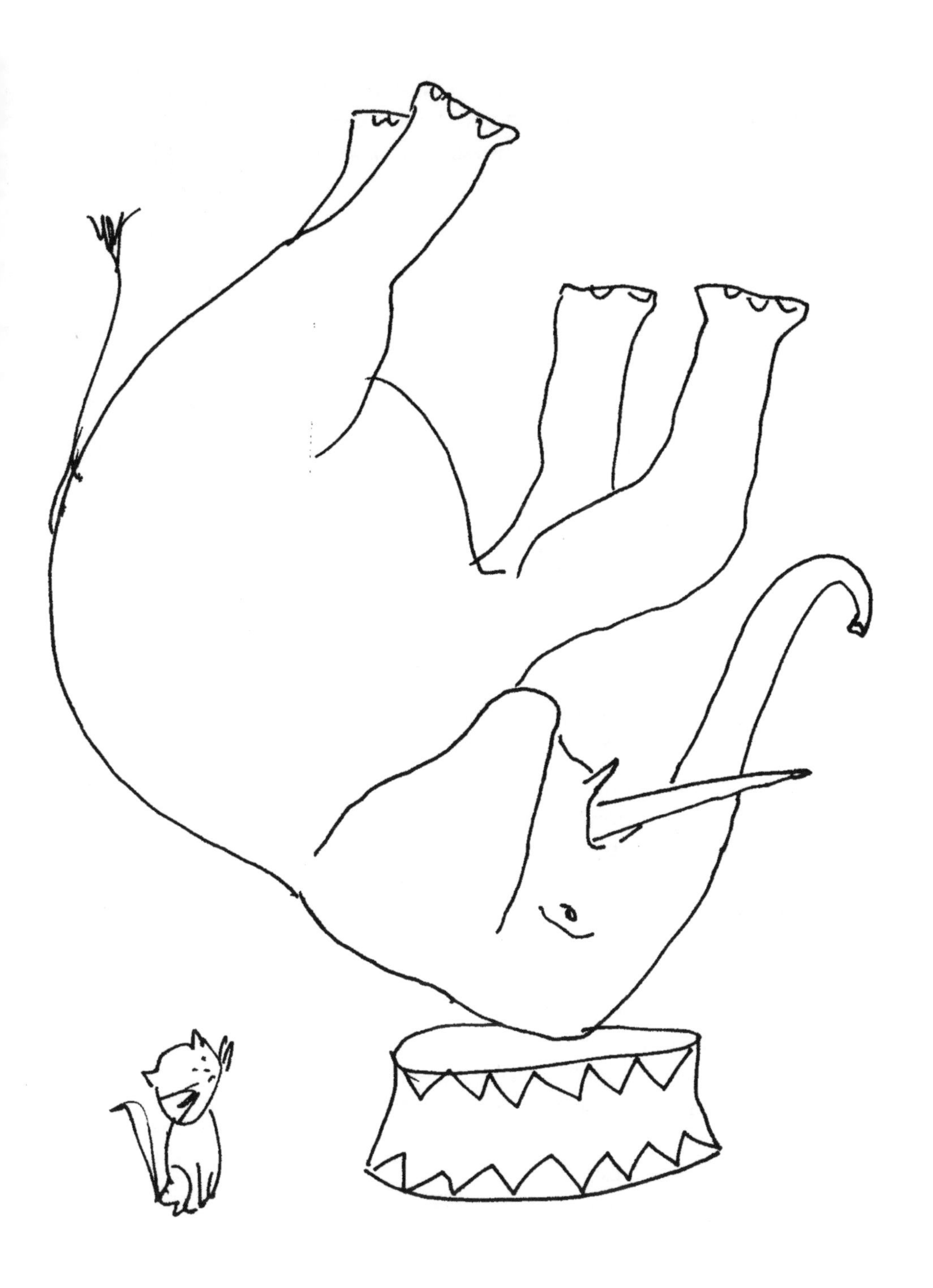

The only animal that has been taught to stand on its head is the elephant.

* Pets which go out at night in Ohio, USA, must have lights attached to their tails. (Presumably known as tail lights.)

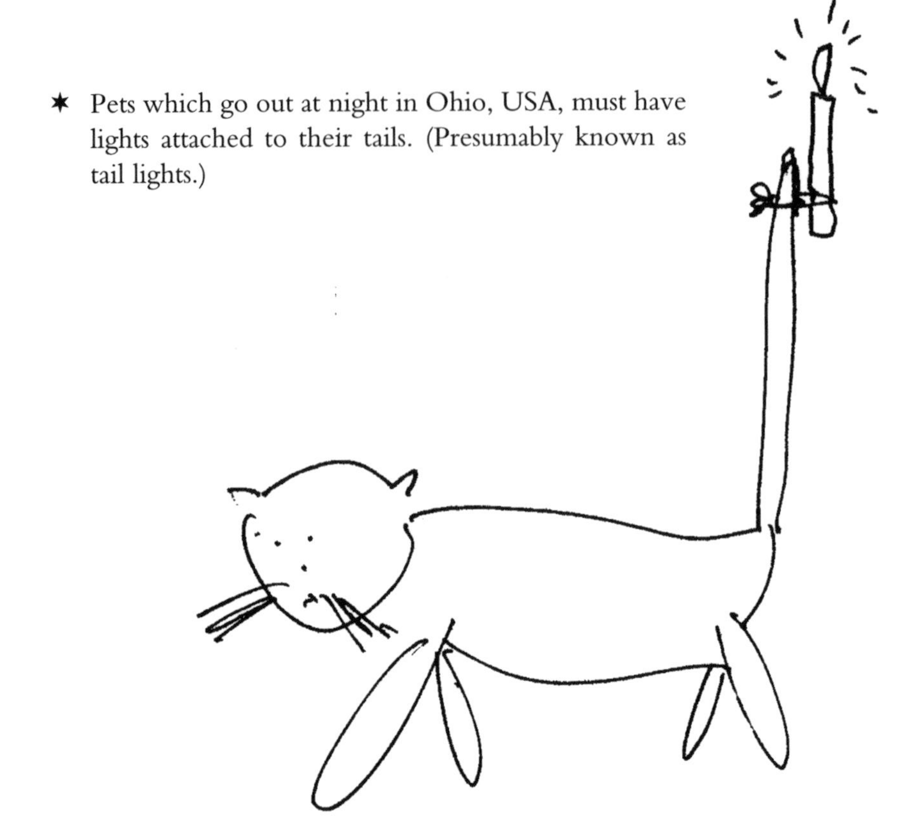

* Contrary to what most people believe, the vampire bat doesn't give a painful bite to its victim before sucking the blood from the victim's body. When a vampire bat extracts blood from its victim, very often its victim doesn't even know it's happening as the mammal has painkilling saliva. The bat also extracts blood from its victim ever so gently. The vampire bat uses its blade-like fangs to make a tiny incision and laps up the blood that seeps out – it does not suck the blood out. The major risk of being bitten by a vampire bat is catching rabies.
* A horse's heart can weigh up to 11lb (4.98kg).
* An earthworm has five hearts.
* The reason why we don't see baby pigeons is because pigeons first leave their nests when they are approximately 35-days-old. By that time, of course, they look fully-grown.
* Rats can and do kill cats.
* The testicles of an octopus are contained in its head.
* The male midwife toad carries eggs on its back until they are ready to hatch. Sometimes, the eggs are from more than one mother.

HIPPOPOTAMUSES

- There are two species of hippopotamus that make up the family Hippopotamidae: the pygmy hippopotamus and the common hippopotamus. The common hippopotamus is the larger of the two species, and is the third largest land animal after the elephant and the white rhinoceros.
- The common hippo can be found in wetland and grassland in East and South sub-Saharan Africa. The rare pygmy hippopotamus can be found in wetland and tropical forest in West Africa.
- The common hippopotamus has a greyish-black coloured barrel-shaped body with a large head, a huge mouth and short legs. The pygmy hippopotamus is about the size of a domestic pig – barely a fifth of the weight of its large relative – and has a much smaller head than the common hippopotamus.
- The hippo's eyes, ears and nostrils are positioned so that the hippo is able to see, hear and breathe with just the top of its head visible above the surface of the water.
- The hippo is able to seal its nostrils underwater.
- The common adult hippo is over 11ft (3.35m) long and can weigh as much 7,055lb (3,200kg). The pygmy hippo is approximately 5ft (1.52m) long and weighs around 606lb (274.87kg).
- The name 'hippopotamus' means 'horse of the river'. The name was given by the ancient Greeks who mistakenly believed that the hippo was related to the horse.
- Amazingly, the hippo's closest living relative is the whale. The two are believed to have had a common ancestor and to have split 54 million years ago.
- The female hippo is called a cow. The male hippo is called a bull. The baby hippo is called a calf.

A pair of hippopotomii

- Common hippos live in temporary groups called schools. Pygmy hippos lead a solitary existence and do not live in groups.
- Hippos feed mostly at night. The common hippo's diet mainly consists of grass (the occasional killing of prey has been reported). The pygmy hippo's diet is more varied. Pygmy hippos usually eat fruits, grasses and ferns.
- Hippos do not use their teeth to crop vegetation – they use their broad mouths.
- Although it is a huge mammal, the common hippo doesn't eat very much compared to other large mammals. The common hippo consumes around one and a half per cent of its body weight in food a day.
- Hippos usually mate in the water. It is the dominant males who have mating rights over the females.
- The common hippo's pregnancy lasts for approximately eight months: the pygmy hippo's pregnancy lasts around six and a half months.
- Baby hippos may be born on land or under water.
- The hippopotamus gives birth to one young.
- At birth, baby hippos weigh 50-100lb (22.67-45.35kg).
- Baby hippos can walk, run and swim five minutes after birth.
- Baby hippos stay with their mothers until they have fully matured at around eight years of age.
- The common hippo can open its mouth approximately 150 degrees. When a hippo appears to be 'yawning', it is usually showing a rival its huge teeth in a display of aggression.

- The baby hippo's main predators are hyenas, lions and leopards. Occasionally baby hippos fall prey to crocodiles.
- The baby hippo drinks its mother's milk underwater, but it can only take a few drops at a time because it hasn't yet learnt how to hold its breath under the water for longer than a few seconds.
- The adult hippo's main predators are other hippos and humans.
- The common hippo can live to 45 years in the wild, and the pygmy hippo can live to 35 years.
- The dagger-like canine teeth in the common hippo's lower jaw can grow to 20in (50.8cm) long.
- The common hippo's skin is approximately 1½in (3.81cm) thick and, if removed, would weigh about a ton.
- Hippos are often pictured with birds on their backs. These waterbirds are not a nuisance to the hippo; they are actually very useful in that they eat the parasites from the hippo's skin.
- Some common male hippos can be extremely territorial. If a male hippo invades another male's territory without acting submissively then a vicious fight will probably ensue. There will be a lot of splashing, and the hippos will bite each other with their tusk-like teeth. Males also fight each other over mating rights. Males intimidate each other by expelling copious amounts of faeces and catapult them indiscriminately with their tails. In these rather bizarre faecal battles, the winner is regarded as being the hippo who produces and spreads the greatest amount of excrement in the shortest possible time. Diarrhoea rules! Even more amazing, bull hippos also do this to attract females. (They probably regard the courting human male's use of foul-smelling aftershave with equal distaste).
- In addition to using their faeces as a weapon, hippos also practise something called 'muck spreading' where they spread their faeces over many square yards by wagging their tails vigorously. It is thought that one of the reasons hippos do this is to help them to find their way back home. However, some experts believe that hippos muck spread as a way of marking their territories.
- Hippos can walk under water on riverbeds.
- A hippo's day is divided into two halves: the common hippo spends most of the day submerged in water (coming out occasionally to bask in the sun), and the night is spent feeding on land.
- The hippo has to spend much of its time submerged in water to help keep its skin moist because it loses moisture from its skin at a rapid rate. A hippo exposed to the sun will dehydrate much faster than any other mammal.
- Hippos can float in the water by filling their lungs with air. This helps to reduce their body density.
- Although they are good swimmers, hippos cannot deal with rapid currents and must, therefore, swim in slow moving waters.
- It is a myth that hippos sweat blood. Indeed, hippos cannot sweat at all. Hippos

excrete large amounts of secretions from underneath their skins. This turns reddish brownish in colour when exposed to air, giving the appearance of blood. This fluid is thought to protect the hippo's skin from the sun whilst also acting as an antibacterial agent to help clean any wounds the hippo may have acquired during fights.

- Hippos are hunted by humans for their meat and for their tusk-like teeth.

Animals Use Tools

Some humans like to believe (rather arrogantly) that only they can think and use tools. Many allegedly eminent scientists still deny that animals can make tools. There is no doubt that this viewpoint makes them very popular with the meat industry and with scientific laboratories where animals are used in experiments.

The truth is rather different.

The truth is that many animals (and birds) use sticks and stones as implements to help them in their daily lives.

- Insects use small stones to pack the dirt firmly over and around their nests.
- Spiders use stones to keep their webs steady when the weather is stormy.
- Orang-utans and baboons use sticks and stones as weapons.
- Monkeys use stones to help them crack nuts. In one zoo, a monkey who had poor teeth kept (and guarded) a stone hidden in its straw for nut cracking. That monkey had a tool which it regarded as its own property.
- Chimpanzees drum on hollow logs with sticks in order to send messages to one another.
- Monkeys know how to use sticks as levers.
- The Indian elephant will break off a leafy branch and use it to sweep away the flies.
- Ants know how to keep grain in a warm, moist atmosphere without the grain sprouting.
- A lurcher called Red at the Battersea Dogs Home in London, England, startled staff by using his teeth to open the spring-loaded catch on his kennel. He would wait until the staff had gone home and locked up for the night before escaping. Once free, he would then pad along the corridor and free his chums before leading them to the food store for midnight feasts. This happened a dozen times before the humans found out how the animals were escaping.
- At Oxford University, a crow called Betty picked up a piece of wire, used her beak to shape it and bent it into a hook to lift food from the bottom of a vertical pipe. Once she had learned how to do this, she made other hooks to extract food from places she couldn't reach with her beak or claws. She did this without being shown how to do it.

- Chimpanzees routinely use tools such as twigs and stones to help them hunt and gather food. Scientists from Cambridge University observed animals for several months in southern Senegal. Chimpanzees were observed making spears out of tree branches and then using their spears to catch small wild animals such as bush babies (creatures the size of squirrels). Most of the spear hunting is done by female chimpanzees. The chimpanzees first selected a branch of the right length, then removed the leaves and trimmed off extra branches. The chimpanzees then used their teeth to whittle the end of the spear to a sharp point. The chimpanzees used one hand to direct the spear – much as a human will.
- Gorillas use branches to test the depth of water they intend to wade through.
- Gorillas use giant leaves as napkins to clean their fingers and faces after eating – particularly when they've been eating messy fruits.
- Gorillas, normally nomadic animals, will use twigs and leaves to make overnight nests in trees or on the ground.
- Crows are cunning birds who have great skills with tools. They have been seen using their bills to whittle twigs into hooks and using leaves as probes to extract grubs from crevices. A study published from experts at the University of Auckland has shown that, like humans and some other larger animals, crows can use a combination of tools to achieve what they want. The birds use logic and reasoning to decide how best to get what they want. So, for example, they will use one tool (a short stick) to create or obtain a second tool (a longer stick) which they need to reach food. Some humans (including most lawyers and nearly all politicians) would find this beyond them.
- Monkeys use tools to dig up roots, crack seeds and dig insects out of holes in trees. Two scientists from Cambridge watched wild capuchin monkeys in the Sierra da Capivara National Park in Brazil and discovered that their use of tools is widespread. Stones were used as spades to dig up roots or other food. And the monkeys used stones to crack open seeds, to break tubers into smaller more manageable pieces for eating and to open hollow branches. They also used stones to crush lizards and to break the outer hard skin of cactus plants in order to get at the soft, edible inside of the plant. The monkeys were seen to use a stone in one hand while using the other hand to scoop away debris. So, for example, when digging, the spade would be used with one hand and the other hand used for moving away loosened soil. Most remarkable of all, perhaps, was the fact that the monkeys were seen to improve their tools. When using twigs to probe tree holes or crevices in rocks in order to reach honey, insects or water they would modify the twigs by breaking off leaves or stems to make them more useful.

Horses (Domestic)

- Domesticated and wild horses belong to the Equidae family, and can be found throughout the world. The Equidae family also includes asses and zebras.
- Horses are thought to have first been domesticated at around 4000–3000 BC
- There are considered to be approximately 207 different varieties of horse. This figure also includes ponies.
- Horse breeds are classified by size and build: heavy horses, light horses and ponies.
- A young horse is called a foal until it is weaned. From the time it is weaned until it is four-years-old, a young male horse is called a colt, and a young female horse is called a filly. A mature female horse is called a mare. A mature male horse is called a stallion. A mature male horse that is used for breeding is called a stud. A castrated mature male horse is called a gelding. The mother of a horse is called a dam, and the father of a horse is called a sire.
- A horse's height is measured in hands. One hand is 4in (10.16cm). A horse is measured from the ground right up to the withers (the highest point of the shoulder). Outside Britain and America, the measurement of horses is more commonly made in centimetres.
- A fully-grown small horse is called a pony. By definition, a pony is any horse whose height does not exceed 14.2 hands.
- Young female horses reach puberty at around 15 to 24 months old.
- It is not unknown for a stallion to reject a mare as a sexual companion if her coat happens to be the wrong colour.
- A mare's pregnancy lasts for approximately 11 months.
- Mares usually give birth to one young.
- Foals are born well-developed and are walking around within an hour of birth.
- Domestic horses are weaned from four and a half to six months of age.
- Horses are herbivores and, in the wild, they mainly feed on grasses and shrubs. Horses feed for approximately 16 hours a day.
- Horses can live 30 years or more. However, the average lifespan of a horse is 20–25 years. Thoroughbreds tend to die slightly earlier than crossbreeds.
- Horses are herbivores and, in the wild, they mainly feed on grasses and shrubs. Horses feed for approximately 16 hours a day. The oldest horse that ever existed lived to be 62-years-old. His name was Old Billy, though it is not known at what point the 'Old' was added.
- Horses are herbivores and, in the wild, they mainly feed on grasses and shrubs. Horses feed for approximately 16 hours a day.
- Up until the age of ten years, a horse can be aged correctly by looking at its teeth.
- Horses sleep for less than three hours a day.

- Horses have three patella ligaments which allow them to lock themselves into a stable, standing position. This enables them to relax their other muscles, and allows them to sleep while standing up without any risk of falling down.
- A horse with a black and white coat is referred to as a piebald. A skewbald refers to a horse that has patches of white with any other colour except black.
- The thoroughbred is familiar with most people for its prowess on the racecourse, and is the most valuable of all breeds of horse. The thoroughbred originated in England in the 17th and 18th centuries. This magnificent horse has an average height of around 16 hands and weighs approximately 1,066lb (483.52kg).
- By the time they are five-years-old, many thoroughbreds are already retired from the racecourse.
- The thoroughbred can run at speeds of 40mph (64.37km/h).
- The largest breed of horse is the shire horse, which weighs approximately a ton (1.02 tonnes) and can stand up to 17.2 hands high. The smallest breed of horse is the falabella, which stands at 7.5 hands high. The falabella is not considered a pony but a miniature horse. This is because the falabella has the proportions of a horse.
- Horses are social animals and, in the wild, live in herds. A typical herd includes a dominant older mare, a stallion who protects the herd, two to four other mares and their young.
- Horses hate to be by themselves and, being herd animals, enjoy the companionship and the protection of other horses. A horse kept singly is not a truly happy horse.
- Horses have one toe on each foot, protected by a hoof. Horses' hooves grow continuously – about 0.2in (0.5cm) a month – and are largely composed of keratin.
- The four natural speeds for horses are walking, trotting, cantering and galloping.
- It is not natural for domesticated horses to jump. If left to their own accord, horses would prefer to walk around obstacles rather than jump over them. Training horses to show jump is a lengthy and complicated process.
- The horse's vocal repertoire includes: nickering, squealing, snorting, screaming and neighing.
- Horses are thought to have their own unique 'neigh'.
- The mane on the domestic horse's neck falls to the side, but the mane on other species stands erect.
- Horses cannot vomit.
- A mule is a cross between a female horse and a male donkey. A cross between a male horse and a female donkey is called a 'hinny'. All species in the horse family can interbreed but their offspring are usually sterile.
- Bizarre neck movements that are repeated endlessly for hours at a time (such as weaving or head circling) usually indicate that the horse is unhappy and is bored with its environment.

- A horse usually swishes its tail quite violently when it is feeling angry.
- You can tell a lot about the mood of a horse by the way its ears are positioned. For example, if a horse appears to have its ears flattened back against its head, it usually means that the horse is feeling aggressive. If the apertures of the horse's ears are pointing to the rider on its back, it usually signifies that the horse is feeling submissive and nervous.
- Horses have two blind spots: one directly behind them and one just in front of them.
- Next time you see a statue of a horse with a rider, take a closer look at the horse's legs. If the horse has all four legs on the ground, the rider died of natural causes. If the horse has one of its front legs in the air, the rider died from his injuries in battle. Finally, if the horse has two front legs in the air, then the subject of the statue died in battle.

Talking Of Horses

There are a number of sayings which revolve around horses. Here are some of the best-known, together with their meanings (and in some cases their origins):

1. A stalking horse
Hunters used to stalk game by hiding behind their horses as they advanced on their prey.

2. To change horses in mid-stream
Attempting to change from the back of one horse to the back of another while crossing a stream is risky. The phrase draws attention to the hazards involved in making a major change in one's plans in the middle of a difficult or important activity.

3. To be on one's high horse
In medieval England, the tallest horses were ridden by people of the highest rank. A high horse gave the rider the chance to look down on people.

4. To ride a hobby horse (to death)
The habit of introducing one's favourite subject into a conversation at every opportunity.

5. Horses for courses
Different skills are suited to different tasks.

6. To find a mare's nest
To discover something new and exciting only to find that, although it might seem attractive, it is of no real value.

7. Straight from the horse's mouth
Experts judge the age of a horse by examining its teeth. An owner who lied about a horse's age when trying to sell it stood the risk of having his deception exposed when the buyer checked the animal's mouth. The phrase 'straight from the horse's mouth' means straight from a source who really knows.

Eight Celebrity Horses

1. Rawhide (The Range Rider)
2. Scout (Tonto)
3. Lucky (Dick West)
4. Diablo (The Cisco Kid)
5. Marshall (Matt Dillon)
6. Trigger (Roy Rogers)
7. Silver (The Lone Ranger)
8. Topper (Hopalong Cassidy)

The Legend Of Black Beauty (probably the best-known celebrity horse of them all)

- The American saddlebred stallion who portrayed Black Beauty in the 1946 film was called Highland Dale.
- Ralph McCutcheon was Highland Dale's owner. It was Ralph McCutcheon, a famous animal trainer in Hollywood, who trained Highland Dale.
- Highland Dale stood 15 hands high.
- The famous stallion was around 26-months-old when he made his appearance as Black Beauty.
- Some of Black Beauty's tricks involved, untying knots, walking lame and playing dead.
- Black Beauty or Highland Dale also starred in the following films: *Giant, The Return of Wildfire, Outlaw Stallion, Wild is the Wind,* and *Gypsy Colt* as well as the popular, long running American television series: *Fury.*
- Highland Dale's favourite treat was carrots.
- Highland Dale suffered from a respiratory disease called heaves. He died at the age of 29.
- In the 1994 version of the film, the horse who played Black Beauty was called Docs Keepin Time. Previously, Docs Keepin Time had a career as a racehorse.
- The movie, *Black Beauty,* was based on a book by English author Anna Sewell.

Animals Are Capable Of Love

Animals are just as capable as human beings of loving their partners, their families, their leaders, their teachers, their friends and others who are important to them. An ape will show exactly the same signs of love and affection when dealing with her baby as a human mother will when dealing with her baby. Both will look longingly, tickle and play with their babies. Both feed their young, wash them, risk their lives for them and willingly put up with their noise and unruly behaviour.

Anyone who doubts that animals love their young should stand outside a farmyard when a calf has been taken away from a cow, and listen to the heartbreaking cries of anguish which result. Cows have been known to trek miles to try to reach a calf from whom they have been parted.

Lewis Gompertz, who lived from 1779 to 1861 and was a potent champion of the rights of blacks, women and the poor (and, indeed, all oppressed human beings), was also a powerful champion of animals. He was a founder of the Royal Society for the Prevention of Cruelty to Animals. In his book *Moral Inquiries On the Situation Of Man And Of Brutes,* Gompertz wrote: 'From some birds we may learn real constancy in conjugal affection, though in most instances their contracts only last for one season, but how strict do they keep this. They have no laws, no parchments, no parsons, no fear to injuring their characters, not even their own words to break in being untrue to each other: but their virtue is their laws, their parchments, their parsons, and their reputation; their deeds are their acts, their acts – their deeds: and from their own breasts do they honestly tear down to line the beds of their legitimate offspring.'

Gompertz described an incident illustrating the wisdom of blackbirds. 'I observed a male blackbird flying about in an extreme state of agitation,' he wrote. 'And on my going to discover the cause of it, the bird retreated from me as I followed it, till it stopped at a nest containing a female bird sitting upon her eggs, near which there was a cat: in consequence of this I removed the cat, and the bird became quiet. After that, whenever the cat was about the place, the blackbird would come near my window and would in the same manner direct me to some spot where the cat happened to be stationed.' Gompertz also wrote about a male blackbird which had bravely attacked a cat which had caught its female partner, and described three incidents which illustrate animal kindness and wisdom. The first concerned two goats which had met each other on a narrow path between two precipices. There was no room for the two goats to turn or pass and so one of the goats lay down, allowing the other to walk over it. The second incident involved a horse who had been hurt by a nail when he had been shod. Finding it painful to walk, he had gone back to the farrier and shown him his hoof. The third incident involved a sheep dog who jumped into freezing cold water and successfully rescued another dog which had been floating on a lump of ice. `I would now fain ask,' wrote Gompertz, 'if all this does not show reason and virtue?'

A woman who keeps rats has reported how when one rat was too ill to fetch food for herself, a second rat brought food from their bowl into the nest where the sick rat was lying and laid the food around her so that she could eat without having to move. Every time the woman tried to pick up the sick rat, the nurse rat, doubtless misunderstanding her motives, bit her hand.

J. Howard Moore, the author of *The Universal Kinship,* described how monkeys may adopt the orphans of deceased members of their tribe, and how two crows fed a third crow which was wounded. The wound was several weeks old, and the two crows had clearly been playing 'Good Samaritans' for all that time.

Charles Darwin wrote about a blind pelican who was fed with fish brought to it by pelican friends who normally lived 30 miles (48.28km) away.

Strong males in a herd of vicunas will lag behind to protect the weaker and slower members of their herd from possible predators.

Many animals are so loyal to one another that if one half of a couple dies, the other may die shortly afterwards – consumed by grief. This has been reported to happen with swans, wolves and oxen.

Before slavery was abolished, black people who fell in love were regarded as enjoying simple 'animal lust' as a result of 'animal attraction'. When black people formed lifelong pairs this was dismissed as nothing more than a response to an 'instinct'.

The same things are, of course, said about animals (with just as little evidence to support it). Animal abusers argue that animals which seem to show love are merely acting according to instinct.

However, the evidence proves that they are wrong and that animals are perfectly capable of feeling complex emotions. Animals are certainly capable of loving.

Kangaroos (Eastern Grey and Red)

* The eastern grey and the red kangaroo belong to the family Macropodidae. The eastern grey kangaroo can be found in eastern Australia and in some parts of Tasmania, and the red kangaroo can be found in Central Australia. The kangaroo's habitat is wide-ranging and includes forests and deserts. The term 'kangaroo' is used generally for any of the large Australasian marsupials of the family Macropodidae, but the word is also used to refer to any of the family's other species such as wallabies and tree-kangaroos.
* Kangaroos are marsupials. Marsupials are characterised by the fact that babies continue to develop outside the mother's womb.
* The red kangaroo is the largest of the kangaroo species as well as the largest living marsupial, weighing as much as 200lb (90.71kg) and standing 6ft (182.88cm) tall or more. Female red kangaroos are less than half the size of males. It is only the male red kangaroo that has reddish fur. The female red kangaroo's fur is a bluish grey.
* The male eastern grey kangaroo can grow to 6ft (182.88cm) in height and weigh up to 145lb (65.77kg) (females are approximately half this size). Another species of large grey kangaroo is the western grey, which is nicknamed the 'stinker' because of its curry-like odour. Western grey kangaroos tend to be brown in colour (as opposed to grey) and leaner in build than eastern grey kangaroos. However, in spite of their colour differences, both species are difficult to tell apart as they look very similar. The major difference in the two species is the reproductive cycle: female eastern grey kangaroos have longer pregnancies, and carry their young in their pouches for longer.
* Eastern grey kangaroos residing in Tasmania have adapted to the cold winters by having thicker fur. They also have darker fur and are slightly smaller in build. The eastern grey kangaroos of Tasmania are called 'forester' kangaroos, and are a protected species.
* The kangaroo has a powerfully built body, a thin neck, large ears, strong hindlegs with muscular thighs, large hind feet, short thin forelimbs and a long tail.
* The female kangaroo is usually referred to as a doe (other names may include: jill, roo or flyer). The male kangaroo is usually referred to as a buck (other names may include boomer or jack). The baby kangaroo is called a joey.
* A kangaroo's tail can grow to nearly 4ft (1.22m) long.

After the kangaroo has given birth, the joey – which is tiny at less than 1in (2.5cm) long – makes the arduous journey (which takes two or three minutes) to its mother's pouch. Once the journey has been made, the joey will then attach itself to one of its mother's four teats where it will receive a steady supply of milk. At around six months, the joey pops its head out from its mother's pouch to have a look at the surrounding world. The joey will spend some time outside the safety of its mother's pouch during the day.

* The kangaroo moves about by using its two hind legs and feet to hop. When hopping at speed, it uses its tail for balance and for steering. When moving about on all fours, the kangaroo uses its tail as a fifth limb (or as a third hindleg).
* Just like cattle, kangaroos also chew the cud; they regurgitate what they have eaten, chew it as cud and swallow it so that it can finally be digested.
* A kangaroo's main diet includes: grass, plants, leaves and shrubs.
* To avoid the daytime heat, kangaroos usually graze in the evenings.
* Despite their huge size, kangaroos eat less than sheep do.
* Kangaroos are social animals and live in groups, often governed by an older, more dominant male who attains his top position by winning fights with other males within the group. The usual collective name for a group of kangaroos is a 'mob' or a 'troop'. There can be 80 or more members in a mob. However, red kangaroos are not as sociable as their grey cousins and tend to live in much smaller groups.
* To increase the chances of giving birth to a baby with good genes, the female kangaroo usually mates with the strongest and most dominant male (called the Alpha male) within the mob.
* During the breeding season, male and female red kangaroos secrete an orange-red powdery substance known as cinnabarinic acid on their necks and chests. This 'blush' is much more obvious in males.
* Approximately 30-33 days after conception, the female kangaroo usually gives birth to one young.
* Several hours before birth, the female kangaroo will spend time licking her pouch to clean it.
* Kangaroos usually give birth by sitting forward with their long tails out in front of them between their hind legs.
* To prevent the joey from falling out, its mother's forward opening pouch contains strong muscles to keep it shut.
* The female kangaroo usually gives birth annually.
* The eastern grey kangaroo is fully weaned from its mother's milk when it is about 18-months-old. The red kangaroo is fully weaned at around 12-months-old.
* Grey joeys tend to stay in their mothers' pouches three months longer than red joeys. This is because greys take longer to develop.
* At around eight-months-old, before it is fully weaned, the baby kangaroo will usually be too big to fit into its mother's pouch. However, it still manages to suckle one of its mother's teats by poking its head into her pouch.
* Shortly after giving birth, the female kangaroo is ready to mate again.
* As the young joey matures, the quality of its mother's milk changes. The mother is able to produce two different kinds of milk from her teats: one kind for the newborn and another kind for the growing joey.
* The female kangaroo is able to suspend her pregnancy. The female usually does

this if she is already carrying a joey in her pouch or if the environmental conditions are not adequate.

* The female kangaroo teaches any young she has to fight. She does this by play fighting with them. It is important for young male kangaroos in particular to learn how to fight because one day they may have to fight off other males while competing for females during the breeding season. They may also have to fight males while competing for seniority within the mob.
* Male kangaroos really do 'box' when they fight. When two male kangaroos begin a fight, they usually link forearms and try to push each other to the ground. If this does not resolve the dispute then they will probably use their forepaws to lash out at each other. Sometimes, one of the kangaroos will resort to leaning back on its strong, muscular tail to give its opponent a powerful kick with its two back feet in an attempt to push its rival away.
* Kangaroos can bound to speeds of over 35mph (56.32km/h).
* The grey kangaroo can cover a distance of 30ft (9.14m) or more in a single leap.
* The kangaroo uses less energy the faster it hops.
* It is thought that kangaroos thump their tails or their hind feet on the ground to startle predators and to warn other kangaroos of danger.
* Some of the kangaroo's enemies include: dingoes, domestic dogs, eagles, snakes and man. Kangaroos are killed for their meat and skins. Many are also killed because farmers believe them to be an agricultural nuisance by destroying crops – particularly wheat crops. In fact, kangaroos affect only five per cent of wheat farms. Sadly, in one year alone, over three million eastern grey kangaroos were shot in Australia.
* Kangaroos can swim and are able to move their hind legs independently in the water. They cannot do this on land.
* Kangaroos lick their forearms to keep cool during the hot weather.
* The kangaroo can go for several months without drinking any water.
* In Australia, kangaroos are the most common large animals to be involved in accidents caused by road vehicles.
* Kangaroos can live to approximately 28 years in captivity.

Myths About Animals

Wolves howl at the moon.

Wolves howl as a warm-up before they go hunting, to find others or to warn off strangers. But they don't howl at the moon.

A swan can break a man's arm with its wing.

Swans aren't really all that strong. You'd have to be a child or quite frail for a swan to break your arm.

Lemmings commit mass suicide by leaping into the sea.
The old myth that lemmings commit suicide by leaping into the sea was apparently given credence by a wildlife documentary made in 1958 which showed lemmings leaping to their deaths. Decades later, the film crew admitted that imported lemmings had been driven (safely) off the cliff edge to fit the myth and the script.

March hares are mad.
There have been many explanations for the fact that hares can be seen to jump around rather more than usual during springtime. It used to be thought that hares mated in March. It was widely believed that all the jumping, boxing and rearing up which can be observed was a sign of males competing and females preserving their honour from unwanted suitors. But hares mate between February and November (and rest the other two months) so there is no reason why mating activity in March should be more obvious than at any other time of the year. The real explanation seems to be that, like many humans, hares simply feel full of the joys of spring during the month of March when the first weak rays of spring sunshine are especially welcome. And, of course, after a winter spent largely indoors, humans are more likely to be out and to spot them.

Cats don't like water and can't swim.
Although cats evolved from creatures living in the barren deserts of Eurasia, cats which are exposed to water when they are kittens grow up to enjoy a nice swim. Abyssinian cats will take a shower with their owners. Turkish angoras and Manx cats are particularly likely to enjoy a swim. The Bengali mach-bagral cat, which lives in the rivers of Burma, Nepal and southern China, is known as the swimming cat. It catches fish with its extra long, hooked claws.

Badgers spread tuberculosis to cows.

We believe it is a myth that badgers spread TB to cows. We believe that the evidence shows that cattle movements spread TB among cows, and that it is cows which give TB to badgers – not the other way round.

Wild animals are often accused of spreading disease to 'farm' animals. Wild badgers are blamed for infecting cattle with tuberculosis, wild boar are persecuted for spreading classical swine fever to commercial pigs, deer have been killed lest they carry foot and mouth disease, and bison are slaughtered lest they spread brucellosis to cattle. Even the hedgehog has been accused of carrying numerous dangerous diseases which might affect people or domesticated animals.

The belief that wild animals are the cause of illness and spread disease among domesticated and farm animals is a well-cultivated but unsubstantiated myth.

Farmers who perpetuate these myths invariably claim that the wild animal concerned has somehow acquired a natural immunity to the disease and is, therefore, able to remain symptom free while still being a threat to farmed animals. We are not aware of any scientific evidence to support this claim. And if the claim were true, it would be scientifically illogical to kill the wild animals because they had successfully developed immunity to a disease.

Farmed animals are weak and susceptible to disease because of the confined, unnatural and stressful conditions in which they are kept and the poor and often unnatural diet they are given.

Is there not a lesson to be learnt from the fact that wild animals, which must fend for themselves and which are deprived of antibiotic cover and the other luxuries afforded to domestic animals, are often much healthier and suffer far less disease even though they are exposed to the same parasites and pathogens as domestic animals?

When wild animals fall ill in large numbers it is usually because of a new problem such as pollution, drought, overcrowding or the invasion of some new pathogen (usually introduced by human beings).

Bats are blind.

Bats can see perfectly well. They use their eyes for navigation and for hunting. The myth that bats are blind originated because many species of bat also use echolocation – radar – to feel their way through the night and to spot prey and predators. But sonar doesn't work well for them over long distances and so they use their eyes.

Mice love cheese.

Cheese is one of the last things mice fancy. It is nothing like their normal natural diet of grain, pulses and fruit. They do, however, like high sugar foods. So if you are trying to attract a mouse, a piece of chocolate (or some peanut butter) would make more sense than a chunk of cheese. In an emergency, mice will eat anything – even their own tails – so a nice piece of smelly cheddar will probably prove attractive to a starving mouse.

OSTRICHES BURY THEIR HEADS IN THE SAND.

Ostriches don't bury their heads in the sand. However, when sensing danger an ostrich will fall to the ground and lay its head and neck on the ground. Because the ostrich's head and neck are lightly coloured and blend in with sandy soil it looks as though the ostrich has buried its head.

GOLDFISH ARE STUPID.

Goldfish have a memory span of up to three months. And they can tell the time.

Goldfish are not stupid

A FALLING CAT WILL ALWAYS SURVIVE BECAUSE IT WILL LAND ON ITS FEET.

A falling cat will twist in the air in an attempt to land feet first but cats who fall from high places are, nevertheless, often injured or killed. When cats fall they stand a better chance of surviving if the fall is of around eight storeys. Once a cat has reached its terminal velocity or greatest speed – which it does after falling five storeys – it can spread its limbs and relax, and be in a better position to absorb the impact when it hits the ground. A cat called Andy who lived with Florida senator, Ken Myer, once survived a fall of 16 storeys, but the record for falling out of a high building is said to be held by a cat which fell 46 storeys and survived.

RATS CAUSED THE BUBONIC PLAGUE WHICH KILLED A THIRD OF EUROPE'S POPULATION IN THE MIDDLE AGES.

It was the fleas which lived on the rats which carried the plague which killed so many people. The plague caused by the fleas carried on black rats killed a quarter of the total population in Europe at the time. (The total death toll was around 25 million.) Rats were rife because between the 12th and 17th centuries, cats were persecuted. The fact that cats' eyes seemed to shine at night convinced superstitious and frightened people that they had demonic powers. Throughout Europe cats were stoned, burnt and hurled from towers because they were feared to have black powers. This was a mistake for which the cat-killers paid a heavy price. When the Crusaders came back from the Holy Land with plague-carrying Asiatic black rats hiding in their luggage, there were no cats left to kill the rats. And so the rats spread throughout Europe. And so did the plague. The result: rather a lot of human beings died. The Black Death has not disappeared. Millions died of the same disease in India and Uganda in the 20th century.

CATS CAN SEE IN THE DARK.

It is a myth that cats can see in total darkness. They can't. However, cats do have very good night vision, and in dim light their vision is much better than that of the average clear-sighted human being.

BULLS ARE MADE ANGRY BY THE COLOUR RED.

It is a myth that the colour red ignites fury in bulls, as bulls are actually colour blind. So waving a blue, white, purple, or even a fluorescent green cape at a bull would still have the same effect as waving a red cape. In the bullring, it is believed to be the flapping movement of the cape that the bull is attracted to (and annoyed by) and not the colour.

WILD ANIMALS (SUCH AS FOXES) KILL FOR PLEASURE.

Foxes are often criticised (by those who hunt them) on the grounds that they sometimes kill large numbers of hens. The implication is that the fox kills for pleasure. (This argument is usually put forward by those who like hunting foxes for pleasure.) The truth, however, is that like other predators who may kill more than they can eat when they have the opportunity, foxes usually try to store the food they have killed.

CATS 'PLAY' WITH THE ANIMALS THEY'VE CAUGHT BEFORE THEY KILL THEM.

Contrary to myth, cats do not 'play' with animals for fun – what may look like 'playing' is part of their learning and training process. Cats like to chase, to catch and then to kill. They kill so that they can eat, and they need to practise their chasing skills. It is, however, important to remember that a cat or a kitten will be just as happy chasing a ball of paper or a piece of string (particularly if it is manipulated in an effective and lifelike manner). This shows that the cat doesn't chase and catch because it enjoys the suffering which is produced – how much 'fun' could there possibly be in 'torturing' a ball of paper or a piece of string?

CHAMELEONS CHANGE COLOUR TO MATCH THEIR SURROUNDINGS.

Chameleons change colour according to their mood rather than to fit in with their background.

CATS USE THEIR WHISKERS TO HELP THEM BALANCE.

It is a pleasant and well-sustained myth that a cat uses its whiskers to help maintain its balance. Whiskers play very little part in enabling a cat to walk along narrow ledges. Whiskers aren't entirely ornamental, however. A cat does use its whiskers to feel its way through gaps.

Animals (Not Just Cats) Show Curiosity

Stand in the street and look up into the sky and the chances are that people walking by will look up too. This phenomenon is called curiosity and although it is rumoured to have killed the cat it is something we regard as basically human.

It isn't.

All living creatures are frequently consumed by curiosity. Even birds.

Bernd Heinrich and Thomas Bugnyar of the University of Vermont in Burlington, USA, sat ravens on a perch in a room in front of one of them. The scientist then moved his head and eyes and stared in another direction. The birds followed his gaze. Sometimes they jumped down from their perch to have a closer look at whatever it was that had caught the man's attention. (This piece of research was conducted after a serendipitous observation made by Dr Bugnyar who noticed that a raven called Hugin got fed up with a tougher raven called Munin who used to bully him and take his food. So Hugin tried a little trick. As soon as Munin started to bully and steal his food he [Hugin] would go over to some empty containers, lift the lids off them and pretend to eat what was inside. Munin would follow to try to find the food that Hugin had pretended to be eating. While Munin was distracted, Hugin would go back to his own food and eat. Eventually, of course, Munin got wise to the trick. But it worked for a while.)

Animals With Pets

Animals have often been reported to have pets of their own. A chimpanzee who was thought to be lonely was given a kitten as a companion. The chimpanzee groomed the kitten, carried it about with her and protected it from harm.

A gorilla called Koko had a kitten companion which she herself named All Ball.

An elephant was seen to routinely put aside some grain for a mouse to eat.

Racehorses who have had goat companions have failed to run as expected when separated from their friends.

Some Animals Which Are Not So Well-known

Addax

Critically endangered desert living antelope with spiral horns. The addax has a pale sandy coat in the summer which turns to grey-brown in the winter. It has a long tail with a black tip. The addax can be found in north-west Africa. The addax can grow to 5½ft (1.68m) long and weigh up to 297.62lb (135kg).

Capybara

There are two species of capybara. These barrel-shaped animals are the largest members of the rodent family. Their eyes and small, rounded ears are set high on their blunt heads. Capybaras can be found in South America. They can grow to 4ft 6in (1.37m) long and weigh around 110lb (50kg). Capybaras are good swimmers and are semi-aquatic. They have partially webbed feet. Capybaras are rather shy animals.

Dugong

A docile, herbivorous large marine animal with a grey torpedo-shaped body, paddle-like flippers and a tail which is fluked like a dolphin's. The dugong can grow to 13ft (3.96m) or more long. The dugong is found in coastal waters from the Red Sea to the south-west Pacific islands. The dugong's muzzle is broad and square. The endangered dugong is also known as the 'sea cow' because of its diet of grass (sea grass in the dugong's case).

Fennec Fox

Found in Africa throughout the Sahara. The fennec fox has a cream yellowish coat with exceptionally large, pointed ears (its large ears help to keep the fox cool in the hot desert sun). Fennec foxes are the smallest of all foxes. Excluding its tail, the often nocturnal fennec fox can grow to 16in (40.64cm) long. The fennec fox has fur on the soles of its feet.

Fossa

Can only be found on the island of Madagascar. This endangered carnivore has a cat-like head and large eyes. The colour of the fossa's short fur is reddish-brown. Excluding its tail (which can grow to 3ft (0.91m)), the fossa is approximately 2ft 13in (0.88m) long. The arboreal fossa is an agile climber, climbing through the trees in pursuit of its main prey – the lemur. Bizarrely, during adolescence, the female fossa develops – what looks like – a fake penis, resembling the male fossa's penis. Once the adolescent female has reached adulthood, her clitoris returns to normal.

Kinkajou

Member of the raccoon family. The nocturnal kinkajou has a prehensile tail which is approximately 22in (55.88cm) long. Excluding its tail, the kinkajou can grow to 30in (76cm) long. The kinkajou's soft, woolly coat varies from yellow to brown. The kinkajou has a very long tongue – up to 5in (12.7cm). The kinkajou can be found in East Central and South America. The kinkajou spends much of its time in the trees and is an adept climber. The kinkajou can use its prehensile tail to hang upside down.

Margay

Member of the cat family. The margay can grow to 31in (78.74cm) long (excluding tail). The slender margay has a tawny coat covered in stripes and black rings with brownish centres. The margay has a long, ringed tail. Margays can descend trees headfirst due to its ankle joints being able to rotate 180 degrees. The margay can be found from North Mexico to North Argentina.

Pangolin

There are seven species of pangolin. Pangolins can grow to 6ft (182.88cm) long. Pangolins' bodies are covered in horny, overlapping scales. Five species of pangolin have prehensile tails. The pangolin looks like a cross between an armadillo and an anteater, but it is not related to either. Pangolins live on ants and termites, which they lap up with their very long tongues. Pangolins can be found in Asia and Africa. Pangolins do not have any teeth. Pangolins are capable of rolling up into balls when threatened.

Sugar Glider

Blue-grey marsupial. The sugar glider is approximately 5.9in (15cm) long (excluding its tail). The sugar glider has a membrane on each side of its body, stretching from its front legs to its back legs. This little marsupial can be found in Australia, New Guinea and Indonesia. The sugar glider is capable of 'flying' from one tree to the next as far as 145ft (44.19m) away. The sugar glider has a long, bushy tail which acts as a rudder during glides.

Zorilla

Member of the weasel family. The zorilla has a skunk-like appearance. The zorilla can grow to 15in (38cm) long (excluding its tail). The zorilla has four striking white stripes running down its black coat. Zorillas can be found in sub-Saharan Africa. When the zorilla feels threatened, just like the skunk, it will spray its enemy with a nasty-smelling liquid from its anal scent glands.

Koalas

- The koala is the only member of its family, Phascolarctidae. The koala can be found in eucalyptus forest and woodland in eastern Australia and in some southern parts of Australia.
- The koala bear is not actually a bear – it is a marsupial. Marsupials are characterised by the fact that their young continue to develop outside the mother's womb.
- The cute koala has a bear-like body; a large head; a broad face; large, round tufted ears; a big leathery black nose; short powerful limbs and no tail except for a very short rounded stump. The koala's coat is made up of soft brown-greyish fur with a whitish coloured neck and chest.
- Koalas can weigh up to 33lb (14.96kg) and grow to 32in (81.28cm) long.
- Koalas feed almost entirely on eucalyptus trees.

- The koala spends approximately four hours a day eating.
- There are hundreds of different types of eucalyptus tree, but the koala will only feed on a small percentage of them.
- Koalas consume approximately 17.63oz (0.5kg) of foliage a day, which they grind down into a fine paste with their specially adapted teeth.
- To aid digestion, the koala swallows gravel or soil.
- Eucalyptus leaves are toxic to most other herbivores, but a koala's liver is adapted and can break down the toxic substances in the leaves.
- The koala lacks energy and, therefore, spends up to 20 hours a day sleeping. The reason for the koala's lack of energy is simple: the food it eats contains very little energy value as well as very few nutrients. The koala's lack of zest is also compounded by the fact that it has hardly any fat on its body and, consequently, no stored source of energy.
- The koala has five digits on each of its forepaws. Two of those digits are opposable to the other three, which gives the appearance of the koala having two thumbs on each forepaw. The koala's unusual forepaws, combined with the needle-sharp, curved claws on its hind feet, enable it to climb and grip branches with great expertise.
- The koala's closest relative is the common wombat of eastern and south-eastern Australia.
- The female koala is two-years-old when it commences breeding.
- During the breeding season, which occurs in the Australian summer, male koalas produce a growling bellow. They bellow in this way to call out to females in the area and to intimidate other male competitors. Some of the females emit loud wailing sounds if they are frightened or are being troubled by any of the males.
- It is usually the older, more dominant males who are successful at mating the female koalas.
- A koala's pregnancy lasts for approximately 35 days.
- The koala usually gives birth to one young.
- Like the baby kangaroo and other young marsupials, a young koala is called a 'joey'.
- The young koala is the size of a jellybean, approximately less than 1in (2.5cm) long when it is first born. The young koala then makes the journey to its mother's rearward-opening pouch. Once in the pouch, the baby koala will latch itself onto one of its mother's nipples – and there it will remain until its development is complete. At around seven to eight months, the baby koala will leave its mother's pouch for good and will spend most of its time – for approximately a further five months – clinging to its mother's back.
- When the koala becomes too big to fit into its mother's pouch, it will continue to suckle by poking its head into her pouch.

The koala spends nearly all of its time in eucalyptus trees, and sleeps usually by wedging itself in the fork of a tree.

- During the weaning process, which begins at around five months, the baby koala eats its mother's faeces. The mother's faeces are expelled in such a way that they contain partially digested leaves and, more importantly, micro-organisms which will enable the baby koala to digest eucalyptus leaves once it is fully weaned.
- At around six-months-old, the young koala is fully furred.
- The average lifespan of the koala is 12-18 years.
- Koalas do most of their feeding at night.
- Koalas are usually solitary animals, only getting together during the breeding season.
- Amazingly, koalas do not suffer from parasites. The eucalyptus oil on the animal's fur acts as an insecticide.
- Domestic dogs, owls and wedge-tailed eagles are just some of the koala's predators.
- Like all animals that live in dry countries, koalas can go for long periods without water. Koalas receive most of their moisture from eucalyptus leaves.
- The koala is a protected species.
- Koalas used to be extensively killed for their pelts. In one year alone, two million pelts were exported. Thankfully, this barbaric practice has long since been banned. Now, the koala's main threat to its survival is disease, loss of habitat and forest fires.

Seven Animals Which Mate For Life

1. Badger
2. Beaver
3. Fox
4. Gibbon
5. Mongoose
6. Orang-utan
7. Pigeon

Animals As Carers: How Animals Help People

It is well known that animals help people in a number of different ways. People who would otherwise be lonely but who share their lives with a dog or a cat often suffer far less from illness than those who do not have an animal to talk to, play with or sit with. Stroking a cat can help reduce blood pressure. Talking to a budgerigar can help stave off depression. Watching goldfish swimming around a tank can ease anxiety. And walking the dog can help ease aching joints and improve cardiovascular fitness.

But here are some other examples of how compassionate, thoughtful, imaginative and caring animals can and do help people:

- In their excellent book *When Elephants Weep,* Jeffrey Masson and Susan McCarthy report how a man called John Teal, who was working with endangered musk oxen, was at first alarmed when some dogs approached and the musk oxen snorted, stamped and thundered towards him. Before Mr Teal could move to escape, the oxen formed a defensive ring around him and lowered their horns at the dogs. It turned out that the musk oxen were protecting their new human friend in exactly the same way that they would protect their calves from predators.
- The life of a man in Boston, USA, was saved by his dog Belle who had been trained to call for help. The man, who was diabetic, had a seizure and collapsed. The dog then bit into the unconscious man's cell phone and called the emergency services on 911.
- Dogs can be used to help diabetic patients by using their keen sense of smell. The dogs can detect abnormalities in a diabetic's blood sugar level. The specially trained dog periodically licked her owner's nose to check his blood sugar level. If she was worried (could smell ketones), she would paw and whine at him until he took action to put things right. 'Every time she paws at me in that way I grab my meter and test myself,' said the man. 'She's never been wrong.'
- Dogs have also been trained to detect cancer by smell. And early studies are showing impressive results. A dog's nose has 220 million cells associated with its sense of smell. Humans have just 5 million. (It is for this reason that dogs are used to sniff out drugs, explosives and human remains.) Some experts now even claim that dogs can be trained to smell cancer cells in human beings. Dr Armand Gognetta, a skin cancer specialist, has reported that a grey-haired Schnauzer called George, who has been trained to detect skin cancer cells in humans, has a success rate of nearly 100 per cent. George was trained after a medical journal had described how another dog had kept sniffing at a mole on her owner's leg – ignoring a number of other moles. A biopsy had revealed that the mole which had attracted attention had been malignant.
- Dogs have been reported to be sensitive to impending epileptic seizures. No one knows how they do this but dogs are sensitive to seizures about forty minutes before they occur. Dogs can therefore be trained to offer early warnings – enabling their owners to take the appropriate precautions for their safety.
- Many pets know (presumably through some sixth sense such as extra sensory perception) that their owners are going to be in danger. Wildlife writer George Laycock has described how a collie whose owner worked in a factory making explosives, saved his owner's life. Every day the collie walks to work with the man. But one day, the dog began to whine and sat down in the road. The dog would not budge. Eventually the man left the dog and went to work alone. The collie went back home and crawled under the man's bed. He stayed there all

day, whining. That day a tremendous explosion destroyed the factory – and killed the collie's owner.

- Cat owners have reported that when they are feeling ill their cat will make much of a fuss of them – purring loudly and rubbing against them when they are feeling unwell.
- It has frequently been reported that dogs who are separated from their owners will sense when something terrible has happened. Author Sandra Collier reports that when a friend was taken seriously ill while on holiday, her dogs – left at home in the care of another friend – began howling in the middle of the night. The dogs howled continuously. It was later discovered that the dogs had started howling at the moment their owner had fallen ill.
- Writer Ernest Thompson Seton got caught in two wolf traps while working in the wilderness. At nightfall, a pack of hungry wolves gathered around him. The leader began to growl and snap at Seton who was trapped and helpless. As the wolves were about to attack, Seton's dog Bingo suddenly appeared and killed the leader of the wolf pack. Bingo then dragged a tool to Seton that enabled him to undo the traps and free himself. The really strange thing is that the dog had not been taken on Seton's expedition. At home he had whimpered and acted strangely. Eventually, despite attempts to detain him, he headed into the dark to find the endangered Seton.
- Four New Zealanders were swimming off Ocean Beach near Whangarei on New Zealand's North Island when dolphins swam close to them in tight circles and herded them to safety. One of the swimmers, a lifesaver, tried to escape from the dolphins but was herded back into the group – just as he noticed a 9ft (2.74m) great white shark swimming towards the group. 'The dolphins had corralled us up to protect us,' said the lifesaver. The swimmers spent the next 40 minutes surrounded by the dolphins before the shark disappeared and they were allowed to swim back to shore. The dolphins had sensed the danger to the human swimmers and had taken action to protect them, just as they would protect their young. Later, two of the dolphins were butchered by poachers.
- Animals have been known to give food to hungry humans. Koko the gorilla, who learned to communicate with humans through sign language, gave medical advice to a woman who complained of indigestion. Koko told the woman to drink orange juice. When the woman revisited ten days later and offered Koko a drink of orange juice, Koko would not accept the drink until assured that the woman felt better.
- A Border collie woke a young mother from a deep sleep and led her to her baby's cot. The baby was choking on mucus and had stopped breathing.

LIONS

- Lions belong to the family Felidae. Lions can mainly be found in parts of sub-Saharan Africa, but a small number survive in the Gir Forest Sanctuary in India.
- There are five subspecies of lion. They are: the Asiatic lion, Masai lion, Angolan lion, Transvaal lion and the Senegalese lion.
- Lions mainly inhabit open savanna and grassy plains.
- Excluding the tail which is approximately 3ft (0.91m) long, the lion can grow to 7ft (2.13m) or more in length.
- A fully-grown male lion can be 4ft (1.22m) high at the shoulder and weigh as much as 550lb (249.47kg). Male lions can be 50 per cent heavier than female lions.
- It is the male lion that has a mane around its head, neck and shoulders: the female does not have a mane. A lion's mane is usually fully-grown by the time it is five-years-old.
- The lion's mane (which weighs very little) makes the lion look larger than he is. This helps to scare off other male rivals and, if a fight should occur, helps to protect the lion's head and neck from its opponent's teeth and claws.
- The lion's mane becomes darker with age.
- The female lion is called a lioness. The male lion is called a tom or a lion. The baby lion is called a cub, lionet or whelp.
- A group of lions is called a pride. A pride can include 30 members or more.
- A typical pride consists of 4–12 females (who are related to one another), their young offspring and several males who are nearly always unrelated to the females.
- Lions are primarily nocturnal animals, and do their hunting at night. However, if they are really hungry, they have been known to hunt during the daytime.
- Lionesses do most of the hunting. Lionesses hunt small animals such as warthogs on their own, but they will band together to hunt large prey (such as gazelles or giraffes) which they cannot easily catch and kill on their own. It is normally the male lions who dominate the carcass and eat first within the pride. It is usual for all the members of the pride to share the kill; however, lions tend to be reluctant when it comes to sharing small kills with the rest of the pride.
- Lions are carnivores. The lion's diet includes: antelopes, zebras, buffaloes, warthogs, gazelles, wildebeest, giraffes, small animals, birds, reptiles and carrion. Lions have also been known to eat young rhinos and young elephants.
- Lions can run at speeds of 35mph (56.32km/h) or more. A lot of their prey can run faster, and this makes hunting difficult. Added to this, lions do not have the stamina to run at high speeds for more than a few hundred yards. So if a lion can steal another animal's prey to avoid having to hunt – it will.
- The lioness has a one in four chance of succeeding in catching its prey. This means that many cubs starve to death during their first 12 months of life.

A Lion's Pride

The lion he sits there full of valour
Guarding his territory
This wonderful beast of the African plains
Has risen through victory

The lion he bathes in the African sun
Watching all around
The members of his pride know he is ready
To defend at any sound

The lion he governs all those in his realm
It is to him they must adhere
His confidence of spirit and magnificent might
Cause any challenger to fear

The lion he revels in his majestic glory
For he knows that he is king
His knowledge is power his power is knowledge
That only time can bring

The lion he sits there all faded and worn
The years no longer his friend
He knows that his days are soon to be numbered
His pride he cannot defend

The lion he sits there still full of valour
Guarding his territory
This wonderful beast of the African plains
Has fallen from victory

Donna Antoinette Coleman

- If the availability of prey is scarce, or the prey is too large for one or two lions to catch, lions will hunt together in groups. Lions hunt by creeping up to their prey as close as they possibly can and then, when they are approximately 90ft (27.43m) away, they will launch an attack at their victim. One of the methods lions use to kill their prey is to leap at their victim and use its powerful front paws to break its victim's neck.
- Studies have shown that females prefer to mate males with big manes. This is probably because a large mane might be an indicator of good genes.

- Male lions need to eat up to 22lb (9.97kg) of meat a day. Females need 18lb (8.16kg) of meat a day.
- A lion is capable of consuming a quarter of its body weight in one sitting.
- A lioness may copulate hundreds of times during her time of oestrus. Oestrus can last four days or more.
- The lion usually keeps guard over his mating partner to try to prevent other males from mating with her.
- The lioness's pregnancy lasts approximately 100-119 days.
- The average litter size is two or three cubs.
- Lionesses give birth any time of the year. When the baby cubs are born, they weigh about 4½lb (2.04kg).
- Once the lioness has given birth to her cubs, she will usually keep them away

from the rest of the pride until they are six to eight weeks old. This is thought to help the bonding process and to ensure that mum and cubs get used to one another's unique scent.

- It is not unusual for several female lions of a pride to give birth within weeks of one another. And it is not unusual for female lions to suckle cubs belonging to other females in the pride.
- Females with cubs of similar ages will often form crèches within their pride, where the mothers will help one another in looking after their young.
- The baby cub is dependent on its mother for the first two years of its life.
- Hyenas, leopards, martial eagles and pythons are just a few of the predators likely to threaten young cubs.
- If the young male lions do not leave their natal pride of their own accord then they are driven out by the rest of the pride by the time they are around two to four years of age. The young related male lions who leave the same pride tend to stay together, hoping one day soon to take over a pride they can call their own.
- A male lion who is no longer part of a pride, and is unable to form a coalition with other lions is a pitiful sight, especially if the male is past its prime and his pride has been taken over by younger, stronger males. These poor lone, nomadic lions will try their utmost to form alliances with other nomads but if they are unsuccessful then the rest of their days are destined to be fraught with danger and hardship. The already difficult task of hunting prey is made much more difficult if the lion is by itself.
- Young lionesses are often allowed to stay on in their natal pride but sometimes they can be forced to leave by the other members of the pride if being there is likely to put a strain on the pride's resources. Like the males, they too will try to form alliances.
- The males of the pride are always on the lookout for other males who want to take over their pride. Huge fights may ensue, with the males of the pride fiercely defending their territories – sometimes to the death. If the intruders are successful at driving the males away from their pride (which is sometimes the case, especially if the pride males are old) the successors will then kill and eat some of the cubs who are in the pride. They do this to stop the mother or mothers from lactating, thus, bringing the females into heat much earlier so that they can be mated with as soon as possible.
- Although male lions will fiercely fend off any male outsiders, they tend not to fight one another within the pride.
- Lions can live to 18 years in the wild.
- Lions may spend as much as 20 hours a day resting.
- A lion's roar can be heard up to five miles (8km) away. Both male and female lions roar, but it is the male lion who has the loudest roar. Lions usually roar to announce that they are in control of their territory and to warn other lions

nearby. Males also defend their territory by patrolling and scent marking with their urine.

- ♦ Unlike most cats, lions do not mind the water and can become good swimmers.
- ♦ In some parts of Africa, fur balls coughed up by lions are worn as talismans.
- ♦ Habitat destruction and hunting have seriously threatened the magnificent Asiatic lion with extinction.

'As long as people will shed the blood of innocent creatures
there can be no peace, no liberty, no harmony between people.
Slaughter and justice cannot dwell together.'
ISAAC BASHEVIS SINGER (1904–1991)

THE ELEVEN MOST POPULAR HOUSEHOLD PETS

1. Goldfish
2. Dog
3. Cat
4. Hamster
5. Guinea pig
6. Rabbit
7. Mouse
8. Budgerigar
9. Rat
10. Gerbil
11. Chinchilla

FAMOUS PEOPLE AND THEIR (NOT SO FAMOUS) ANIMALS

- ✱ Wolfgang Amadeus Mozart owned a starling whom he taught to whistle the theme of the last movement of his G Major Piano Concerto (K453).
- ✱ Scottish writer, Sir Walter Scott, was a great animal lover who kept many pets throughout his lifetime. One of Sir Walter's favourite pets was a hound called Maida, who was painted alongside Sir Walter so frequently that the poor hound would walk away in disgust as soon as he saw an artist put brush to paper.
- ✱ Oliver Cromwell owned a greyhound called Coffin-Nail.
- ✱ Sir Winston Churchill loved animals – particularly dogs and cats. Nobody ate in Sir Winston Churchill's house until his pet dogs had been fed.
- ✱ The Roman poet, Virgil, had a pet fly. When the fly died, Virgil held a funeral for it at his home.

- American poet, Carl Sandburg, kept goats of which he was very fond. One evening, when it was bitterly cold, Carl Sandburg let 15 of the goats into his house in Michigan and played the guitar to them.
- American President, John Quincy Adams, used to keep silk worms during his time in power.
- French Poet, Gerard de Nerval, used to take his pet lobster for walks.
- Julius Caesar is believed to have owned a giraffe.
- British poet, William Wordsworth, owned a dog that would bark furiously if the rhythm wasn't right when one of his master's poems was read aloud.
- American writer, Gertrude Stein, disliked the author Ernest Hemingway so much that she taught her dog to jump up and bark by waving a handkerchief in front of the dog's face whilst saying: 'Play Hemingway! Be Fierce!'
- George Orwell, the English novelist and essayist, and author of *Animal Farm* and *1984,* once owned a pet goat called Muriel.
- Charles IX, King of France, owned 36 miniature greyhounds. The former French King's greyhounds all wore matching red and green collars made out of velvet.
- British author, J. R. Ackerley, owned an Alsatian called Queenie. One day, Queenie accidentally bit his master's hand after they were both scuffling for a rotten apple core on the ground. Later, when she saw Ackerley's hand bandaged up, Queenie was so upset that she skulked to 'the darkest corner of the bedroom and stayed there for the rest of the afternoon.'
- American novelist John Steinbeck's dog ate half of the first draft of his manuscript, *Of Mice and Men.* And when Steinbeck's novel received bad reviews, he decided that his dog was a good literary critic and, thus, promoted the canine to be 'lieutenant-colonel in charge of literature.'
- In 1945, Jerome Napoleon Bonaparte – the last of the Bonapartes – tripped up over his dog's lead and died.
- The Roman emperor, Caligula, saw to it that his favourite horse had his own house to live in, complete with furniture. Caligula's horse even had his own slaves.
- Dorothy Parker, American short-story writer and poet who was famous for her robust sense of humour, named one of her dogs after US President, Woodrow Wilson, because it was – as Dorothy Parker once put it – 'full of shit'.
- Frederick the Great, the King of Prussia, had a painting made in honour of the spider that saved his life. The spider fell into Frederick's drinking chocolate which the cook had poisoned. (And Frederick, of course, didn't drink the chocolate.)
- Paul Gallico's novel, *The Snow Goose,* was based on a factual story of a goose that used to visit British painter and naturalist Sir Peter Scott's home during the winter months.
- British poet, Walter Savage Landor, had a dog called, Pomero. When the dog died, the family cat lay upon Pomero's grave night and day.

* American writer and cartoonist, James Thurber, owned a dog that was so aggressive that when the dog died, James Thurber had a 'Beware of the Dog' sign put up above its grave.

* When a dog belonging to the famous American painter, James Abbott McNeill Whistler, became ill, Mr Whistler called out a very notable doctor to take a look at his dog. Although the doctor treated the dog respectfully and carefully, he was outraged that he should be called out to look at a dog, and he decided to have his revenge. The following day, Mr Whistler received an urgent message from the doctor to come to his house immediately. Of course, Mr Whistler thought the worst and started to think that perhaps it was bad news about his dog. Once he arrived at the house, the doctor greeted him by saying: 'Good morning, Mr Whistler. I wanted to see you about painting my front door.'
* Charles Dickens owned a terrier called Snittle Timbery.
* American general, George Patton, owned a bull terrier called William the Conqueror.
* The famous characters Benjamin Bunny and Peter Rabbit were based on Beatrix Potter's own pet rabbits, Benjamin Bouncer and Peter Piper.
* Whenever American author, Ellen Glasgow, used to travel away from home, she would send postcards to her pet dogs.

* Albert Schweitzer, Alsatian-born German philosopher, theologian, missionary doctor and organist, owned a gentle wild boar that used to attend church.
* Audrey Hepburn's Yorkshire terrier dog was called Mr Famous.
* The legendary American animator, Walt Disney, owned a pet mouse called Mortimer. It was Mortimer who was the inspiration for the cartoon character, Mickey Mouse. Walt Disney originally wanted to call the now legendary screen mouse Mortimer, but his wife – thankfully – objected to the name.
* Shortly after Mary Queen of Scots was executed at Fotheringhay Castle, one of her dogs was found to be hiding underneath her clothes. When the dog emerged, he laid himself down in the blood between his mistress's body and her severed head.
* Abraham Lincoln was the first American President to bring a cat into the White House.
* FBI chief and crossdresser, J. Edgar Hoover, owned a dog called Spee De Bozo.
* American explorer, Richard Byrd, owned a white fox terrier called Igloo.
* Alexander the Great hated cats.
* Elizabeth I introduced the death penalty for anyone who possessed greyhounds but who was not a gentleman.
* When Queen Victoria arrived back to Buckingham Palace after her coronation in Westminster Abbey, one of the first things she did was give her much loved dog a bath.

Mice (Wood Mice)

- The wood mouse (also known as the long-tailed field mouse) belongs to the family Muridae, and is one of the most widespread of European mammals. The wood mouse can be found in Europe, North Africa and Central Asia.
- The wood mouse can grow to just over 4in (10.16cm) long. The wood mouse's tail can also grow to just over 4in (10.16cm) long.
- The wood mouse has a long snout, prominent eyes and long, rounded ears. On the upper part of its body, the wood mouse's fur is usually dark yellow-brown in colour with a band of darker fur running from its head down the length of its upper body. Its flanks are yellowish and the underside of the wood mouse's fur is white/grey. A little golden patch can sometimes be found on the wood mouse's chest.
- As their name suggests, wood mice tend to live in woodlands. However, woodlands are not the only place they can be found. Wood mice also inhabit fields, parks, mountain-sides, hedgerows, sand-dunes, moorlands and domestic gardens. During the winter, they may also inhabit buildings.
- In any place they inhabit, wood mice usually hide away in underground burrows,

where they make nest chambers for their young and keep their supply of food for the winter. Nevertheless, it is not uncommon for wood mice to make their nests above the ground, inside wall cavities or inside tree holes. Unless they are in buildings occupied by people, wood mice will not live alongside house mice. It is unusual for the wood mouse to stray further than 650ft (198m) from its burrow.

☞ Wood mice are very adept climbers and can climb trees with great ease.

☞ The wood mouse is often only active at night, which means that it is rarely seen during the daytime.

☞ The wood mouse – with its large hind feet – bounds along the ground like a miniature kangaroo. It is capable of leaping 3ft (0.91m) into the air.

☞ The wood mouse's diet usually includes: shoots, buds, seeds, nuts, fruits, berries, fungi, insects, insect larvae and snails. Wood mice have even been known to steal honey from beehives.

☞ The wood mouse has many predators including: cats, foxes, badgers, stoats, pine martens, weasels, kestrels and owls. And, of course, human beings kill vast quantities of mice. Vivisectors use vast numbers of mice in their laboratories.

☞ The wood mouse's tail skin can easily slip off. If a predator catches the wood mouse by the tail, the tail skin slides off allowing the wood mouse to scurry away to safety.

☞ The wood mouse's breeding season usually starts in spring and lasts into autumn – depending on abundance of food.

☞ The female wood mouse likes to be groomed by the male before mating with him.

☞ The wood mouse's pregnancy lasts around 26 days.

☞ The average litter of the wood mouse consists of five to six young.

☞ The baby mice are born blind and naked, and weigh less than 0.07oz (2g).

☞ The young mice are weaned at around 21 days.

☞ Wood mice may have about four litters of young a year.

☞ In the wild, wood mice live on average for about six months. They can, however, live for as long as two years if conditions are good.

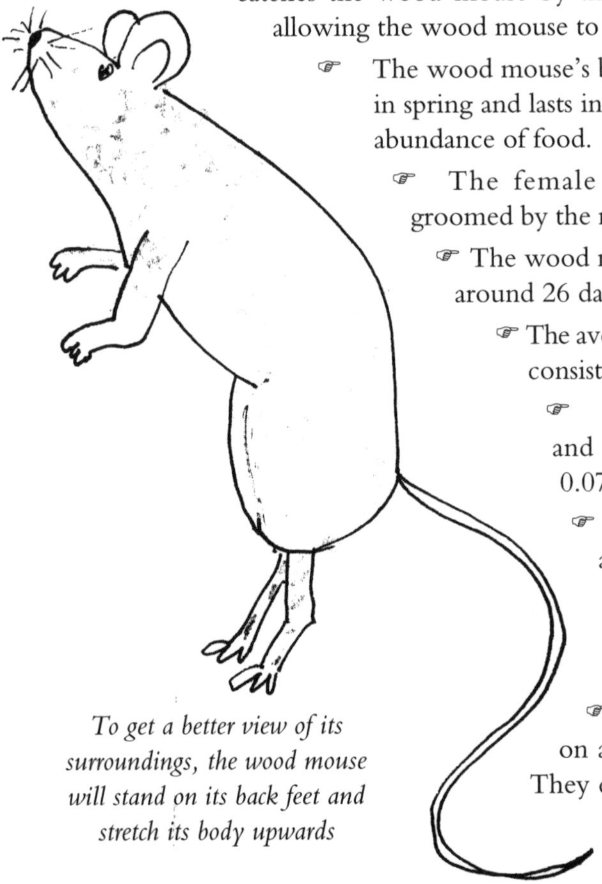

To get a better view of its surroundings, the wood mouse will stand on its back feet and stretch its body upwards

- ☞ If a female wood mouse who has babies is alarmed, she will run off with her babies hanging on tightly by their mouths to each of her teats. This method of escape is far more efficient than carrying her babies one by one to safety.
- ☞ Wood mice often groom themselves when they are frightened.
- ☞ The wood mouse is a solitary animal, but it will sometimes share its nest with other mice during the winter months.
- ☞ The wood mouse does not hibernate. Instead, it goes into a torpid state, using up less energy throughout the cold months when food is likely to be scarce.
- ☞ There is sometimes confusion about the differences between the wood mouse and the house mouse. The two most obvious differences involve colour and smell. The adult house mouse does not have greyish white underparts – although its underparts can be pale brown or even a dusky grey in colour. The colour contrast between the upper and underparts is not so evident as it is in the wood mouse. And, unlike the wood mouse which hardly smells at all, the house mouse has a strong, musky odour. When the two mice are compared, the other obvious differences are the eyes, ears, hind feet and tail. The wood mouse has more prominent eyes, larger ears, larger hind legs and a longer tail. The tail on the wood mouse is lightly haired: the tail on the house mouse is hairless.
- ☞ Tannins and saponins are harmful to mice but if eaten in the right proportions, the dangers of one substance cancels out the toxicity of the other. Mice manage to eat just the right amounts of the two, getting the balance right so that they survive.

How To Catch A Mouse Without Killing It

When a mouse took up residence in our home recently, our first thoughts were to find a way of catching the mouse without having to kill it. We tried several times to catch the mouse using commercial, humane mousetraps – which trap the mouse inside a box as soon as it reaches for the bait. Unfortunately, these traps didn't work – our mouse was far too clever.

After a week of living with our incontinent, smelly mouse, a relative passed on this wonderful tip on how to catch the mouse without killing it.

The items you will need are:

1. An unused biscuit tin
2. A thimble
3. Half a slice of bread (if that)
4. Some peanut butter

Fill the thimble with bread. Push the bread in quite tightly so that the mouse will have to pull at the bread to get it out of the thimble. Smear a very tiny amount of peanut butter onto the bread. You must not put too much peanut butter onto the bread otherwise the mouse will fill itself up on the peanut butter and leave the bread untouched (mice only eat small amounts of food).

Place the thimble on the floor and balance the biscuit tin on top of the thimble. You should face the open end of the thimble to the inside of the biscuit tin. The tin should be balanced on the very edge of the closed end of the thimble (so that it's almost about to fall off).

The mouse is attracted to the smell of the peanut butter and crawls underneath the biscuit tin to get at the source of the smell. It licks the tiny amount of peanut butter and then starts to eat the bread inside the thimble. Because the thimble has been tightly packed, the mouse has to pull at the bread. This causes the thimble to slip completely inside the biscuit tin, thereby trapping the mouse.

Mice usually come out at night so, if you put your trap down before going to bed, by the morning your mouse should be safely trapped inside the tin. Slide a thin piece of hardboard beneath the tin (so that the mouse cannot escape), and free your mouse a good distance away from your house and any other occupied buildings. (If you don't free the mouse a good distance away from your home, the mouse will come back for more of your lovely peanut butter).

Always wash your hands well after handling mice, and wipe down any areas in your house where the mouse may have been. Mice have a tendency to urinate everywhere, and their urine can carry some unpleasant diseases.

Animals Have Much Better Survival Instincts Than People

There has, for centuries, been a belief that animals can detect impending natural disasters before they happen. For example, there is good evidence that many animals know when earthquakes and tsunamis are imminent.

1. Just before the tsunami crashed into southern India in 2005, animals ran from the coast to the safety of a nearby hilltop. A herd of antelope stampeded from the shoreline ten minutes before the waves hit. In Sri Lanka, where 30,000 people were killed, all the wild animals (elephants, leopards, deer, etc) managed to survive at the Yala National Park on the coast. The animals all escaped before the waves hit. Throughout the area there was only one report of a dead animal as a result of the tsunami.
2. In California, it has been reported that horses will not let people ride them when earthquakes are due.
3. In China, in 1975, snakes emerged from hibernation to escape being buried when an earthquake hit the city of Haicheng.
4. The Chinese Government has published an official booklet describing animal signs that precede and, therefore, predict earthquakes. Tell-tale signs include

cattle and horses refusing to enter their corrals, rats leaving their hiding places and running around wildly, and fish jumping out of the water.

5. Before major earthquakes and floods, small mammals leave their burrows and cattle migrate to high ground.
6. Desert tortoises in Nevada dig shallow holes in rocky soil to catch rain when they sense that there is a storm coming.
7. Sheep will run for shelter when they sense bad weather coming. The sky may be blue – with no signs of an impending storm – when they start running.
8. Cats can predict earthquakes. When an earthquake is coming, a cat will do everything it can to get out of any building. A cat which has kittens, will take the kittens with it. In the hours before an earthquake hits, cats get extremely agitated. They have often been seen scratching at doors to be let out, or simply hurrying outside. The Chinese always used to rely on cats to predict earthquakes and other natural disasters. It is likely that cats are more sensitive to faint tremors or changes in magnetic fields than people are.

No one yet knows how animals do this. Do they hear the rumblings of an earthquake? Do they feel the changes in the earth's electromagnetic field? Or do they sense a change in atmospheric pressure? Whatever the explanation, it seems reasonable to conclude that if you see animals running from somewhere you should leave too. If your cat suddenly picks up its kittens and heads for the door maybe you should follow.

How A Spider Constructs A Web

THE SPIDER FIRST FLINGS OUT A LINE OF SILK with a blob of glue on the end. When the blob of glue catches on a leaf, twig or wall, the spider pays out a new thread and lets its weight pull down the thread a little. It then makes the second anchor point before dropping, still spinning silk, to make a third anchor point. The spider then fills in the maze, using these three guy ropes as the framework.

Monkeys

- Monkeys evolved in Africa and are categorised into two primate groups: Old World and New World monkeys. The Old World monkeys are found in Asia and Africa. The New World monkeys are found in Central and South America.
- There are a number of anatomical differences between the Old World and the New World monkeys. New World monkeys usually have round nostrils that are spaced wide apart, whereas Old World monkeys usually have narrow, downward pointing nostrils that are spaced closer together. Old World monkeys

do not have prehensile tails (tails that are capable of grasping), whereas some New World monkeys do. And New World monkeys don't have hard patches of bare skin (ischial callosities) on their buttocks. Many Old World monkeys do.

- There are believed to be over 200 different species of monkey.
- The mandrill, found in West Central Africa, is the largest monkey in the world. It is easily recognised by its vibrant red and blue face (the coloration in females and juveniles is more subdued). Mandrills can grow to 32in (81.28cm) long and weigh over 55lb (24.94kg). The male mandrill's brightly coloured face becomes even brighter when he is excited. Mandrill males have yellow beards. Unlike many other species of monkey, mandrills do not live in trees.
- When a female mandrill is ready to mate, her bottom swells and becomes bright red.
- The pygmy marmoset, found in South America, is the smallest monkey in the world; its body length is 4-6in (10.16-15.24cm) long. It is so small that it can fit into the palm of a human hand.
- The pygmy marmoset feeds in an extraordinary way. It gouges holes in tree bark with its large incisors, and marks the holes with its scent (sometimes urinating in the holes). The marmoset then returns to the holes later on to feed on the sticky sap.
- Dusky titi monkeys have an unusual way of maintaining their relationships with their partners and of declaring their territories. Before sunrise, the loved-up couples entwine their tails and perform a duet together.
- Most monkeys are arboreal (relating to or living in the trees). Arboreal monkeys use all four of their limbs to leap from tree to tree.
- Baboons with their dog-like heads are Old World monkeys and, unlike many other monkey species, do not live in trees.
- The Guinea baboon is the smallest of the baboon species: the olive baboon is the largest.
- There are striking differences in appearance between the male and female white-faced saki monkeys. The male's coat is black all over but with a pale face and a black nose. The female's coat is greyish brown in colour with a black face and a pale stripe on either side of its nose.
- The massive pendulous nose of the Old World male proboscis monkey can be 3in (7.62cm) or more in length. The proboscis monkey's nose keeps on growing even in adulthood. Female proboscis monkeys have smaller noses. And the young have small, upturned noses. Females prefer to mate with males with big noses – the bigger the better. It is the female proboscis monkey that usually initiates sex. She lets a male know that she's interested by pouting her lips at him.
- The male proboscis monkey sometimes displays its erect penis to frighten off intruders.
- The loudest monkeys are the howler monkeys. Their vocal sounds can be heard more than 1½ miles (2.4km) away. Male howler monkeys usually howl at the

beginning and at the end of each day. They do this to find out where their competitors are so that they know what they will have to do in order to defend their territories.

- Some of the monkey's predators include: wild dogs, hyenas, jackals, cheetahs, lions, leopards and snakes.
- The Celebes macaque money has a hairy crest along its crown. The crest rises when the monkey becomes excited.
- Japanese macaques (also called 'snow monkeys') that live in the mountains in northern Honshu in Japan have learned to survive further north in the colder weather than any other primate except man. Winter can be devastatingly cold with temperatures dropping as low as -15C. Japanese macaques, who have fluffy, grey-coloured coats, huddle together to keep warm. Japanese macaques living in the mountains of West Tokyo have learned to warm themselves by bathing in the hot springs where they live.
- Just like human children, young Japanese macaque monkeys enjoy making snowballs in the snow.
- Monkeys often groom one another. Grooming not only helps to keep their coats in good condition but also serves to strengthen bonds and ease tensions. Monkeys have been known to use grooming as a commodity to barter with other monkeys. For example, female baboons and patas monkeys will trade grooming with females who have young for a chance to caress their infants.
- Vervet monkeys have different alarm calls for different predators.
- The bald uakari monkey (the only short-tailed New World monkey) has hairless crown and a red face. The redder the male bald uakari monkey's face, the more attractive he is to females. When excited, the bald uakari monkey wags its tail just like a dog.
- The spider monkey has the most dextrous prehensile tail of all the New World monkeys. The spider monkey's heavily furred tail, which can grow to 36in (91.44cm) long, is able to support the monkey's whole weight.
- Monkeys are highly social animals and live in clans that may include several hundred individuals.
- The Hanuman langur monkey is revered by Hindus because it is thought to be descended from the monkey-god Hanuman. Hanuman langurs are so revered by the local people that troops of langurs are allowed to run freely about villages, towns and temples.
- In contrast to the outgoing Hanuman langurs, their relatives the golden langurs are reclusive. So much so, that nobody was able to photograph them until 1953.
- Monkeys are omnivores. Their diets include: small animals, lizards, insects, fruit, seeds, vegetation, roots, eggs, sap and honey,
- Almost all monkeys eat and move about during the daytime and sleep at night.
- Silvered leaf monkeys have silver-black shaggy coats but have babies who have bright orange coloured coats.

- Colobus monkeys living in the mountains and tropical forests of equatorial Africa can leap up to 30ft (9.14m) to reach the branches of trees that are lower down.
- Night monkeys are able to see in the dark, and are the only truly nocturnal monkeys. Night monkeys are also called 'owl monkeys' because of the hooting noises they make during the night. It is often the males who make the hooting noises. They tend to do more hooting when there is a full moon in the sky.
- Vervet monkeys living on the Caribbean island of St Kitts, steal leftover drinks from alcohol-serving bars. In fact, five per cent of vervet monkeys living on the island have now become hardened binge drinkers.
- Barbary apes (or Barbary macaques) are the only wild monkeys in Europe. They live on the Rock of Gibraltar. According to legend, Gibraltar Rock will remain under British rule as long as the Barbary apes are there. The Barbary ape was incorrectly named because it was originally mistaken for an ape because, like the apes, it does not have a tail.
- All five species of mangabey monkey have light-coloured eyelids. It is thought that they communicate with one another by fluttering their eyelids.
- Monkeys show aggression by exposing their teeth.
- Patas monkeys can run to speeds of 35mph (56.32km/h).
- Most species of monkey give birth to one young. However, tamarins and marmosets usually give birth to twins.
- Marmosets are capable of giving birth every five months.
- A group of monkeys is called a troop.
- In captivity, monkeys can live for 45 years or more.

Artistic Animals

We don't usually think of animals as having artistic natures. But this is simply because of our prejudices. When a bird takes bright objects to decorate its nest we tend to dismiss this as pointless theft. When a human being collects bird feathers to decorate a room or a hat they are said to be showing artistic tendencies. Here are half a dozen well-documented examples of animals exhibiting artistic tendencies:

- Monkeys prefer looking at pictures of monkeys to pictures of people and prefer looking at animated cartoons rather than at still pictures.
- Naturalist, Gerald Durrell, wrote about a pigeon who listened quietly to most music but who would stamp backwards and forwards when marches were being played, and would twist and bow, cooing softly, when waltzes were played.
- A gorilla enjoyed the singing of tenor Luciano Pavarotti so much that he would refuse to go outdoors when a Pavarotti concert was being shown on television.
- Animal abusers have for years dismissed birdsong as merely mating calls. But it is now suspected that birds sing to give themselves pleasure.

- ✐ Numerous apes have painted or drawn identifiable objects while in captivity.
- ✐ When a young Indian elephant was reported to have made numerous drawings (which were highly commended by artists who did not know that the artist was an animal), other zoo keepers reported that their elephants often scribbled on the ground with sticks or stones. When an Asian elephant got extra attention because of her paintings, nearby African elephants used the ends of logs to draw on the walls of their enclosure.

How To Survive An Encounter With A Lion

Here are our suggestions offered with absolutely no guarantees:

1. As much as your instinct will tell you to do so – do not run. Running away from a lion is one of the worst things you can do. Running only acts as a trigger for the lion to attack. You will never be able to outrun a lion.
2. Stare the lion in the eyes – do not avert your gaze. Always keep eye contact.
3. Make yourself look as huge as possible. Do not crouch down, as lions like their target to be unthreatening.
4. Shout at the lion as loudly and as fiercely as possible. Shouting is likely to distract a lion.
5. If the lion attacks you then aim for its eyes. With a male lion you can try grabbing its testicles. (If you dare!)
6. Naturally, the best prevention from an attack by a big cat is avoidance. When travelling to countries where lions roam, use your common sense. Stay in your vehicle. Or if you're travelling on an elephant's back, then don't get off until you know that you're 100 per cent safe.
7. It is advisable not to take dogs with you into the wilds where lions or cougars are likely to be. Taking a dog with you may increase your risk of attracting a mountain lion or a cougar.
8. Never wander into the wilds by yourself.
9. Good luck!

Orang-utans

- ✱ Along with gorillas and chimpanzees, orang-utans are great apes. They belong to the family Hominidae. Orang-utans are generally found in the lowland swamp forests of Borneo and Sumatra.
- ✱ There are two subspecies of orang-utan: the Sumatran and the Bornean. The Sumatran is thinner with a paler coat; thicker, longer hair and a longer face.

* Generally, orang-utans spend most of their lives in the trees; they are the world's largest arboreal mammals. Male orang-utans can grow to 4½ft (1.37m) tall and weigh 185lb (83.91kg) or more. Female orang-utans are much smaller.
* The orang-utan's coat varies from orange-red to brown. Orang-utans have very long arms that can be over 6½ft (1.98m) long. They also have long, curved fingers and toes giving a hook-like appearance to their hands and feet, this makes it easier for them to grip tree branches. Orang-utans move through the forest by swinging a tree branch back and forth using their heavy weight until they can reach the next tree.
* Adult male orang-utans have large, fatty cheek pads and large, inflatable laryngeal pouches or sacs. Females also have laryngeal pouches but they are not as pendulous as those seen on males. (Adult males also have more pronounced beards). The larger the male's cheek pads, the more attractive he is to females. Bornean orang-utans' laryngeal pouches are larger than the Sumatran orang-utans' laryngeal pouches. Bornean orang-utans' cheek pads curve forwards whereas Sumatran orang-utans' cheek pads lie flat.
* Orang-utans share 97 per cent of their DNA with human beings. However, of the great apes (gorillas and chimpanzees), the orang-utan is the least related to humans.
* The orang-utan's diet includes: fruit (which makes up a large proportion of its diet), plants, bark, honey, termites, nestling birds, eggs and small animals.
* Orang-utans are the world's slowest breeding animals. Bornean females give birth on average every eight years.
* Orang-utans usually give birth to one baby. They have a gestation period of around nine months.
* The baby orang-utan weighs approximately 2.2lb (1kg) at birth.
* Mother and baby share an extremely close bond with each other; the mother will carry her baby around with her continuously during the first year of its life.
* Orang-utans are usually fully independent by the time they are ten-years-old.
* In her lifetime, the average female will give birth to three or four young.
* Orang-utans dislike the rain, and will often protect themselves from the weather by using leaves as 'umbrellas'.
* 'Orang-utan' is Malaysian for 'person of the forest'.
* Every night, the orang-utan makes a nest for itself out of leaves and twigs in the crown of a tree, usually with a roof to shelter itself from the rain. Females share their nests with their young offspring. Adult males who are too heavy to rest in the trees, tend to make their nests on the forest floor. It takes the orang-utan approximately five minutes to make its night-time nest.
* In the wild, adult orang-utans without young are rather solitary animals. This is especially true of the orang-utans living in Borneo. Orang-utans living in Sumatra tend to be more social.
* Orang-utans are highly intelligent animals and are capable of making and using

tools. They shape sticks to extricate the seeds from large fruits. They also use sticks to probe for insects in tree holes, or to extract honey from bees' nests. They use twigs as toothpicks to clean their teeth. Orang-utans can also learn sign language.

* Male orang-utans – with the aid of their laryngeal sacs that they inflate with air, thereby adding resonance – make loud bellowing noises which can sound quite terrifying. These loud bellowing noises or roars can be heard up to 0.93 miles (1.5km away). Orang-utans make these loud roaring sounds to discourage other males from getting too close. If a strange male intrudes upon another male's comfort zone, the resident orang-utan may try to frighten the intruder away by shaking and breaking tree branches. If the intruder does not retreat then sometimes a fight will ensue. Fights sometimes result in deep wounds which eventually lead to scarring. Orang-utans also use their laryngeal sacs to make a defensive noise which has been described as a burping sound.
* Orang-utans have been known to live for over 60 years in captivity.
* Examinations from fossils of orang-utans dating back 40,000 years ago show that orang-utans are approximately one third smaller today than they were back then.
* When on the ground, orang-utans tend to move around on all fours. Unlike chimpanzees and gorillas, which walk on their knuckles and on the soles of their feet, orang-utans usually move around on clenched hands and on clenched feet that are bent inwards.
* The orang-utan is an endangered animal and is close to extinction in the wild. Habitat destruction and hunting are the main reasons for the declining numbers. Female adult orang-utans are killed so that their young babies can be sold on as pets.

Gift Giving Among Animals

Giving gifts is part of the mating ritual among all sorts of animals. Even insects do it. Crickets and cockroaches give nuptial gifts (usually edible) designed to help win a mate and prolong copulation.

Cockroaches give the female of their species (and choice) a tasty uric acid paste they have stored up for the occasion. Male scorpion flies build mounds of dried saliva which the females find irresistible. While the female eats the dried saliva, the male has his wicked way with her.

Often a female will select her mate according to the size or quality of the gift she is offered.

Male fireflies proffer a protein boost with their sperm. The quality of the protein boost is advertised by the intensity of the firefly's glow.

The male dance fly will offer a prospective lover a tasty insect nicely wrapped in silk. (Crafty dance flies will offer fairly rough-looking insects very nicely wrapped. The female of the species will respond better to an appetising gift in a beautiful wrapping than to a spectacular gift which isn't very well wrapped.)

Animals And Sex

- Pigs have penises shaped like a corkscrews. They ejaculate a pint of semen whenever they have sex.
- When the male honeybee ejaculates – he explodes. His genitals remain inside the female to stop her mating again.
- The female pig has an orgasm which lasts for 30 minutes.
- Buffalo sex lasts five seconds.
- The female chimpanzee sometimes has sex with eight different males in just 15 minutes.
- Some breeds of snail have sex only once in a lifetime.
- Female giant pandas urinate on the ground near a tree to attract males. And males urinate or wipe their bottoms on the trunk. To show their virility and strength, males place their marks as high as possible on the tree trunk. They do this by doing a handstand.
- A lioness on heat wants sex every half an hour, non-stop, for five days and nights.
- Female funnel web spiders eat their males after sex. But some males produce a knockout gas which leaves the female too limp to eat – but capable of sex.
- One species of firefly lures a male, has sex with him and then eats him alive. She does this because the male produces a natural biochemical defence against spiders – a major predator. The female doesn't have this defence and so she eats the male to immunise herself.
- The desert rat has sex up to 122 times an hour. (Except when Mrs Desert Rat complains of a headache.)
- Prostitution has been observed among some animals. If a baboon offers herself sexually to a male, she may contrive to steal his food and he may let her keep the food in exchange for sex.
- Chimpanzees get sex over and done with in seven seconds. The elephant takes only 30 seconds. A ferret can usually manage eight hours of sex, and the average sex session between marsupial mice lasts 12 hours.
- Just before two porcupines have sex, the male sprays his female mating partner from head to toe with his urine.

Orcas (Otherwise Known As Killer Whales)

- Orcas, like dolphins, belong to the family Delphinidae, and are one of the most widely distributed mammals on the planet. Orcas can be found throughout most of the world's oceans.
- Whales, along with porpoises and dolphins are collectively known as cetaceans. There are two types of cetaceans: toothed and baleen. The orca belongs to the toothed variety.
- The orca is black in colour with a white underside and white patches above each eye. It has a distinctive grey marking (known as a saddle-patch) on its back. It has a powerful tail and a dorsal fin around the middle of its back which can grow to 7ft (2.13m) long. It also has pectoral fins on either side of its body. The whale uses these pectoral fins for stopping, steering and for changing direction.
- The male can grow to 30ft (9.14m) long and weigh over 4.5 tons (4.56 tonnes).
- The orca has lungs – not gills, which means that it is unable to breathe underwater. When underwater, the orca frequently comes to the surface of the water for air. And before taking in air through its nostril/blowhole which is situated on the top of its head, the orca blows out stale, moist air (not water). This can fire upwards about 9ft (2.74m). The orca's blowhole is kept shut under water by strong muscles.
- To help keep their bodies warm, orcas have a thick layer of blubber underneath their skins. This layer of blubber is also a store of energy.
- The orca's diet includes: fish, cephalopods, aquatic mammals and birds. Inside one orca, scientists found the remnants of 14 seals and 13 dolphins.
- In order to keep healthy, the orca has to eat approximately 551lb (249.92kg) of food every day.
- Orcas use echolocation to detect their prey. The orca emits sound waves which produces an 'echo' if it hits any object up to 300ft (91.44m). With echolocation, the orca is able to pick up the size of its prey, its body structure and even how fast it is travelling.
- Despite having extraordinarily sharp teeth with which to grip and rip open their prey, orcas are unable to chew their kill.
- An orca's pregnancy can last as long as 17 months.
- A baby orca is called a calf.
- The orca usually gives birth to one young.
- A newborn calf weighs approximately 330lb (149.68kg) and can be as much as one third as long as its mother's body.
- Calves usually remain with their mothers for life.
- Around half of all calves die within a year of being born.

- The father does not participate in bringing up its calf.
- The mother's milk contains approximately 42 per cent of fat and is very rich. This is to help the calf to quickly develop a thick layer of blubber underneath its skin.
- Just like the bottlenose dolphin, the mother will go for a whole month without sleep so that it can take care of its baby. Going for a whole month without sleep enables the mother to keep her vulnerable calf safe from predators and to help keep her calf warm until it develops enough blubber to keep out the cold.
- Orcas are very acrobatic and often leap high out of the water. This form of water activity is called 'breaching'. Orcas also raise their heads vertically out of the water – a manoeuvre called 'spy hopping'. It is thought that orcas spy-hop because they are surveying their surroundings for potential prey.
- Orcas communicate to one another using a variety of sounds which include: squeals, clicks and whistling sounds.
- Orcas are social animals and live in family groups called pods, which may consist of as many as 50 individuals.
- When hunting, it is not uncommon for one pod to combine forces with another pod.
- Each orca pod is reported to have its own dialect.
- Male orcas live to approximately 60 years of age. Female orcas can live to more than 90 years of age.
- Orcas can swim at 30mph (48.28km/h) or more.
- The orca excretes oily mucus from its eyes, which helps to cleanse and protect them.
- Orcas can dive to depths of 200ft (60.96m) or more.
- It is widely believed that, like other whales, orcas have no sense of smell.
- When orcas want to rest, one half of their brain is used for breathing control and steering in the water, while the other half of the brain is in a relaxed state.
- The orca's more common name, the 'killer whale' has led to this beautiful mammal being totally misunderstood by mankind. Amazingly, there is no recorded instance of an orca killing a human being in the wild. The orca acquired the name 'killer whale' because of its remarkable hunting skills.
- Humans are the main threat to orcas. Orcas are at risk from fishermen, boat propellers, polluted waters (caused by man) and food shortages (caused by man).

Animals As Teachers

There is now no doubt that animals actively teach their young in order to pass on skills which many traditionally regarded as being 'nothing more than instinct'.

So, for example, we have watched an adult cat giving lessons to orphan kittens for which he had taken responsibility. The adult cat, teaching the art of stalking, would edge forwards and then stop and look over his shoulder to see if the kittens were following in the correct style. After the lesson had gone on for some time, the kittens started playing behind the adult cat's back. They got away with it for a couple of times but on the third occasion, the adult cat saw them. He reached back and gave them both a clip with an outstretched paw. The kittens weren't hurt but they certainly paid attention to what they were being taught.

Animal Young

General terms:

Calf: the young of large animals such as: antelopes, camels, cows, elephants, elks, giraffes, hippopotamuses, moose, rhinoceroses, whales, etc.

Chick and fledgling: young of any bird.

Cub: young of carnivorous animals such as: bears, wolves, foxes, lions, tigers, etc.

Foal: young of horse-like animals (donkeys, zebras, etc). Male offspring are known as colts, and female offspring are known as fillies.

Fry: young of most fish.

Kid: young of goats and related animals such as antelopes and some deer.

Kit and kitten: young of fur bearing mammals.

Note: overlap is common. A fox is small, carnivorous and dog-like – and so its young can correctly be referred to as kits, kittens, cubs, pups or puppies.

Specific Terms For Young Fish

Clam	spat
Cod	codling, sprag, scrod
Eel	elver
Herring	brit
Mackerel	spike, blinker, tinker
Mussel	spat
Oyster	spat
Salmon	alevin, grilse, parr, smolt

Commonly Used Specific Terms For Young Animals

Antelope	calf
Ass	foal
Beaver	kit
Cow	heifer (female)
Deer	fawn
Donkey	foal
Elephant	calf
Fox	cub
Hare	leveret
Hippototamus	calf
Hog	grice, piglet, shoat, shote
Horse	foal, colt (m), filly (f) yearling
Lion	cub, lionet
Llama	cria
Pig	piglet
Rabbit	bunny, kitten
Rat	pup
Rhinoceros	calf
Sheep	lamb, lambkin, cosset

Specific Terms For Young Birds

Chicken	cockerel (male), pullet (female)
Duck	duckling
Eagle	eaglet
Goose	gosling
Hawk	eyas
Hen	pullet
Owl	owlet
Peafowl	peachick
Pigeon	squab
Swan	cygnet
Turkey	poult

Otters (European)

- Together with minks, polecats and badgers, otters are members of the weasel family (Mustelidae). The European otter can be found in North Africa and in most of Eurasia south of tundra line. There are 13 species of otter but, of all the species, the European otter has the largest geographical range.
- Due to a history of persecution, loss of habitat and the accumulation of agricultural pesticides, the European otter became scarce in the 1960s. But in recent years, cleaner rivers and the reintroduction of otters have slowly produced an increase in the population in some areas. Otters are common along the Scottish west coast and on the Shetland and Orkney Islands.
- The predominantly aquatic otter has a flat head; a broad muzzle; small, rounded ears (with an acute sense of hearing); small eyes; a long body; a long, thick tapered tail; short legs and five clawed, webbed toes. The otter's streamlined body and rudder-like tail (which can grow to 16in (40.64cm) or more in length, and which is used for propulsion under the water) help to make the otter an excellent swimmer and diver. Although adept in the water, the otter cannot stay under the water for longer than 40 seconds.
- The otter can weigh 33lb (14.96kg) or more. And its body can grow to just over 3ft (0.91m) long.
- The otter's underfur is very dense, about 450,000 hairs per sq. inch (70,000 hairs per sq. cm). The underfur acts as insulation by trapping air against its skin. This helps to protect the otter's body from the cold. The top layer of the otter's coat consists of long, thick guard hairs which help to keep the otter's underfur dry. The fur on the otter's throat and belly is much paler than the brown fur on the rest of its body.
- The otter's sleek fur contains an oily secretion which helps to keep it waterproof. The otter has to groom regularly in order to maintain the waterproofing efficiency of its fur.
- Otters tend to reside near marshes, streams, rivers, freshwater lakes and some coasts. Generally, they live anywhere near water where food is abundant and they can live undisturbed.
- The female otter is called a bitch. The male otter is called a dog. The baby otter is called a cub.
- The otter has stiff, sensitive whiskers which it uses to detect prey when underwater, especially if the water is murky, or it is after dark. Otherwise, the otter relies on its sight to hunt for prey.
- Otters can close their ears and nostrils when underwater.
- Otters feed mainly on fish but they also feed on crayfish, eels, frogs, birds, small mammals, shellfish, molluscs and carrion. Every day, otters have to eat up to 15 per cent of their body weight in food.

- Otters are mostly solitary animals, usually only coming together during the breeding season.
- The otter's pregnancy lasts for approximately 60-65 days.
- Otters can give birth any time of the year. Although in places where the winters are harsher, the young are more likely to be born in the spring.
- The otter's average litter is two or three young. The baby cubs weigh approximately 3.5oz (99g) at birth.
- The cubs are usually weaned after about four months.
- As soon as the cubs are old enough, it is not unusual for the female otter to drag her reluctant offspring into the water to encourage them to swim.
- After birth, the cubs usually stay with their mother for a year or more.
- Otters are often nocturnal animals, but otters who reside near coastlines tend to be more active during the daytime.
- Otters are very shy and elusive animals.
- To get a better view of its surroundings, the otter stands upright on its hind feet and tail.
- Otters are playful animals and love games. They enjoy play fighting, sliding down well-used mud or snow 'chutes' into the water and chasing each other, especially during courtship. It is usually the young otters who play games. The adults, who have to spend much of their day searching for food, don't have a lot of time for play.
- Otters sometimes communicate with one another by whistling.
- Like nearly all species of otter, the European otter has scent glands below the base of its tail, which it uses to communicate with other otters. The otter also leaves its droppings (called spraints) as scent markers on prominent places within its territory.
- The otter is a land animal who spends a good deal of its time in the water. It is not uncommon for the otter to travel great distances overland (often at night). When travelling on land, the otter has an awkward, bounding gait.
- The otter goes inside its den – called a holt – to rest. The otter's holt is usually well-concealed by vegetation within a bank-side or under overhanging tree roots. The otter's holt is rarely far away from water.
- Otters are territorial animals with riverbank territories stretching as long as 12 miles (19.31km) or more.
- Otters in captivity have been known to live in excess of 20 years.
- The European otter is a protected species in almost all European countries, and is one of the most threatened mammal species in Europe. The otter used to be hunted to remove the competition threatening fishermen. Also, the otter used to be hunted for sport and for its fur. The main threats to otters today include: habitat loss, water sports and the pollution of rivers.

Ten Songs With An Animal In The Title

1. You Ain't Nothin' But A Hound Dog – Elvis Presley
2. Crocodile Rock – Elton John
3. What's New Pussycat – Tom Jones
4. Eagle – Abba
5. Eye Of The Tiger – Survivor
6. Little Red Rooster – Rolling Stones
7. Frog Chorus – Paul McCartney
8. Dog Eat Dog – AC/DC
9. Rockin' Robin – Jackson Five
10. Crazy Horses – The Osmonds

Pandas (Giant)

- Scientists were confused for many years as to whether the giant panda belonged to the racoon family or to the bear family, but recent DNA tests have shown that it almost certainly belongs to the latter – the family Ursidae. The giant panda can be found in the Sichuan, Shaanxi and Gansu provinces of central and western China. It lives in temperate, tropical, and mountainous bamboo forest.
- The giant panda has black and white markings all over its large body – it has black shoulders, forelimbs, hindlimbs, nose and ears. It also has black oval eye patches. The rest of the panda's body is white.
- There is another panda called the red panda (also known as the lesser panda), which is sometimes included with the giant panda in the two-member family, Ailuridae. The red panda does not look anything like the giant panda. The red panda is much, much smaller than the giant panda and looks like a racoon. The red panda has white markings on its face, reddish brown fur and a long tail. Recent genetic studies suggest that the red panda belongs to the racoon family. The giant panda and the red panda were once thought to be closely related because of the number of similar characteristics they share.
- Giant pandas can weigh as much as 330lb (149.68kg) and grow to 5ft 6in (170cm) tall when standing upright. (The red panda reaches only about 3ft (0.91m) in length – including its tail.)
- The diet of pandas mainly consists of bamboo shoots, bamboo leaves and bamboo stems. Pandas consume a staggering 80lb (36.28kg) or more of bamboo a day. This is because they cannot digest cellulose, so they need to eat a lot of bamboo in order to obtain enough energy from their food. Pandas are primarily vegetarian but they do occasionally eat fish, rodents, small birds and insects. They also feed on other plants as well as bamboo.

- Pandas spend about 10-12 hours of their day eating.
- Owing to their lack of energy-producing diets, pandas need to conserve their energy as much as they can, which means that they will rest whenever possible. To minimise heat loss from their bodies, pandas will try to keep their heads (from where they lose a lot of their heat) warm while resting. One of the ways in which they do this is by propping their heads up on one of their hind legs while sleeping.
- The panda has a pseudo-thumb on one of its forepaws, which has evolved from its wrist bone. The panda's pseudo-thumb comes in very useful when handling bamboo stems to eat.
- Pandas do not hibernate in winter.
- Pandas can sometimes be seen sliding on their backs down slopes. This might have a practical purpose, such as getting rid of debris from their fur or it might just simply be for fun.
- Pandas are solitary animals, preferring to live alone. Once young pandas are old enough, they will leave their mothers to go off to live by themselves.
- It has been reported that pandas use 11 different vocalisations to communicate with one another. For example, when female pandas are ready to mate, they usually make bleating sounds to attract male pandas in the area.
- To attract members of the opposite sex, females usually urinate on a tree trunk at ground level while males either urinate or rub their anal glands higher up against the tree trunk. And to prove to the females just how virile and vigorous they are, the males try to place their secretions on the trunk as high as they possibly can. One of the ways in which they do this is by standing on their heads.
- Pandas have a very short mating season. Male and female adult pandas only get together for a couple of days a year during the breeding season (March to May).
- Male pandas often fight one another to mate with females in oestrus, and it is usually the dominant males who have priority over the females.
- The giant panda's pregnancy lasts for approximately five months.
- The average size of a panda's litter is just one or two cubs. If a panda gives birth to twins, very rarely do both cubs survive. Twins are more likely to be born to pandas living in captivity.
- The mother gives birth to her baby in a den, such as a cave or the base of a hollow tree.
- At birth, the baby panda weighs approximately 4-7oz (113-198g), about the size of a small rat.
- Panda cubs may stay with their mother for three years or more.
- Some of the baby panda's natural predators include: dholes (Asian wild dogs), golden cats, weasels, martens and stoats.
- Infant mortality is high with less than 50 per cent of cubs surviving more than six months.

- Young pandas are good climbers and will climb trees to escape predators.
- Pandas are fully mature by the time they are three-years-old.
- Females mate every two to three years. Occasionally, the male will kill a female's cubs in order to prevent the cubs competing with his own offspring and to bring her into season more quickly.
- The adult panda's 'home range' can extend to 3.5 sq. miles (9.06 sq. km). Within its 'home range', the panda has an area of less than a third of a square mile (half a square kilometre) which is called a core area. Pandas (especially females) tend to concentrate a lot of their activity within their core areas.
- In captivity, a panda can live 20-30 years.
- The panda is an endangered species.
- There are reputed to be less than 1,000 giant pandas living in the world today.
- The main danger to adult pandas is man. Poaching and destruction of the animal's bamboo habitat have contributed to the decline of the panda population.

Animals Enjoy Playing

We accept that cats and dogs like to play (though, quite erroneously, we often assume that it is because we have taught them how to do it) but many people reject the notion that other animals play. When it is pointed out that sheep and lambs like to play the same sort of games that children play, cynics claim that this is anthropomorphic. A few minutes observation will, however, confirm that lambs play tag, king of the castle, hide and seek, and even enjoy running races. Even fully-grown sheep enjoy playing together – abandoning their more active games only when arthritis prevents them from moving easily. The problem is that most people never stop to watch. And the people who do have the opportunity to watch, farmers and hunters, don't like to admit that the creatures they kill so readily are sentient and playful. And so they sustain their ignorance by refusing to see what they look at.

Pigs (Domestic)

- Pigs belong to the family Suidae, and are native to North African, Asian and European forests.
- Pigs inhabit every continent in the world with the exception of Antarctica.
- The uncastrated male pig is called a boar. The female pig who has had one weaned litter is called a sow. The female pig is called a gilt up to the time her first litter is weaned. The juvenile pig is called a piglet.
- The wild boar is the ancestor of the domestic pig.
- The large white domestic pig can weigh 1,122lb (509kg) or more.

- Pigs are omnivores, eating meat and plant matter. Today, most domestic pigs are fed on commercial feed. In their natural conditions, pigs eat little and often – and are not the greedy animals most people are led to believe.
- Pigs need a good supply of water to drink otherwise they will die of salt poisoning. A suckling pig needs at least 4-7 gallons (18.18-31.82 litres) of water a day.
- The large white pig, which is the pinkish white coloured animal most people think of when asked to describe a typical pig, has evolved from the native pigs of north-western Europe and imported pigs from Asia.
- The female pig's pregnancy normally lasts just under four months.
- Sows usually have large litters of ten or more piglets.
- The baby piglet weighs approximately 35-70oz (992-1,984g) at birth.
- If female pigs are kept indoors and do not have access to soil then piglets are likely to be anaemic when they are born.
- Each piglet usually has its own teat to suckle from, and each piglet will fiercely defend its teat from its siblings.
- Piglets grow very quickly on their mother's rich milk. By the time the piglets are three-weeks-old, they will have gained up to five times their birth weight.
- The weaning of piglets is complete at around 12-weeks-old.
- The few sweat glands a pig possesses are in its nose, which may help to keep its nose cool but, unfortunately, do not do much to help cool the rest of its body. (Knowing this really makes the phrase: 'Sweating like a pig' sound rather silly.)
- Since they are unable to cool their bodies by sweating, pigs try to keep cool in the hot weather by wallowing in water or mud. Pigs also wallow in mud to protect their skins from sunburn, dryness and from any nasty bug bites. Large white pigs have to be especially careful about sunburn because their sensitive skins are more vulnerable to the sun's rays.
- The Gloucestershire old spot pig has black-coloured spots on pale skin. Many years ago, Gloucestershire old spot pigs were called orchard pigs. This was because they used to live in the cider orchards of the Severn Vale. Traditional belief has it that the spots were bruises caused by wind-fallen apples. 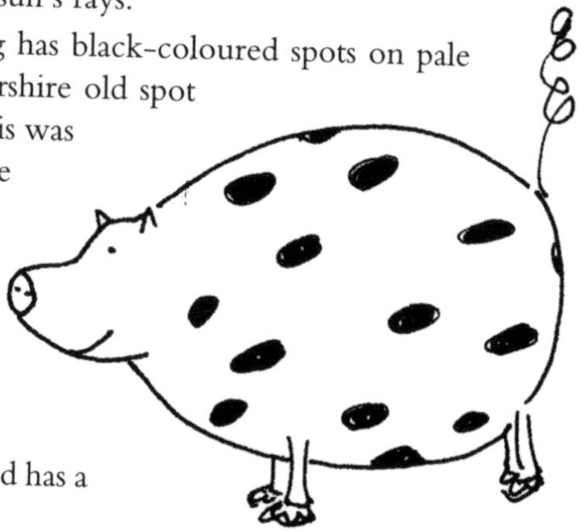
- A purebred Vietnamese potbelly pig has a straight tail. A Vietnamese potbelly pig that has been crossbred has a curly tail.
- The cruel practice of putting a ring through a pig's nose is to stop it from following its natural instinct of 'rooting' (turning up the ground with its snout in search of food). Farmers don't like pigs rooting because they think it damages pasture land.

- Pigs are capable of closing their nostrils. They usually do this while rooting so that their nostrils do not get clogged with dirt.
- Contrary to popular belief, pigs are very clean animals. Unlike many animals they invariably have a toilet area a good distance away from their eating and living quarters. If you have a pet pig who lives with other animals, it is important that your pig does not have to share his living quarters with other animals' droppings.
- The natural lifespan of a domestic pig is around 12 to 18 years.
- The British saddleback pig is black all over except for a light coloured band which extends around the pig's shoulders, down the front legs and feet. Unlike the large white pig which has erect ears, the saddleback has droopy ears.
- Pigs use around 20 different vocal sounds to communicate with other pigs.
- Pigs have an amazing sense of smell and are capable of smelling something buried in the ground from about 20ft (6.09m) away. This is why they are used to sniff out truffles which are underground. Truffles (which are an edible fungi) are an expensive delicacy.
- Pigs sleep for around 13 hours a day.
- Up to 18 months of age, a pig can be aged accurately by looking at its teeth.
- Pigs are highly sensitive and intelligent animals and are much easier to train than a dog. Pigs are believed to be among the most intelligent animals in the animal kingdom.
- Pigs have two functional and two non-functional digits on each foot.
- Because pigs are such intelligent animals, they are more likely to suffer from depression or become aggressive if there is a lack of mental stimulation or emotional fulfilment in their environment. So, for instance, a pig who is kept in a small enclosure or isn't surrounded by other pigs is likely to become depressed.
- Pigs love eating acorns but can become overexcited and aggressive if they eat too many. In the English New Forest area in the autumn of 2006, a bumper harvest of acorns meant that local pigs became aggressive and chased people who were walking nearby with their dogs.

Talking of Pigs

There are a number of sayings which revolve around pigs. Here are some of the best-known, together with their meanings (and in some cases their origins):

1. Pigs in clover
People who have more money than manners are sometimes described as pigs in clover.

2. A pig in a poke/to buy a pig in a poke
The word 'poke' originally meant 'bag'. So a pig in a poke that was taken to market and sold might, when the purchaser had time to open the poke, turn out to be a cat. Buying a pig in a poke is to take a risk and buy something unseen.

3. A pig of a day
A difficult or unpleasant day.

4. To cast pearls before swine
To waste gifts on those who are incapable of appreciating them.

5. In a pig's eye
Expressing scornful disbelief

6. Make a pig of oneself
To eat too much.

7. To make a pig's ear of
To handle ineptly.

8. On the pig's back
Living a life of ease.

'No man should be allowed to be President, who does not understand hogs.'
Harry Truman (1884-1972)

'There exists perhaps in all creation no animal which has less justice and more injustice shown than the pig.'
Sir Frances Bond Head (1793-1875)

Animal Markings

- Animals who eat meat and must kill other animals to survive (predators such as tigers) usually have blotchy or striped coats. The markings are there to break up the animal's outline and to provide natural camouflage.
- Large vegetarian animals who have few or no predators and no need to catch prey (animals such as elephants, rhinoceroses, hippopotamuses, gorillas) have no markings on their coats or skins.
- Polar bears are white (so that they can't be seen against the ice). Lions, fast-

moving, strong predators who don't need to worry about being attacked but do have to worry about creeping up on their prey, are sandy brown because they spend much of their time on sandy plains.)

☞ Animals who are likely to be eaten by predators (prey such as giraffes) also have blotchy coats to provide them with camouflage in their natural surroundings.

☞ Animals which tend to hunt at night (badgers) or which are often hunted at night (zebras) usually have black and white coats. At night, everything is in shadow, and black and white markings provide the best camouflage.

☞ Animals (such as zebras) which live in long grasses often have striped coats.

Polar bears

- The polar bear – along with the other bears – belongs to the family Ursidae, and can be found throughout Arctic regions.
- Polar bears are the largest of the bear species. The mature male polar bear can weigh as much as 1,700lb (771kg) and grow to over 10ft (3.05m) long. Male polar bears are usually twice the size of female polar bears.
- Polar bears have huge bodies; small heads (in comparison to their large frames); short tails; and big paws that have long, non-retractable claws. The polar bear also has small ears. Small ears help to minimise heat loss.
- The skin underneath the polar bear's white or yellowish thick coat is black.

This is to help absorb the heat from the sun's rays much more efficiently, as black is the most heat absorbent colour.

- Underneath the polar bear's skin is a layer of blubber, which is just over 4in (10.16cm) thick. This helps to protect the bear from the harsh arctic weather as well as providing an energy storage. The polar bear is so well insulated from the cold, that it loses almost no body heat.
- The polar bear's pale coat is due to a lack of pigmentation within the hair shaft; the coat's white colour is a result of reflective light. The polar bear's coat is made up of hollow hairs which are believed, by many experts, to help trap ultraviolet light from the sun which is then passed to the skin and converted into heat. (Other experts suspect this could be a myth but have offered no alternative explanation for the hollow hairs.)
- Oxidisation of seal oils, pollutants and exposure to the sun's rays during the summer months can stain the polar bear's coat yellow.
- In Latin, the polar bear is called Ursus maritimus which means 'sea bear'.
- The polar bear does not have any eyelashes.
- The polar bear can run at speeds of 25mph (40.23km/h).
- Polar bears cannot run for long periods at a time, otherwise they would overheat. To cool down, polar bears usually roll their bodies around in the snow.
- Polar bears are excellent swimmers and can swim under water. The polar bear's nostrils close underwater, allowing it to hold its breath for as long as two minutes.
- The polar bear can swim at 6mph (9.65km/h).
- Polar bears can dive under water to a depth of more than 16ft (4.88m).
- Polar bears are thought to have evolved from brown bears some 100,000 to 250,000 years ago.
- The polar bear's diet includes: seals (especially ringed seals), narwhal, caribou, small mammals, seabirds, waterfowl, carrion, seaweed and other vegetation. Polar bears also like to eat belugas and walruses.
- Polar bears have a remarkable sense of smell, and can locate a seal's breathing hole from up to ¾ mile (1.2km) away. Polar bears are patient hunters and will wait for several days near a seal's breathing hole for the right moment to attack. When the moment is right, and the seal comes up for air, the polar bear will usually knock the seal out by striking it with its powerful paw before grabbing the seal out of the water with its strong jaws.
- The polar bear mating season is between April and June.
- Female polar bears mate about every three years. They are ready to mate shortly after their cubs have left to fend for themselves.
- Males that are ready to mate will sometimes kill a female's cubs in order to bring her into season.
- Females are usually about five to six years old when they start to breed.

- In some parts of the arctic, pregnant females go for as long as eight months without food. They live off the fat that they have acquired during the summer months.
- The female polar bear gives birth to her young in a den made out of snow. (The only place in the world where polar bears dig dens in the permafrost rather than in the snow is on the land to the south-west of Hudson Bay near Churchill, Manitoba).
- The polar bear's litter consists of one to four cubs (two cubs is usual).
- Cubs weigh around 21-25oz (595-707g) at birth.
- The polar bear cubs will stay in the den until they are approximately four-months-old. By the time they are ready to leave the den, the cubs will have grown quite rapidly due to their mother's milk, which has a high-fat content.
- The polar bear's average lifespan in the wild is 15-18 years.
- Polar bears do not hibernate. Although, females who are giving birth do spend their time in the den in a torpid state (they reduce their heart and breathing rates and lower their body temperatures).
- Of the bear family, the polar bear is the bear that is most likely to kill humans. However, polar bears usually only attack human beings out of hunger.
- Polar bears are solitary animals, but they do tolerate one another's company quite well.
- Churchill, Manitoba in Canada is known as the 'Polar bear capital of the world'. Many tourists go to visit Churchill each year to catch a glimpse of the beautiful, white bears.
- Female polar bears who have lost their cubs have been known to adopt another female's cubs. There have been occasional reports of females switching their litters.
- Although the polar bear is no longer in danger of extinction, thanks to the 1973 International Agreement On The Conservation Of Polar Bears, the main threat to the polar bear comes from man-made problems: hunting, pollution and global warming.

Animals Can Be Vain And Self-Conscious

Animals have often been reported to show signs of vanity, self-consciousness, embarrassment and other allegedly exclusively human emotions. Here are a few examples:

- Chimpanzees have been observed using a TV video monitor to watch themselves making faces. The chimpanzees were able to distinguish between a live image and a taped image by testing to see if their actions were duplicated on the screen. Chimpanzees have even managed to use a video monitor to help them apply make-up to themselves (humans find that this is a difficult trick to learn). One chimpanzee has been reported to have used a video camera and monitor to look down his own throat – using a flashlight to help the process.

- Male baboons with worn or broken teeth yawn less than male baboons with teeth in good condition – unless there are no other males around, in which case they yawn just as often. It seems fair to assume their behaviour is at least partly governed by vanity.
- One gorilla who had a number of toy dolls used sign language to send kisses to her favourite puppets and dolls. But every time she realised that she was being watched she stopped doing this – presumably through embarrassment.
- When a bottlenose porpoise accidentally bit her trainer's hand she became 'hideously embarrassed', went to the bottom of her tank with her snout in a corner, and wouldn't come out until the trainer made it clear that she wasn't cross.
- Wild chimpanzees show embarrassment and shame and may show off to other animals whom they want to impress.
- People who live with cats will have probably noticed that if a cat falls off a piece of furniture, it will immediately do something else as though pretending that the fall didn't take place at all – often beginning to wash itself.
- Elephant keepers report that when elephants are laughed at they will respond by filling their trunks with water and spraying the people who are laughing at them.
- Many dog owners have reported that their animals make it clear that they know when they have done wrong. A dog which feels it has done something wrong may go into a submissive position before its pack leader (or 'owner') knows that the animal has done something 'bad'.

Rabbits (European)

- The European rabbit belongs to the family Leporidae, and is native to south-west Europe and possibly north-west Africa.
- The European rabbit is the ancestor of all breeds of domestic rabbit.
- The male rabbit is called a buck. The female rabbit is called a doe. The baby rabbit is called a kitten.
- The rabbit's coat has three layers of fur and is usually greyish-brown in colour with an orange-coloured nape and a white-greyish underside.
- The rabbit has a dark tail with the underside being white. This 'tail flag' is believed to exist in order to make it easier for other rabbits to see when one of them is fleeing from danger, as rabbits usually run (in a zigzag motion) with their tails erect.

* The European rabbit can weigh as much as 5.5lb (2.49kg) and have a body length of up to 19.7in (50cm).
* Rabbits have an almost 180-degree vision. This is because their prominent eyes are situated on the sides of their heads enabling them to detect potential predators quickly.
* There is sometimes confusion about the difference between rabbits and hares. Here is how to differentiate between the two:
  - a. rabbits are smaller than hares.
  - b. hares have longer ears with black tips.
  - c. rabbits have shorter hind legs than hares.
  - d. hares have a more upright stance.
  - e. rabbits usually have their tails erect when running – hares do not.
* Rabbits live in burrows. Large colonies of rabbits live in warrens. (Burrow is to warren as village is to town, and burrows can grow together into a warren just as villages can grow together into a town). A warren consists of a number of underground burrows connected to one another by tunnels. Several hundred rabbits can occupy one warren. Depending on the size of the warren, warrens may have as many as sixty entrance holes.
* Rabbits are social animals and live in strict hierarchical groups, with less dominant rabbits (subordinates) living in less 'luxurious' parts of the warren. The leadership of the top ranking males in the group is often challenged by the less dominant males in the group, which may result in fighting with lots of leaping at and kicking one another.
* Rabbits are essentially nocturnal and crepuscular in their habits. ('Crepuscular' means they go out a lot in twilight, just before it gets dark.) However, when they don't feel persecuted, they do become partially diurnal.
* Rabbits feed close to their warrens. It is not usual for rabbits to stray more than 450ft (137m) from their homes.
* Rabbits feed on grasses, vegetation and crops – usually staying within their habitat range. And they occasionally eat earthworms and snails. If food is scarce during the winter, rabbits will also feed on bark from young trees.
* When rabbits are feeding, there is often one rabbit standing guard to watch out for predators.
* Rabbits – usually old bucks – thump their hind feet on the ground to warn other rabbits of nearby predators.
* The rabbit's predators include: foxes, stoats, weasels, badgers, cats, polecats, buzzards and golden eagles. Weasels, badgers, buzzards and golden eagles usually attack young rabbits.
* Rabbits squeal loudly when threatened.
* When food has been digested and is then excreted, the rabbit will eat its droppings which are normally soft and contains proteins and vitamins. The second time around, the rabbit's droppings are hard and are not eaten.

* Rabbits have to groom their fur regularly otherwise it becomes matted and may lose its ability to provide insulation during wet and cold weather.
* Rabbits have scent-secreting glands under their chins and in their groins. These are important for sexual communication.
* Rabbits are sexually mature before they are six-months-old.
* The rabbit's pregnancy lasts for approximately 30 days.
* The doe has a special breeding nest which may be in a short, purpose-built dead-end burrow called a 'stab' or a 'stop'. The mother usually conceals the entrance of the burrow when leaving the young by themselves in the nest.
* Nests are made up of moss and grass and are lined with fur stripped from the mother's underside. It does not hurt the mother too much when plucking fur from her body as her hormones help to loosen it.
* The average rabbit's litter consists of three to seven young.
* A doe can give birth to as many as 12 young in one litter.
* Baby rabbits (or kittens) can weigh around 1oz (28g) at birth.
* Rabbits really do live up to the cliché of 'breeding like rabbits'. When the rabbit density is low, it is not uncommon for a doe to produce around 30 babies or more a year. Since each new female baby can start breeding within six months, it isn't difficult to see how the rabbit population can explode.

* Baby rabbits leave their nests when they are about three-weeks-old.
* Rabbits are weaned at around 21-days-old.
* Once they're old enough, young male rabbits usually leave their mothers. Female rabbits tend to stay close to their mothers.
* Over three-quarters of rabbits die before reaching their first birthday.

- When encountering strange baby rabbits, females may attack or even kill them. It is not unknown for males to go out of their way to protect any related or, indeed, unrelated baby rabbits from attack.
- The buck plays no part in bringing up its young. However, the buck does have a role to play in protecting the females and young in his group from any outsiders.
- Most does are pregnant again after only several days of giving birth.
- Rabbits can live about 10 years in the wild.
- A virus called myxomatosis killed a high percentage of the rabbit population in Europe in the 1950s. Myxomatosis originated in central South America, where it exists naturally, and was originally introduced into both Australia and Europe to control the rabbit populations. A French landowner caused this hideous disease to spread by inoculating two of his rabbits with the myxoma virus, which he obtained from Switzerland. The landowner believed that the disease would go no further than the grounds of his estate but in just a few years, myxomatosis killed massive numbers of rabbits. The rabbits died horribly with fever and skin tumours. Myxomatosis is still killing rabbits in the wild.

RHINOCEROSES

- The rhinoceros belongs to the family, Rhinocerotidae. There are five species of rhinoceros: Indian, black, Sumatran, Javan and white.
- Of the five species of rhino, the white rhino (of which there are two subspecies) is the largest. After the African and the Asian elephant, the white rhino is the largest of all land animals.
- The white rhino can weigh over 2 tons (2.03 tonnes) and grow to over 13ft (3.96m) in length.
- The smallest species of rhino is the Sumatran. The Sumatran rhino weighs around 0.78 tons (0.8 tonnes) and is about 8-10ft (2.38-3.04m) long.
- White and Indian male rhinos tend to be noticeably larger than females of the same species whereas in both sexes of other species of rhino, there is hardly any difference in size.
- White and black rhinos can be found in Africa: the white rhino in north-east and South Africa and the black rhino in sub-Saharan Africa. The Javan, Indian and the Sumatran rhino can be found in Asia. Rhinos inhabit savanna, swampy grassland and forest.
- All five species of rhino are at risk of extinction. The rarest of the species is the Javan rhino. Poaching is the main reason for the massive reduction of the rhino population. Rhinos are usually poached for their horns because of the ridiculous belief that rhino horns have medicinal and aphrodisiac properties. Rhino horns are also used for the handles of ceremonial daggers.

- The white rhino is not white in colour and the black rhino is not black in colour. In fact, both rhinos are greyish in colour. The white rhino got its name from the Afrikaans word 'wijde' which means wide. The word refers to the fact that this variety of rhino has wide lips and a wide mouth. The English then mistook the word for 'white', and so the white rhino was named.
- Unlike the African species, the Asiatic species (in particular the Indian rhino) have what looks like armoured-plating on their bodies where the skin is divided by deep skin folds.
- The closest relatives to rhinos are tapirs.
- The rhino's vocalisations include: squeals, honks and snorts.
- The rhino's (depending on species) diet includes: grass, plants, shrubs, crops, twigs, shoots, bulbs and fruit. Rhinos are herbivores.
- The White rhino has a blunt, broad mouth, giving it the ability to graze very close to the ground. The black rhino has a prehensile hooked upper lip, which is ideal for removing leaves from bushes. The white and the black rhino do not have canine or incisor teeth. Both species of rhino use their lips to feed.
- White rhinos usually eat grass whereas black, Javan and Sumatran rhinos are primarily leaf eaters. Indian rhinos on the other hand eat grass and leaves.
- In captivity, white rhinos have been observed drinking up to 18 gallons (82 litres) of water a day.
- Rhinos love water and are good swimmers.
- Rhinos often spend many hours wallowing in the mud, especially during the heat of the summer. Bathing in mud not only helps rhinos to keep cool but it also protects their skins from biting insects.
- Rhinos usually stick to a rigid routine where they follow the same trail every day at the same time, spraying their tracks with urine along the way.
- A rhino's skin is like any other mammal's. It is the tissue underneath the skin that is thick. The tissue underneath the skin is approximately 0.78in (2cm) thick.
- Rhinos can run at 30mph (48.28km/h) or more.
- Javan and Indian rhinos only have one horn – though female Javan rhinos are hornless. Instead of a horn, female Javan rhinos may have a small stump. The other species of rhino have two horns, with the larger horn at the front and the smaller horn situated behind it. In the black rhino, the rear horn can be just as long (or even longer) as its front horn.
- The rhino's horn is made of compacted keratin (the same stuff that human nails are made from). The rhino's horn can grow to more than 4ft (1.22m) in length.
- Female white rhinos often indulge in affectionate horn rubbing with one another.
- If the rhino's horn becomes broken, it will grow back.
- A rhino uses its horn for:
  a) obtaining food and water (for example, digging)

b) charging at enemies in self-defence
c) fighting with other rhinos during the mating season
d) steering their young while on the move
e) giving dance-like displays during courtship
f) showing affection to their loved ones

- Male rhinos (particularly male black rhinos) have a tendency to fight one another. Fights can be vicious and many wounds are inflicted. So vicious is the fighting that around half of all black rhinos die from wounds obtained during fights.
- Adult rhinos are largely solitary animals, especially mature males. However, immature rhinos and females without young tend to be a little more gregarious by forming pairs or temporary groups. Of all the species of rhino, the white rhino is the most sociable.
- Of all its senses, the rhino's sense of smell is its best: the volume of its nasal passages is bigger than its brain. The rhino also has very good hearing: their large, tubular ears are capable of swivelling to detect sounds. The rhino's poorest sense is its eyesight; its small eyes – placed on either side of its head – provide rather poor vision.
- Female Indian and white rhinos first give birth at around six to eight years old. Black rhinos give birth a little earlier than this.
- Rhinos have amazing stamina when it comes to mating. Copulation in rhinos may last as long as an hour or more (this includes multiple ejaculations). During copulation, the adult female (called the 'cow') usually carries on walking around as normal while the adult male (called the 'bull') struggles on his hind legs to stay attached to his mating partner.
- After a pregnancy of approximately 15-16 months (seven to eight months in the Sumatran rhino), the rhino usually gives birth to one young.
- At birth, the baby rhino weighs 51-143lb (23.13-64.86kg) (depending on species).
- Rhinos usually give birth every two to four years.
- The hides of young rhinos usually have a pinkish hue.
- Just before she gives birth, a rhino mother will usually drive her existing calf away.
- The baby rhino's main predators are lions and hyenas.
- When white rhinos feel threatened, the group may defend themselves and their young by forming a circle where they face outwards with their rumps touching one another's.
- White rhinos are reported to be more placid and timid than black rhinos.
- The Sumatran rhino is the hairiest of all the species of rhino. The Sumatran is thinly covered with a coat of dark, straggly hair. For this reason, the Sumatran is also called the 'hairy rhinoceros'.
- Longevity varies in the different species of rhino. White and Indian rhinos can live 45 years or more.
- 'Rhinoceros' means 'nose horn' in Greek.

Animal Camouflage

Animals who hunt, or who are hunted, are often camouflaged. To us their camouflage may sometimes seem rather ineffective, perhaps too showy, but the effectiveness of their camouflage has to be considered in relation to the perspective of the animals concerned. Even big animals such as lions and tigers are much closer to the ground than most humans are, and so the colour and shapes of the environment in which the animals will have to survive are different to the colours and shapes we see.

Strange But True (Part 5)

- Baboons who are at the bottom of the dominance ladder will behave submissively and in a sycophantic manner in order to earn favour and to move up the ladder. Climbing the dominance ladder will give them greater access to the big perks such as an early crack at dinner or a mating opportunity. (Apart from the absence of an inflation-proof pension and a BMW, there is not much difference between the behaviour of a baboon and the behaviour of an executive working for a large multinational corporation.)
- The box jellyfish does not have a brain.
- The beaver can cut down a 6in (15.24cm) diameter tree – using its strong incisors – in less than an hour.
- Over a million animal species have been named, but the total number of species may be as many 30 million. Most of the undiscovered animals are in the tropics. Many are undoubtedly becoming extinct before we find them.
- The anaconda snake does not lay eggs like other snakes, it gives birth to its young. The anaconda may have 75 live young at one time.
- Animals frequently display a sense of fun. Even insects can, on occasion, have a mischievous sense of humour. The Venus flytrap is one of the few carnivorous plants. We have, on several occasions seen Venus flytraps decorated with spider webs. In each case, the spider had built a web right across the plant – effectively taking out the competition.
- In its lifetime, a crocodile may grow up to 50 sets of teeth.
- An Australian box jellyfish can kill a man in three minutes. Its tentacles are armed with stinging cells which – when brushed against – fire out tiny, poisonous barbs or harpoons.
- The six spot burnet moth (which flies by day not by night) is packed with cyanide.
- Crocodiles kill more people in Africa than lions do.
- The bombardier beetle fires off a chemical spray as hot as boiling water when faced with enemies. It can fire the spray in any direction.

- The only mammals known to have levels of cancer similar to those of humans are the last few beluga whales. These animals are confined to the heavily polluted industrial waters of the Saint Lawrence estuary in eastern Canada.
- In the absence of another animal prepared to do it for them, many animals will reduce their anxiety levels by grooming, hugging and stroking themselves.
- The animals closest to man are the following species of great apes: chimpanzees, gorillas and orang-utans.
- When faced with danger, it takes American badgers about one minute to burrow their way to safety.
- The black widow spider's venom is 15 times more deadly than the rattlesnake's venom.
- Pigs love affection and are amazingly loyal

- The harvest mouse weighs less than a small coin.
- With the exception of humans, the house mouse is the most widely distributed mammal worldwide.
- In the spring of 2006, one of the world's oldest known living creatures, Harriet the tortoise, died in Australia aged 175 years. Harriet was born in 1831, the year Charles Darwin embarked upon his historic journey aboard HMS Beagle.
- There are no spiders in Antarctica.
- The swan has over 25,000 feathers on its body.
- Horse whisperer Monty Roberts spent years as a teenager watching feral mustangs. He saw how the horses communicated with one another; observing what signals they used and how they settled disputes. He later used those techniques to help him persuade horses to cooperate with him instead of 'breaking

them'. With apparently mystical skills, Roberts surprised observers by showing how he could get a wild horse to cooperate with him within 30 minutes of meeting it.

- The lifespan of a spider can range from three months to 30 years.
- Horses take less than a minute to copulate.
- A stallion's penis is about 20in (50.8cm) long.
- A quarter of cat owners admit that they have blow-dried their cat's fur after a bath.
- Some female cats act as midwives to other cats giving birth. They will chew through the umbilical cords and help clean the newborn kitten.
- Humans are the only animals who regularly drink milk from another animal.
- Grizzly bears are capable of sheering off a 12-millimeter steel bolt.
- Ravens make special calls to attract wolves and foxes to the site of dead animals. The birds know that if they can get the bigger predators to break up the carcass they can still have access to a good deal of meat but will be saved much of the work. In addition, ravens can count, can shape leaves into special tools for extracting grubs from crevices in trees and are believed by scientists to have an innate capacity for logical thought.
- A kangaroo's fart contains no methane.
- An ostrich can kill a lion with a single kick.
- The ostrich is the largest, heaviest living bird and can run at 43mph (69.20km/h).
- The wild white cattle of England are thought to be living descendants of animals who lived in the country in prehistoric times.
- Most animals will not eat animals of their own species. They know it isn't healthy to do so. Bovine spongiform encephalopathy (BSE), aka mad cow disease, was caused by feeding meat from cows to cows (which are vegetarian animals).
- Tarantulas do not spin prey-catching webs.
- Sharks can't stop moving. The great white, maku, basking and blue sharks have to keep moving to stay live. But they have a central generator organ that allows them to swim while they are unconscious. This enables them to sleep as they swim.
- The ferret's scientific name, Mustela putorius furo, means 'musk-bearing stinking, thief'.
- Rats' teeth are more than five times as hard as steel.

Seals (Common)

- True seals, fur seals, sea lions and walruses are collectively known as Pinnipeds. These marine mammals are divided into three families: the Odobenidae or walrus, the Otariidae or eared seals and the Phocidae or true seals. The common seal belongs to the last family, along with 17 other species. The two main differences between true seals and eared seals is that true seals lack external ear flaps and are unable to bring their hind flippers forward.

- Common seals can be found throughout the northern Hemisphere.
- The common seal has a rounded head; no external ear flaps; a short, blunt snout; nostrils (which form a V-shaped pattern) and white whiskers (called vibrissae). The common seal's body is torpedo shaped, with two front flippers (each containing five large, black claws) and two powerful hind flippers. A fully-grown adult seal can weigh as much as 600lb (272.15kg) and grow to 6ft in length. Mature males are about 25 per cent heavier than female seals.
- The common seal is able to see much better underwater than on land.
- The common seal usually occupies estuaries, sea lochs and shallow coastal waters. Common seals can be seen basking – often with their backs arched and heads and hind flippers raised – on sandbanks at low tide. The common seal also likes to bask on rocks near deep water. If they find a favourable spot, they will often return to it day after day.
- The common seal is rather cumbersome on land and is better adapted for moving in the water. However, the structure of the seal's body suggests that at one time it used to be a terrestrial animal, living on the land and able to walk about on all four separate limbs. Now, the seal is almost marine – but not exclusively so. For the seal has retained its covering of fur and, unlike other marine animals, it likes to spend some of its time on land.
- The common seal propels itself in the water with its hind flippers using side-to-side strokes, and manoeuvres itself in the water with its front flippers.
- The common seal's coat is variable in colour. The seal's coat can be white, pale grey, dark grey, pale brown, dark brown or black. The common seal's coat also has a speckled appearance with lots of distinctive various-sized blotches and spots. These distinctive markings are unique in each individual. Underneath the seal's skin is a thick layer of blubber, which helps to insulate the seal's body from the harsh weather and to provide energy when the need arises.
- The common seal is also referred to as the harbour seal.
- The common seal is a carnivore and feeds primarily on fish. Common seals will also eat squid, octopus, sand eels, molluscs, shrimps and crustaceans such as crabs.
- The mature female seal is called a cow. The mature male seal is called a bull. The baby seal is called a pup, a calf or a cub.
- Both courtship and mating usually takes place in the water.
- Common seal pups are born during the best weather of the year in order to increase their chances of survival. Pups can be born any time between May and July.
- The female seal often gives birth in a quiet spot on land (or ice) close to the sea.

- The female common seal usually gives birth to one pup a year. Although it's rare, twins have been documented. When twins are born, the mother usually allows the weakest one to die because she is unable to provide for them both.
- Common seal pups weigh approximately 22lb (10kg) at birth.
- The pup is able to swim within hours of birth.
- The common seal pup is usually born with a similar coat to its parents. Unlike some other species of seal pup, their yellowish-white coat called lanugo is usually shed in its mother's womb. If the common seal pup is born with its lanugo (which is rare), then it is shed shortly after birth.
- Seal pups grow very quickly on their mother's rich milk. By the time they are weaned, some pups have trebled their birth weight.
- After the pup has been weaned, usually at around four to six weeks, the mother will leave her pup to fend for itself.
- Common seals moult once a year.
- Common seals can live 30 years or more.
- Some of the common seal's predators include: orcas (otherwise known as killer whales), sharks and polar bears.
- Common seals have a reputation of possessing very placid and shy natures.
- Common seals are playful animals and can often be seen making dolphin-like leaps out of the water.
- Common seals are usually very quiet mammals, probably the quietest of all seals. The seal's occasional vocalisations include: grunts, growls, yelps and coughs. The baby seal tends to make wailing noises when calling for its mother.
- Common seals either sleep floating in the water or on the seabed. If the seal wishes to sleep on the seabed then it must decrease its buoyancy in the water by reducing the amount of air it takes into its body, which is seems to do automatically.
- Observers claim that common seals can survive enforced dives of 300ft (91m) and can remain under water for about half an hour.
- The common seal's eyes are constantly lubricated by tears that emerge from the corners of its eyes. These tears often fall down the seal's cheeks which makes the seal look as if it has been crying.
- The seal is able to close its nostrils and ears when it is underwater.

Animals Can Communicate

Many observers have dismissed animal noises as simply that (noises), but scientists who have taken the time and trouble to listen carefully to the extraordinary variety of sounds made by different animals have concluded that animals really can communicate with one another.

Here are a few examples illustrating the ability of animals to communicate effectively:

1. Scientists studying whales have found that there are patterns of what can only be described as speech in the noises they make.
2. Bees can communicate the direction, distance and value of pollen sources quite a distance away.
3. It is generally assumed that parrots merely repeat words they have heard without understanding what they mean. This is not true. In their marvellous book *When Elephants Weep,* authors Masson and McCarthy report that when psychologist Irene Pepperberg left her parrot at the vet's surgery for an operation, the parrot – whose name was Alex – called out: 'Come here. I love you. I'm sorry. I want to go back.' Another parrot, in New Jersey, America saved the life of its owner by calling for help. 'Murder! Help! Come quick!' cried the parrot. When neighbours ran to the scene of the crime they found the parrot's owner lying on the floor, unconscious, bleeding from a gash in his neck. The doctor who treated the man said that without the parrot's cries he would have died. The same parrot woke his owner and neighbours when a fire started in the house next door.
4. Rabbits communicate by thumping on the ground with their hind feet. They can 'talk' to one another in this way over distances of 600ft (183m).
5. Human beings who have taken the time to do so have found that they have been able to communicate well with all other primates.
6. Animals can communicate in ways we haven't really begun to understand. British biologist Rupert Sheldrake conducted an experiment in which he simultaneously recorded humans at work and their dogs at home. The moment the human left work, the dog, waiting at home, headed for the door. This worked even if the human left work at a different time each day. For example, the daughter of one dog owner reports that their dog always rushed to the door exactly twenty minutes before her mother arrived home. And it didn't matter what time the mother left work. The dog always knew. We know a number of people who have reported similar skills among cats.
7. It is also by no means unusual for human beings to receive messages from animals. British author Sir H. Rider Haggard once described how he had dreamed that his dog Bob was lying dead in a clump of weeds near some water. 'The next day,' wrote Haggard, 'Bob was found dead in just such a place. He had been hit by a train at the same time that I'd had my dream.'

Sheep (Domestic)

☺ Sheep belong to the family Bovidae, and can be found throughout most of the world. Sheep have been domesticated in Europe, Central Asia and the Middle East since around 5,000 (BC).

- ☺ Some of the familiar breeds of sheep include: Welsh Mountain, Hampshire Down, Suffolk, Dorset Horn, Scottish blackface and the Cheviot.
- ☺ The endangered Asiatic mouflon sheep is thought to be the ancestor of all domestic sheep breeds.
- ☺ Like cattle and various other animals, sheep are ruminants – they chew the cud.
- ☺ Sheep are herbivores. When in pastures, sheep feed mainly on grasses.
- ☺ Sheep may spend up to 12 hours a day eating.
- ☺ Sheep will not eat grass contaminated with another sheep's dung. It is cruel, therefore, to have too many sheep grazing in one field.
- ☺ Rhododendron is just one of the number of plants that is harmful to sheep.
- ☺ The average natural lifespan of a sheep is eight to nine years. Very few sheep are allowed to live this long.
- ☺ Sheep are born with long tails. For hygiene purposes, a sheep's tail is normally docked soon after birth. This is necessary today because a sheep's diet is different to that of its predecessors. A modern sheep eats lush, green grass and produces messier droppings with a result that its tail becomes dirtier and attracts flies. When the sheep's faeces were hard, the tail merely provided rudimentary protection for the area.
- ☺ Sheep are very gentle, sentient animals. They also love affection and hate to be by themselves.
- ☺ Sheep are closely related to goats. And just like their close relatives, sheep have 'rectangular' pupils.
- ☺ Sheep have a field vision of 270 degrees.
- ☺ Even though a sheep's wool contains lanolin which helps to protect it from the elements, sheep dislike the rain. If there is any natural shelter available, they will usually hide under that until the rain stops. Sheep also seek shelter from the sun on hot days. But with the cutting back of hedgerows, many sheep on pasture land have no natural shelter at all.
- ☺ Sheep hate walking through water.
- ☺ Rams (uncastrated male sheep) rarely use their horns in self-defence against other animals; they mostly use them for ritual battles with other rams. However, rams will sometimes chase and head-butt humans.
- ☺ Hebridean rams can grow as many as six horns.
- ☺ Sheep are not very good at protecting themselves. They tend to flock together in large groups for self-preservation. A sheep's herding instinct is so strong that all it takes is for several sheep in the herd to start running, and the rest of the herd will usually follow.
- ☺ Sheep become upset and anxious when separated from other sheep.
- ☺ There are over one billion sheep on earth.
- ☺ Sheep are about eight-months-old when they are ready to start breeding.
- ☺ A ewe's pregnancy lasts for approximately five months.

- ☺ On average, most breeds of sheep give birth to one or two young.
- ☺ At birth, a baby lamb weighs between five and ten per cent of its mother's weight.
- ☺ The bond between twin lambs is believed to be so strong that they have even been known to finish off each other's 'baas'.
- ☺ Depending on the breed of sheep, a fleece can weigh up to 20lb (9.07kg).
- ☺ The fleece from one sheep will, on average, produce three jumpers.

- ☺ Sheep are usually shorn of their wool once a year around late springtime.
- ☺ Contrary to popular belief, sheep have good memories and are intelligent animals.
- ☺ Sheep's milk contains twice as many minerals as cows' milk.
- ☺ If sheep roll onto their backs, they may be too heavy to get back up again. They may die as a result. This is one of the reasons why it is important for farmers to check on their flocks regularly.
- ☺ Sheep often form individual friendships with each other, and if one of them should die then the remaining sheep usually suffers enormous grief.
- ☺ Ewes and lambs who have been separated will recognise each other when put into the same field some years later.
- ☺ Fashionable couturiers sometimes use skin and wool taken from newborn or foetal lambs. This requires the lamb to be killed at or even before birth. Sometimes the mother is also killed so that the unborn lamb can be removed from the womb.

☺ Lambs regularly play games such as tag and king of the castle. Older sheep enjoy games too.

☺ Sheep are now known to have excellent powers of recall and are far better at identifying individual humans than humans are at identifying sheep. Moreover, sheep are now known to share similar thought patterns to those of people. When shown pictures of human faces, sheep can tell the difference between them and can remember at least ten human faces for more than two years. They also recognise and remember at least 50 friends within a flock using the same visual cues that we use when identifying other people. Sheep learn new faces very quickly and use part of the brain's temporal lobe to do this (just as people do).

☺ Sheep respond emotionally to things around them. For example, showing a sheep a picture of a friendly face makes the sheep feel happy.

☺ 'We may have underestimated the complexity of a sheep's social environment, and, indeed, their intelligence,' says Professor Keith Kendrick of the Babraham Institute for agricultural research, based near Cambridge. 'Sheep have developed the same kind of sophisticated social recognition skills normally only thought to exist in man and other higher primates. The presence of such skills raises questions as to whether we have underestimated the importance and complexity of their social needs and intelligence.'

Two Strange Experiences

One of us (VC) has had a number of experiences exhibiting the strange powers animals can have. Here are his accounts of two specific experiences. These accounts were written down immediately after the events described.

'Driving through Devon I stopped for petrol. I was alone. I was alert, awake and not at all tired. The only other vehicle at the petrol station was one of those huge lorries used to transport sheep from farms to abattoirs. The lorry was parked to one side – about twenty or thirty yards away from the petrol pumps.

As soon as I got out of my car I heard the sheep bleating in the lorry. The sound was clear and distinctive. As I filled my car with petrol the sound made by the sheep continued. When I had finished filling my car I went into the kiosk and paid for the petrol. On my way back to my car I suddenly stopped, drawn towards the lorry. The baaing had become louder and more insistent. It suddenly occurred to me that one of the sheep might be in special distress. Animals in these lorries are crammed together so tightly that one sometimes gets a leg caught in between the slats of the lorry wall. Maybe I could help.

I walked over to the lorry and looked inside. As soon as I looked inside the baaing stopped. And I could see that the lorry was completely, utterly empty.

There was not one sheep inside it. Nor were there any sheep anywhere else nearby. There were no other lorries and no sheep in nearby fields.

The explanation?

Could the lorry have still been carrying the pain of all those sheep who had been transported in fear and anguish to their death?

Whatever the explanation may be, this story is absolutely true.'

'I was sitting alone in the car while Donna Antoinette popped into a shop near Barnstaple. I heard a hefty kicking sound coming from the rear of the car. I looked round and could see nothing. There was no one nearby. There was not even any other car nearby. The hefty kicking sound came again. It was definitely coming from the boot of the car. The car (a large, heavy saloon) rocked slightly with the kicking. I got out of the car, walked round to the back of the car and opened the boot. I was convinced that at some point an animal must have climbed into the boot. I was so convinced about this that I opened the boot carefully and kept my distance in case the animal leapt out. There was nothing alive in the boot and nothing in there that could have caused any noise. I got back into the car. After Donna Antoinette returned and we drove away, I explained to her what had happened. She reminded me that I had that morning picked up an urn containing the ashes of Karen – a pet sheep who had recently died. Karen's ashes were still in the car boot. Donna Antoinette also quickly reminded me that while alive, Karen always used to kick my leg quite sharply when she wanted more attention. This story is absolutely true.'

By No Means Stupid

'One March I got my ride on mower out from the shed where it had been stored for the winter and started up the engine ready to drive it across the courtyard towards the garden. As I started up the engine I watched four pet sheep, who were grazing in their field, prick up their ears and start to run. I watched as they ran for several hundred yards and then stood waiting at the very spot where, the previous summer, I had dumped the grass cuttings I had taken from the lawns. It slowly dawned on me that the sheep had, after a gap of five or six months, recognised the sound of the lawnmower's engine (differentiating it from the numerous other engines they would have heard in the intervening period), recognised that the sound of the engine meant that I was about to start cutting the grass, remembered that they liked munching a handful of grass cuttings, remembered where I had dumped the grass cuttings some five or six months previously when I had last cut the lawns, and had instantly run round the field to be in position ready for the first batch of cuttings of the season. I know a good many human beings (most of them politicians) who could not have drawn such an accurate conclusion from one piece of information (the starting up of a lawnmower engine).'

Vernon Coleman

Squirrels (Red Squirrel)

- Squirrels belong to the family, Sciuridae. The Eurasian red squirrel can be found in gardens, parks and woodlands throughout Europe and parts of Asia. The Eurasian red squirrel is the only species that is native to Britain, with the vast majority living in Scotland.
- There are only two species of squirrel living in Britain: the red squirrel (Eurasian red) and the grey squirrel (eastern grey).
- In Britain, the red squirrel population has decreased dramatically over recent decades. This diminution is blamed on the introduction of the grey squirrel brought over from America in the late 1800's. Although there have been many theories, nobody really knows for sure why this should be so. One of the theories suggests that the grey squirrel eats food that the red squirrel might have eaten (the grey squirrel seems to be better at obtaining food than the red squirrel). If this is true, then it is exacerbated by the fact that there are 16 grey squirrels for every one red squirrel. However, some experts argue that food competition isn't a problem, as the reds prefer to feed from different types of trees to the greys. The fact that there is a larger population of grey squirrels than red squirrels may be a result of the fact that grey squirrels are hardier and eat a wider variety of foods. Grey squirrels have also been blamed for spreading disease to some of the red squirrel populations, causing them to die out altogether in some areas.

There are, however, some experts who argue that the grey squirrel is totally blameless for the reduction in the number of red squirrels remaining. They believe that red squirrels were already in decline when the grey squirrel was introduced into Britain. The grey squirrel isn't the only mammal to be blamed for the decline of the red squirrel. Man's destruction of some of their natural habit has also been held responsible for the squirrel's dwindling numbers.

- In Britain, the red squirrel is protected by law.

- The native British red squirrel's coat is usually brownish-red in colour. The underside neck and the belly of the squirrel are white. In the winter months, the red squirrel's back usually changes to a brownish-grey colour. Red squirrels also develop more prominent ear tufts in the winter.
- Red squirrels are approximately 8-10in (20.32-25.4cm) tall and weigh an average of around 10.5oz (290g). The grey squirrel is slightly taller at approximately 10-12in (25.4-30.5cm) tall, and weighs an average of around 18oz (510g). The red squirrel's bushy tail can grow to 8in (20.32cm) or more.

Who Stole My Nuts?

Who stole my nuts?
The squirrel demanded
When I capture the culprit
I'll see he's remanded

There were acorns and beech nuts
And cob nuts galore
When I find out who stole them
I'll start a small war

I know where I put them
It was just about here
I tell you quite firmly
Of that I am clear

They were under the oak tree
Two steps to the left
And now that they're gone
I feel quite bereft

Or could it just be
Now here's a strange thought
That the tree that they're under
Is not the same sort

And ten minutes later
There's a glorious screech
As the squirrel declares
They're under this beech!

Vernon Coleman

- The red squirrel uses its long, bushy tail for balance and as a 'rudder' when jumping. Squirrels also use their tails as signalling devices. If it is nervous about something, the squirrel will usually twitch its tail to warn other squirrels to keep their distance.
- By the end of the summer, most red squirrels' tails will have bleached in colour.
- Red squirrels moult their coats twice a year, except for their tails and ear tufts which are only moulted annually. However, this twice a year moulting of tails and ear tufts is unique to squirrels residing in Britain and Ireland.
- A squirrel's nest is called a drey. Dreys may be shared by more than one squirrel, especially in the winter when it is cold.
- The squirrel's drey is usually set in the fork of a tree near the trunk, about 18ft (5.49m) or more off the ground. The drey is spherical in shape with hardly any visible entrance, and is about the size of a football. The drey is usually constructed from twigs. Moss, leaves or grass usually line the inside of the nest. Squirrels sometimes use tree cavities as their nests.
- Squirrels normally have more than one drey. Probably as a safety net just in case one of their dreys becomes damaged and to reduce parasite infestation in the nests.
- The red squirrel's diet includes: seeds from conifer cones, hazelnuts, tree flowers and shoots, berries, sap, fungi, insects, birds' eggs and, occasionally, nestlings.
- Without food, squirrels can only live for a few days.
- Contrary to popular belief, the red squirrel does not hibernate.
- When on the ground, red squirrels are never very far away from trees. This is because squirrels are not adept at running at high speeds when chased by predators and must, therefore, rely on trees to escape from their enemies. Squirrels are very well adapted to climbing and have long, needle-sharp curved claws which help to grip the tree bark when they are ascending or descending down trees. The squirrel is able to climb down a tree headfirst.
- Foxes, stoats, dogs, cats, pine martens and buzzards are just some of the squirrel's predators.
- Squirrels have excellent eyesight and a broad field of vision, which enable them to spot any nearby predators.
- Long before the cold winter arrives the squirrel buries supplies of nuts in the ground. Before burying the nuts, the squirrel usually bites the shell of each nut and smears it with its scent by rubbing its face on it or by licking it. Doing this makes it easier for the squirrel to find its food supply later on by using its sense of smell as well as its memory. Unfortunately, when winter arrives and food is scarce, squirrels do not always find their hidden stores of food (called caches).
- Surprisingly, red squirrels are more likely to die from starvation in the summer than they are in the winter.
- Squirrels can swim.
- The squirrel is only active during the day, and goes to its drey to rest at night.

- The mating season begins around January. When on heat, the female will distribute her scent and make vocalisations to attract males. The female will then lead the males (five at the most) on a chase which can go on for up to ten hours in some cases. She does this to assess each male's stamina and strength in order to see which male is likely to make the most suitable breeding partner. It is usually the experienced, dominant male – the one that is always closest by in the mating chase – who is allowed to mate with the female.
- The squirrel's pregnancy lasts for approximately seven weeks.
- The squirrel's average litter contains three young. The mother gives birth and rears her young in a specially built drey.
- The male plays no part in the rearing of its young.
- The squirrel's young are called kittens.
- Baby squirrels are born toothless and hairless and weigh around 0.28-0.42oz (8-12g). The baby squirrel is fully furred by the time it is three-weeks-old.
- A healthy squirrel usually produces two litters a year.
- Sadly, over 50 per cent of baby squirrels do not reach their first birthday. Their demise is usually due to starvation.
- Baby squirrels leave their nests when they are about two-months-old.
- The squirrel's average lifespan is around three years, but they can live to reach six or seven years.
- In Russia, the red squirrel is hunted for its winter coat.

Longevity Of Ten Birds (Maximum Recorded Age)

- Blue tit – 10 years
- Buzzard – 26 years
- Herring gull – 36 years
- House sparrow – 12 years
- Kestrel – 17 years
- Mute swan – 22 years
- Pheasant – 8 years
- Tawny Owl – 18 years
- White stork – 26 years
- Woodpigeon – 16 years

Animals And Pain

Scientists deny that animals suffer pain. (If they did not, they would not receive permission to perform so many painful and cruel experiments.)

Scientists claim that the evidence for this assertion is the fact that animals don't react in the way that people do when they might be in pain. People in pain often cry out or show other signs of distress but animals often remain quiet and will suffer great pain apparently stoically.

The reason for this is simple. As far as animals are concerned, there is often no advantage to them in showing humans that they are feeling pain. On the contrary, there are good reasons to disguise that they are in pain. Wounded animals try to hide their pain from predators, and human beings are predators. Animals know that if they show that they are in pain (and, therefore, weak) they will be more vulnerable to attack. In addition, animals who live in hierarchical societies (such as lions) may lose status if they appear to be ill.

However, if they are loved and well cared for, animals will show their pain and distress to those whom they trust.

Note: Curiously, the same scientists who deny that animals ever feel pain frequently perform laboratory experiments designed to test new painkilling drugs on animals. Indeed, all painkilling drugs are tested on animals. If animals feel no pain, what is the point of the experiments? How can they possibly work? And if animals do feel pain, isn't this yet more evidence that animal experimentation is cruel and barbaric?

Tigers

- ➔ The tiger belongs to the family Felidae, and is the largest member of the cat family.
- ➔ The tiger can be found in forests, grasslands and swamps in India, South-East Asia, China and Siberia.
- ➔ The female tiger is called a she-tiger. The male is simply called a tiger. The baby tiger is called a cub.
- ➔ There were eight subspecies of tiger but three of these have become extinct since the 1950s. The five subspecies remaining are the Bengal, Chinese, Indo-Chinese, Siberian and Sumatran tigers. All five subspecies are endangered.
- ➔ Of all the subspecies, the Siberian (aka Amur) tiger is the largest.
- ➔ The most common subspecies of tiger is the Bengal.
- ➔ Tigers can weigh as much as 660lb (299.37kg) and can grow to 10ft (3.05m) long. The length includes the tail, which is approximately 3ft (0.91m) long.

- ➔ The tiger is a solitary animal and – unless it is with its cubs – usually lives alone in the wild.
- ➔ Tigers are nocturnal hunters, but, now and again, they have been known to go after prey during daylight hours if they are exceptionally hungry.
- ➔ Tigers are carnivores.
- ➔ The tiger usually hunts alone unless the tiger is a mother with her cubs. Although, occasionally, a tiger will hunt with its mate during the breeding period.
- ➔ The tiger does not chase its prey but stalks and ambushes it. The tiger's striking orange coat, adorned with black stripes, gives it good camouflage protection by breaking up its body against the dense vegetation where it stalks. The tiger tries to get as near to its prey as it possibly can without being seen. It does this by crouching and slowly creeping closer and closer towards its victim. Once the tiger is no more than 100ft (30.48m) away, it makes an attempt to rush at its prey. Owing to its huge size, the tiger cannot run for long periods, so making a bid for its prey further than this will usually result in failure. This isn't helped by the fact that the tiger's prey can usually run much faster than the tiger. The tiger usually attacks its prey from the side or from the rear. The tiger then seizes its prey by the shoulders using its strong forelimbs and sharp claws, and bites its victim on the neck or throat with its powerful jaws.
- ➔ The tiger probably has a fewer than one in ten chance of making a kill, which means that it has to spend a lot of its time hunting. However, the female tiger who has mouths to feed is a little more successful at killing prey because, undoubtedly, she tries harder.
- ➔ Studies suggest that a tiger without cubs will make, on average, up to 50 kills a year.
- ➔ The tiger will eat just about anything that crosses its path. The tiger's diet includes: deer, wild cattle, wild pigs, monkeys, sloth bears, small mammals, birds, fish and reptiles. Sometimes, young rhinos and young elephants are killed and eaten. On rare occasions, tigers have been known to kill and eat leopards, usually leopards who have been troubling, worrying or threatening tiger cubs.
- ➔ Loss of habitat resulting in loss of wildlife has forced some tigers to kill and eat domestic cattle, making tigers unpopular with farmers.
- ➔ Once a kill has been made, the tiger usually drags the carcass near to a body of water. This may involve dragging the carcass for several miles.
- ➔ A tiger is often reluctant to leave its dead prey until every morsel of meat has been devoured from the carcass. If the tiger has to leave its kill, to drink water for example, the tiger will take great care to hide the carcass from any scavengers who might be lurking nearby. Tigers have been known to eat 75lb (34kg) of meat in one evening.
- ➔ Although solitary animals, tigers have been seen sharing their kills with other tigers.

- Tigers reach sexual maturity between the ages of three and five years of age.
- A male tiger will mate a female tiger as many as 100 times in 48 hours.
- A female tiger's pregnancy lasts for approximately 15 weeks.
- The tiger's litter contains two or three cubs.
- At birth, a typical cub weighs just over 2lb (0.90kg).
- The male tiger does not participate in the rearing of its cubs. But it will come back to visit the cubs and their mother up to twice a month.
- Tigers usually breed every two years.
- The tiger's home range can be a big as 60 sq. miles (155.4 sq. km); it depends on the breed of tiger and how much food is available.
- The tiger is very territorial, and marks its home range by using a combination of urine and anal gland secretions. The tiger will mark various landmarks in its home range such as rocks, trees and bushes. It will also leave scratches on trees (using its long, retractile claws). The tiger cannot afford to risk another tiger intruding on its home range because if a fight were to ensue, it could be disastrous for both tigers involved. A wounded limb, for instance, could mean a death sentence to a tiger, as it would face even more difficulty in successfully catching prey.
- The tiger's purr is roughly a hundred times louder than that of a domestic cat.
- Unlike the vast majority of domestic cats, tigers love water and can swim very well. Tigers often stand or lie in the water to keep cool during the hot weather.
- The tiger is an endangered species.
- There are reputed to be less than 8,000 tigers living in the world today. Loss of habitat, a reduction in prey and poaching (largely because tiger body parts are valued in some branches of medicine) are thought to be responsible for the decline of the tiger population. Despite evidence proving that the use of tiger body parts in the preparation of medicines is utterly useless, this practice persists and is rooted in the awe that the tiger commonly inspires.
- In the wild, the average lifespan of a tiger is approximately 10-15 years.
- When tigers greet one another they make a noise that sounds rather like fuf-fuf-fuf-fuf. So, if you should one day encounter a tiger, and the tiger staring back at you is salivating and licking its lips with hunger, you could greet the tiger with a hearty fuf-fuf-fuf-fuf. However, we take no responsibility whatsoever if you should receive a negative response from your beautiful orange and black encounter. Readers who 'fuf-fuf-fuf-fuf' at tigers do so at their own peril.
- The commonly photographed white tigers are all descended from a single male Bengal tiger called Mohan who was captured by the Maharaja of Rewa in India. The Maharaja started breeding these tigers in the early 1950s. Most white tigers have brown stripes and are, therefore, not really white.

An Alphabet Of Animals

A	Aardvark
B	Baboon
C	Coyote
D	Dormouse
E	Elk
F	Ferret
G	Gerbil
H	Hamster
I	Impala
J	Jaguar
K	Kangaroo
L	Lemur
M	Mole
N	Narwhal
O	Otter
P	Platypus
Q	Quokka (a species of wallaby)
R	Racoon
S	Shrew
T	Tiger
U	Uakari (a species of monkey)
V	Vole
W	Walrus
X	X-ray fish
Y	Yak
Z	Zebra

'A wild animal living free never poisons itself, for it knows what foods to choose. This is an instinct animals lose when they are domesticated.'

Maurice Mességué

Wolves (Grey)

- Like dogs and foxes, the grey wolf belongs to the family Canidae. Grey wolves are mostly found in Europe, the Middle East, Asia and North America. Wolves usually live in the wilderness or remote areas but may live close to villages if there is plenty of food available.
- There are two species of wolf in existence today: the grey wolf (the larger of the species) and the red wolf. The red wolf is believed to be extinct in the wild.
- The male grey wolf can weigh as much as 176.36lb (80kg) and grow to 7ft (2.13m) long.
- The wolf's coat has two layers. The first layer is made up of short, thick hairs: the second layer is made up of long, coarse hairs. These two layers of fur act as insulation from the cold and wet weather.
- As one would expect by their name, grey wolves are usually grey in colour but the colour of their fur can vary. For example, there are some wolves that are pure white in colour and some wolves that are jet black in colour. Red and brown wolves are also sometimes seen.
- Wolves are social animals and most of them live in packs or family groups. The ones that live alone are usually young wolves in search of their own territory. There may be as many as 20 or more members in a pack. A pack of wolves consists of a hierarchy where the top-ranking wolves (called the 'alpha' wolves) dominate the rest of the pack. The alpha wolves are often a male and a female who are mating partners. However, it is usually only one of them who has the role of pack leader. It is the alpha wolves who get to eat the kill first (taking the best parts), decide when to hunt and which prey to kill. And they are often the only ones who are allowed to mate in the pack. The position of pack leader is constantly challenged and is not a permanent post, since it can change if a new, younger, stronger wolf within the pack makes a successful challenge for the leadership.
- Members of a pack often play with one another to help the bonding process.
- A subordinate wolf will greet a more dominant wolf member in the same pack by lowering its tail and holding back its ears.
- Wolves live in a world of smells; smells are very important to them. Wolves have an incredible sense of smell, far superior to any human's. Just by sniffing another wolf's urine, they are able to detect the reproductive state, sex, age and health of that wolf. They can even tell what the wolf has had to eat and what mood it is in.
- Wolves mainly feed on caribou, moose, elk, bison, musk oxen, deer, sheep, goats and many smaller animals. Wolves have also been known to eat some of the following: birds, fish, snakes, carrion, grasses, fruits and food from rubbish dumps.

- When chasing their prey, wolves can attain speeds of up to 44.73mph (72km/h).
- When prey is abundant, and there are plenty of small animals around, the wolf will usually hunt alone. But when small prey is scarce, the wolf has no choice but to hunt larger animals with other members of the pack. A wolf cannot bring down a large animal by itself; it needs the other members of the pack to help with the kill. Once a kill has been made, the pack members join in the meal.
- If the pack is unable to eat its kill in one sitting, the wolves will dig a hole in the ground to bury the carcass and return to feed on it later. If any member of the pack digs up the carcass, it will urinate in the empty cache to let other individuals in the pack know that the food is no longer there.
- Wolves prefer to attack animals who are weak, sick or young. This is because vulnerable animals are less likely to put up a lot of resistance.
- The wolf rarely eats every day. Wolves are unsuccessful at catching and killing prey about 90 per cent of the time.
- Wolves can smell their prey from over 1.24 miles (2km) away.
- Wolves roll in dead animals to disguise their scent from potential prey, making hunting easier for them.
- Most wolves are around two years of age before they start breeding.
- The female grey wolf's pregnancy lasts for approximately 63 days.
- A few weeks before giving birth, the female will dig an underground den for her newly born pups. She will also build a second den just in case her pups are threatened and she needs to hide them somewhere else.
- The average litter contains five or six pups.
- The female wolf can give birth to as many as 11 pups.
- Wolf clubs are usually born in the early spring.
- Wolves nearly always help one another in the pack. For example, if the mother has to stay in the den with her cubs, the adult wolves will readily bring her food.
- As soon as the pups emerge from their den, at around a month old, the other members of the pack will be there to greet them.
- The pups feed on regurgitated food from their mother.
- Contrary to popular belief, wolves will not readily attack humans. Wolves tend to be afraid of humans and will usually run away from them.
- The domestic dog is the wolf's closest living relative, but it is the grey wolf that is the domestic dog's ancestor.
- Wolves are highly intelligent animals. They are far smarter than the domestic dog. The grey wolf's brain is a third larger than that of the domestic dog.
- Wolves are excellent swimmers.
- Wolves who live in the forest have been reputed to hear as far as 6.21 miles (10km) away.
- It is a myth that wolves howl at the moon. When wolves howl they do it to call the pack together at the beginning of a hunt, or to warn other wolf packs to

keep away from their territory so as to avoid confrontation. When one member of the pack howls, all the other members join in the chorus.

- The grey wolf's howl can be heard from approximately 6 miles (9.65km) away.
- Wolves have territories of at least 60 sq. miles (155.39 sq. km). In some cases, territories can cover as much as 600 sq. miles (1,55.4 sq. km), depending on the availability of prey. Wolves mark their territories by urinating on prominent landmarks (or scent posts) within their habitat. This task is usually undertaken by the dominant wolf (or wolves) in the pack.
- The wolf has 42 teeth.
- The average lifespan of a wolf living in the wild is 8-16 years.
- Wolves usually mate for life.
- Wolves used to be found in Britain but man eventually wiped them out. It is believed that the last wolf in Britain was killed in 1743.
- The two main threats to the wolf's survival are: being hunted by man and loss of habitat (also caused by man).

'I think I could turn and live with animals,
they're so placid and self-contained,
I stand and look at them long and long.
They do not sweat and whine about their condition,
They do not lie awake in the dark and weep for their sins,
They do not make me sick discussing their duty to God,
Not one is dissatisfied, not one is demented with
the mania of knowing things,
Not one kneels to another, nor to his kind that lived
thousands of years ago.'
WALT WHITMAN (1819-1892)

'We declare henceforth that all animals shall enjoy these inalienable rights: The right to freedom from fear, pain and suffering – whether in the name of science or sport, fashion or food, exhibition or service. The right, if they are wild, to roam free, unhurried by hunters, trappers or slaughterers. If they are domestic, not to be abandoned in the city streets, by a country road, or in a cruel and inhumane pound. And finally the right, at the end, to a decent death – not (whether they are endangered or not) by a club, by a trap, by harpoon, cruel poison or mass extermination chamber. We have only one creed – to speak for those who can't.'
(THE FUND FOR ANIMALS, INC.)

Five Insects That Are Named After Mammals

1. Horsefly
2. Rhinoceros beetle
3. Tiger moth
4. Wolf spider
5. Zebra Spider

The World's Greediest animals

1. Lion
A lion will eat a baby elephant at one sitting.

2. Tiger shark
Eats anything it can catch. Known to eat other sharks.

3. Wolverine
The name means 'greedy'. Will eat anything from a whole deer to a bird's egg.

4. Larva of the Polyphemus moth
A caterpillar which eats 86,000 times its own weight in leaves during the first two months of its life.

Zebras

- Zebras belong to the family Equidae. The Equidae family also includes: horses, ponies and asses.
- There are three species of zebra: Burchell's (or common) zebra, Grevy's zebra and the mountain zebra.
- The most common species of zebra is the Burchell's zebra. There are believed to be over 30,000 Burchell's zebra living in Africa. The least common species is the mountain zebra.
- The Burchell's zebra is found in grasslands and savanna in southern and eastern Africa. The Grevy's zebra is found in dry areas and grassland in Ethiopia, Somalia and North Kenya. The mountain zebra is found in the arid, grassland upland plains in western-south Africa and Namibia.

- The Grevy's zebra has a white belly, and stripes that are narrower and more numerous than the other species. The Burchell's zebra has broader flank stripes and does not have a white belly. The mountain zebra's stripes are more vertically arranged on its flanks. The differences in the stripes of the three species are more noticeable on their rumps.
- The zebra's stripes are not uniformed: one side does not match the other.
- The largest species of zebra is the Grevy's zebra which is over 9ft (2.74m) long and weighs approximately 892.87lb (405kg).
- All three species of zebra have long tails with hair at the tips. The zebra's tail can grow to 20.47in (52cm) in length.
- Like horses and donkeys, zebras are odd-toed ungulates with just one toe on each foot capped by a tough, horny hoof.
- The Grevy's zebra was discovered in 1882, and was named after Jules Grevy who was the President of France at the time.
- The young zebra is called a foal. The mature female is called a mare. The male zebra is called a stallion.
- The vocal sounds of zebras include: whinnying, squealing, braying and nickering. Zebras even make barking noises when alerting other members in their group to danger.
- Zebras are able to sense a rainstorm from as far as 62.13 miles (100km) away.
- Zebras are herbivores. Their main diet consists of grasses and sedges. They will also eat: leaves, buds, roots, bark and fruits.
- The zebra's main predator is the lion.
- Every zebra has its own unique pattern of stripes.
- There are a number of theories as to why zebras have stripes. The following are just some of the theories:
  a) so that zebras can recognise one another
  b) to confuse and overawe predators
  c) to control body temperature
  d) to provide camouflage
  e) to stimulate grooming
  f) to keep disease-carrying insects away
- (Of the above theories, the camouflage theory – although a rather prosaic theory – appears to make the most sense to us. We believe that zebras' camouflage exists to protect them at night rather than during the day. The zebra's main predator is the lion, and lions tend to do their hunting after sunset. In dimming light, a zebra's black and white stripes might offer some camouflage protection. Many animals have camouflage protection (albeit not 100 per cent foolproof) from predators, so there's no reason why the zebra should be any different.)
- Burchell's and mountain zebras live in long-term social groups called harems, which usually consist of several females, their young offspring and one dominant male (or stallion). The other males who don't have harems may form bachelor

groups until they find harems of their own. Now and again, one of the zebras will break away from the group to try to steal another male's harem. A vicious fight will ensue with lots of biting and kicking. If the challenger wins, he gets to keep the harem. The loser is thrown out of the harem and left to live alone. Grevy's zebras tend to live in fluid social groups without any fixed hierarchy.

- The stallion checks the sexual condition of the mares in his harem by sniffing their urine. When he has found a mare who is ready to mate, he will usually follow her around and cover her faeces with his own so that her smell will not attract other males in the area.
- The zebra is pregnant for approximately 12 months. But the Grevy's zebra's pregnancy lasts longer than a year – 390 days or more.
- Zebras usually give birth to one foal: twins are rare.
- If, for some reason, a pregnant zebra feels that it is not safe to give birth (for example, because of waiting predators), she is capable of delaying the birthing process for several days.
- The zebra foal is able to get up and walk around within an hour after birth. It is important that the foal is able to get onto its feet as soon as possible because of likely attacks from predators.
- For the first few days after birth, the mother will make sure that no other animal (including other zebras) comes near so that her baby has a chance to 'imprint' itself onto her alone. Imprinting ensures that the foal will follow its mother around, thus making it easier for the mother to protect her baby.
- Female zebras tend to leave their mothers as soon as they have reached sexual maturity at around two years of age. Males tend to leave their mothers when they are around four-years-old.
- When cornered by a predator, the zebra will try to kick and bite its enemy. Amazingly, a zebra can break a lion's jaw with just one kick.
- When chased, the zebra can reach speeds of up to 40mph (64.37km/h); however, they have difficulty maintaining this level of speed over long distances.
- A zebroid is a cross between a zebra and a horse. A zedonk is a cross between a zebra and a donkey.
- In the wild, little long-tailed birds called drongos are often seen sitting on zebras' backs. This is because they like to eat the insects from the zebras' coats. The insects are usually kicked up from the ground by the zebras' hooves.
- To help nurture and maintain relationships, zebras regularly spend time grooming one another.
- Every year, during the dry season in Serengeti in Tanzania, zebras come together in vast numbers to migrate to the Masai Mara in Kenya – a locality where water and food is freely available. The arduous journey to a wetter country involves a trip of many miles, and the travelling zebras often face many dangers from predators, such as lions and (when crossing the Mara River) crocodiles. Zebras usually migrate with wildebeest and other hoofed animals.
- Zebras can live 20 years or more.

- The quagga which became extinct at the end of the nineteenth century is thought (by some experts) to have been a subspecies of the Burchell's zebra. The quagga – which used to be plentiful in Cape Province – was a creamy, pale brown colour on its upper body with stripes only on its head, neck and shoulders.
- Mountain and Grevy's zebra are both classed as endangered. Grevy's zebras are hunted and killed for their attractive coats.

'If modern civilized man had to kill the animals he eats, the number of vegetarians would rise astronomically.'
CHRISTIAN MORGENSTERN

TWENTY ONE REASONS FOR BEING A VEGETARIAN

VEGETARIANISM IS THE FASTEST GROWING TREND in the developed world. Here are 21 reasons why more and more people are giving up eating animals:

1. Avoiding meat is one of the best and simplest ways to cut down your fat consumption. Modern farm animals are deliberately fattened up to increase profits. Eating fatty meat increases your chances of having a heart attack or developing cancer.
2. Every minute of every working day thousands of animals are killed in slaughterhouses. Many animals are bled to death. Pain and misery are commonplace. In America alone, 500,000 animals are killed for meat every hour.
3. There are millions of cases of food poisoning recorded every year. The vast majority of all those cases are caused by eating meat.
4. Meat contains absolutely nothing – no proteins, vitamins or minerals – that the human body cannot obtain perfectly happily from a vegetarian diet.
5. African countries – where millions are starving to death – export grain to the developed world so that animals can be fattened for the dining tables of the affluent nations. This problem is getting worse now that agricultural land is widely used for growing crops to be used as a petrol and diesel substitute.
6. Food sold as 'meat' can include: the tail, head, feet, rectum and spinal cord of an animal.
7. A sausage may contain ground-up intestines. How can anyone be sure that the intestines are empty when they are ground-up? Who wants to eat the contents of a pig's intestines?
8. If we ate the plants we grow – instead of feeding them to animals – the world's food shortage would disappear virtually overnight. One hundred acres of land will produce enough beef for 20 people, but enough wheat to feed 240 people.

9. Every day tens of millions of one-day-old male chicks are killed because they will not be able to lay eggs. There are no rules about how this mass slaughter takes place. Some are crushed or suffocated to death. Many are used for fertiliser or fed to other animals.
10. Animals who die for your dinner table die alone, in terror, in sadness and in pain. The killing is merciless and inhumane.
11. It's much easier to become – and stay – healthily slim if you are vegetarian.
12. Half the rainforests in the world have been destroyed to clear ground to graze cattle to make beefburgers. The burning of the forests contributes 20 per cent of all greenhouse gases. Roughly 1,000 species a year become extinct because of the destruction of the rain forests. Around 300 million acres of American forest have been cleared to grow crops to feed cattle so that people can eat meat.
13. Every year, 440 million tons (449 million tonnes) of grain are fed to livestock – so that the world's rich can eat meat. At the same time, 500 million people in poor countries starve to death. Every six seconds someone in the world starves to death because people in the West are eating meat. Approximately 60 million people a year die of starvation. All those lives could be saved if the starving people were allowed to eat just some of the grain used to fatten cattle and other farm animals. If Americans ate 10 per cent less meat, world starvation would be a memory.
14. The world's fresh water shortage is being made worse by animal farming. And meat producers are the biggest polluters of water. It takes 2,500 gallons (11,375 litres) of water to produce one pound (0.45kg) of meat.
15. If you eat meat, you are consuming hormones that were fed to the animals. No one knows what effect those hormones will have on your health. In some parts of the world as many as one in four hamburgers contains growth hormones that were originally given to cattle.
16. The following diseases are commoner among meat eaters: anaemia, appendicitis, arthritis, breast cancer, cancer of the colon, cancer of the prostate, constipation, diabetes, gallstones, gout, high blood pressure, indigestion, obesity, piles, strokes and varicose veins. Lifelong vegetarians visit hospital 22 per cent less often than meat eaters – and for shorter stays. Vegetarians have 20 per cent lower blood cholesterol levels than meat eaters – and this reduces heart attack and cancer risks considerably.
17. Some farmers use tranquillisers to keep animals calm. Others routinely use antibiotics to stave off infection. When you eat meat you are eating those drugs. In America, 55 per cent of all antibiotics are fed to animals.
18. In a lifetime, the average meat eater will consume 70 lambs, 10 cows, 36 pigs, 36 sheep and up to 750 chickens and turkeys.
19. Animals suffer from pain and fear just as much as you do. Most spend their last hours locked in a truck, packed into a cage with hundreds of other terrified animals and then cruelly pushed into a blood-soaked death chamber.

20. Animals which are a year old are often far more rational – and capable of logical thought – than six-week-old babies. Pigs and sheep are far more intelligent than small children.
21. Vegetarians are fitter than meat eaters. Many of the world's most successful athletes are vegetarian.

The Wisdom of Animals

Animal abusers will sometimes argue that since human beings can speak foreign languages and do algebraic equations, they are inevitably 'better' than animals. What nonsense this is. If we follow this argument to its logical conclusion then we must assume that humans who cannot speak foreign languages or do algebraic equations are in some way second-class and are not entitled to be treated with respect.

Who decides which are the skills deserving of respect?

If we decided that the ability to fly, see in the dark or swim under water for long distances were the skills worthy of respect, there wouldn't be many human beings reaching the qualifying standard.

Cats can find their way home – without a map or a compass – when abandoned hundreds of miles away in strange territory. How many human beings could do the same?

How many humans could spin a web?

Even seemingly simple animals can think.

Turtles have been observed learning a route from one place to another. To begin with they make lots of mistakes, go down cul de sacs and miss shortcuts. But after a while they can reduce their journey time dramatically.

Birds, which might normally be alarmed by the slightest noise, learn to ignore the noise of trains and cars when they build their nests near to railway lines or busy roads.

Even oysters are capable of learning. Oysters which live in the deep sea know that they can open and shut their shells at any time without risk. But oysters which live in a tidal area, learn to keep their shells closed when the tide is out – so that they don't dry out and die. This might not quite rank alongside writing a classic novel but how many human beings can write classic novels?

Animals use reason and experience to help them survive, and they exhibit all of the skills which the animal abusers like to think of as being exclusively human.

All animals accumulate information which helps them to survive and live more comfortably. Moreover, they do it just as man does – by discriminating between useful and useless information and by memorising information which is of value. A puppy who has been burnt on a hot stove will keep away from it just as surely as will a child who has suffered a similarly unpleasant experience. Older fish learn to be wary of lures – and become far more difficult to catch than young ones. Rats learn how to avoid traps, and birds learn where telephone wires are strung (so that they don't fly into them). Arctic seals used to live on inner ice floes to avoid the polar bears but after man arrived and proved to be a worse enemy, they started living on the outer ice floes.

Many animals know that they can be followed by their scent, and act accordingly. A hunted deer or hare will run round in circles, double back on its own tracks, go through water and leap into the air in order to lose its pursuers.

Flocks of parrots will send an advance scouting party ahead to check out that all is well.

Surely, we owe it to animals to treat them with respect and, at the very least, to leave them alone to live their lives on this earth free from our harm?

Darwin wrote that: 'there is no fundamental difference between man and the higher mammals in their mental faculties'. He also argued that: 'the senses and intuition, the various emotions and faculties, such as love, memory, attention, curiosity, imitation, reason, etc of which man boasts, may be found in an incipient, or sometimes even well-developed condition in the 'lower' animals.'

The wonders are unending. The honeycomb and the bird's nest are wonders of architecture. Insect communities practise true and genuinely caring socialism.

Even the seemingly lowly ant has a complex and sophisticated lifestyle. Ants can communicate with one another and recognise their friends. They will clean one another, they play, they bury their dead, they store grain, they even clear land, manure it, sow grain and harvest the grass which they have grown. Ants plant crops and build roads and tunnels.

There are still tribes of men who live almost naked in very crude huts and whose social structures are relatively primitive when compared to, say, the beavers who cut down trees, transport them long distances, dam rivers, construct substantial homes and dig artificial waterways.

Animals have many skills we cannot emulate.

The eagle and the vulture have eyes as powerful as a telescope. The swallow will travel thousands of miles every spring – only to be trapped and shot when it dares to land for a while to rest and to drink.

Many animals, birds and insects can predict the coming of storms far more effectively than our allegedly scientific weather forecasters.

Weight for weight the tomtit has more brain capacity than a human being.

Animal behaviour which seems impressive is often dismissed as nothing more than instinctive. But that seems to us patronising and nonsensical. There is now ample evidence available to show animals can invent and adapt tools according to circumstances. That can hardly be called 'instinctive' behaviour. If a Martian looked down on earth and watched humans rushing about on our routine daily work, might he not describe us as incapable of original thought? Might he not regard us as responding only to instinct?

How cruel and vicious a species we must look to lobsters who are boiled alive, to donkeys who are beaten beyond their endurance, and to all farm animals.

Man is the only being on the planet to kill for the sake of killing; to dress up and turn killing into a social pastime.

Only man gloats over the accumulation of material goods which he does not truly need. Only man needs an army of lawyers to fight over what is right and wrong. Only man has forgotten the meaning of natural justice. And everything we invent seems to turn against ourselves. The aeroplane gave us the ability to drop bombs on one another, the car gave us the traffic jam and pollution, and television gave us the reality TV show.

We have created a hell on this earth for other creatures. Our abuse of animals is the final savagery, the final outrage of mankind in a long history of savagery and outrage. Instead of learning from other animals, instead of attempting to communicate with them, men kill, abuse, torture and torment animals. We destroy the relationships of animals with one another, with their environment and with our own race. We diminish ourselves in a hundred different ways through our cruelty and our ignorance and our thoughtlessness. 'Man's inhumanity to man makes countless thousands mourn and his inhumanity to not-men makes the planet a ball of pain and terror,' wrote J. Howard Moore.

If man were truly the master of the universe, he would use his wisdom and his power to increase the comfort and happiness of all other sentient creatures.

Sadly, tragically, man has used his wisdom and his power to increase the misery of other sentient creatures. Animal abusers imprison millions of animals in cruel and heartbreaking conditions, and ignore their cries of pain and distress on the grounds that animals are not 'sentient creatures'. Sheep and cattle are left out in huge fields in cold, wet weather. They shiver and search in vain for shelter because all the trees and hedgerows have been removed to make the farm more efficient. The animal abusing farmer cares not one jot for his animals: he cares only for his profits.

'Until he extends the circle of his compassion to all living things,' wrote Albert Schweizer, 'man will not himself find peace.'

The merciful man is kind to all creatures.

Learning From Animals

There is much we could learn from animals if only we would open our eyes and our minds. We don't have to experiment on animals – or to mistreat them – to learn from them. Here, are eleven things we could have learned from watching how animals look after themselves and behave towards one another.

✓ We should touch the people we care about as often as we can.

- ✓ When those whom we love come home after being away, we should always hurry to greet them.
- ✓ We should stretch when we get up and always before we start moving about.
- ✓ We could soothe and protect our bodies and our minds by taking regular naps.
- ✓ Whenever we are upset or feel threatened, we should avoid biting when a growl will do just as well.
- ✓ We should forget the bad things that happen. Accept whatever punishment we may deserve. And never waste time on regrets or guilt.
- ✓ Whatever we are doing (and however much fun it was when we started) we should always stop when we have had enough. This is particularly true of eating.
- ✓ We should be loyal.
- ✓ We should never pretend to be something we are not.
- ✓ When someone we love is having a bad day, we should make sure that we sit close by to give them silent comfort.
- ✓ Whatever our age, we should make sure that we devote some time every day to playing.

Other books by Vernon Coleman

Alice's Diary

Alice's Diary, the original memoirs of a very real six-year-old mixed tabby cat called Alice, explains precisely what it's like to be a cat. It's the nearest any of us will ever come to finding out exactly what cats think about themselves, other cats and us.

Until she started to keep this diary, Alice had hardly written anything. She certainly hadn't written anything for publication. But this, her first book, sparkles with wit and fun and a rare enthusiasm for life. She describes everything that happens to her and her half sister Thomasina with a keen eye for the absurd and a rare sense of wisdom.

Whether she is describing her relationship with the human beings with whom she shares her life (described as the Upright in Trousers and the Upright who wears a Skirt), her relationships with her many cat friends or her (not always successful) attempts at hunting, no cat lover will fail to find her story enchanting.

Any cat lover who is fortunate enough to read this book will laugh out loud occasionally, smile frequently and maybe even cry once or twice. Most important of all, perhaps, every reader will, for the first time, have an insight into what it's really like to be a cat.

Over 50,000 delighted readers from around the world have already bought this beautifully-written and illustrated hardback book. Our files are bursting with letters from confirmed fans (of all ages) who tell us how much they have enjoyed *Alice's Diary*. *Alice's Diary* can be yours for only £9.99. Such a remarkable book for such a small price. *Alice's Diary* is an illustrated jacketed hardback (142 pages).

Here is a brief extract from *Alice's Diary*

May 17th: Today I broke a vase. It was a complete accident. I jumped onto the mantelpiece and the vase just fell off. I don't think I touched it at all.

But the last time I broke a vase the Upright who wears a Skirt was furious. So this time I thought I'd stay out of the way for a while. Although it rained steadily all day I didn't go back into the house until it was absolutely pitch dark, and the Uprights had been calling me for several hours.

Sure enough, when I finally got back they were so pleased to see me that nothing at all was said about the vase.

Not that it was really my fault anyway.

Other books by Vernon Coleman

The Cats' Own Annual

The Cats' Own Annual is written as though it's actually by and for cats! Vernon Coleman claims that there is a newspaper for cats called *Cats' Own Paper*, which has been in existence for 100 years and is normally only available for cat subscribers. To celebrate the paper's centenary, Vernon insists that he has been asked to compile an Annual so that 'Uprights' can see the world through a cat's eyes.

The following is only a *hint* of what's inside this wonderful book…

- Reasons why cats are better than dogs
- Facts every cat-lover will want to know
- Favourite methods of transport for cats
- Best things about Uprights
- Worst things about Uprights
- Foods cats really like
- Foods cats really hate
- Famous people who adored cats
- Poems and limericks
- Ways in which cats are superior to Uprights
- An ordinary day in the life of a cat

And much more!

The Cats' Own Annual includes a list of the best things about Uprights (from a cat's point of view). Here's an example…

They have laps. There are few comforts more satisfying than a plump, well-upholstered lap.

And here's an example from the book's list of the worst things about Uprights:

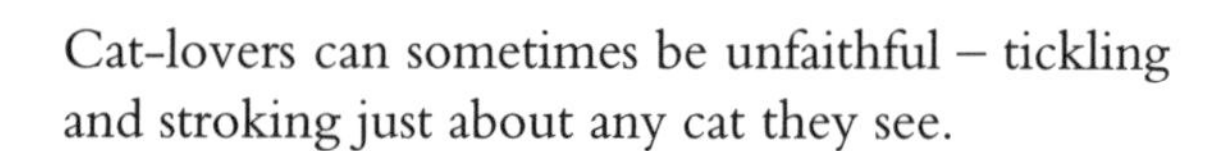

Cat-lovers can sometimes be unfaithful – tickling and stroking just about any cat they see.

Price £12.99 (hardback)
(plus £1 per book towards p&p)

Published by Chilton Designs
Order from Publishing House • Trinity Place • Barnstaple • Devon EX32 9HG • England
Telephone 01271 328892 • Fax 01271 328768

Other books by Vernon Coleman

Cat Fables

Once again, Vernon Coleman has produced a classic gem in this beautifully written and illustrated (with 'cat-toons') cat book. Whether you want this exquisite hardback book with its trademark yellow cover as a gift for yourself, or for friends or relatives, we are certain it will not disappoint. Every one of Vernon Coleman's cat books is a treasure. That is why cat lovers all around the world consider Vernon Coleman's cat books the crème de la crème of cat books, and why they are so sought after by book collectors.

Cat Fables contains 30 delightful stories about cats with a message (or a 'moral') at the end of each story, hence the book is called *Cat Fables* and not *Cat Stories*. Here is just one of the shortest fables from the book just to give you a taste.

The Price Of Everything And The Value Of Nothing

Two cats were walking down the road. They were both new to the neighbourhood. One was very well-groomed and wore an expensive collar. The other was rather unkempt and had no collar. He had a mouse in his mouth. They stopped for a moment to introduce themselves.

'I'm His Highness Rupert Braunton the 5th,' said the cat with the expensive collar. 'I cost £500. How much did you cost?'

The unkempt cat put down the mouse he was carrying. But he didn't answer.

'How much did you cost?' demanded His Highness.

'I'm not sure,' replied the cat without the collar. 'My name is Fred.'

'I bet you didn't cost anything,' said His Highness with a sneer. 'With a name like Fred I suspect that your Uprights were probably paid to look after you.'

Fred didn't say anything.

'I'm insured for more than £500,' said His Highness. 'My Uprights think I'm worth twice that now.'

'Oh,' said Fred.

'I don't suppose you're insured at all, are you?' said His Highness.

'I don't know,' said Fred, who didn't know what insurance was let alone what it tasted like.

'After I won the big cup last month they said my value had doubled,' said His Highness.

Fred nodded.

'Where are you off to?' asked His Highness.

'A cat who lives down the road got knocked over by a car last week,' explained Fred. 'Today is his first day out. I thought I'd go and see how he is.' He looked down at the mouse he'd put down. 'I caught him a fresh mouse. I thought he'd like it.'

'What's the cat's name?' asked His Highness.

'Billy,' said Fred. 'His Uprights call him Billy.'

'Billy!' said His Highness. 'Another common name. Was he a stray?'

'I think so,' admitted Fred.

'So he didn't cost anything either?'

'Probably not.'

'No insurance?'

'I don't expect so.'

'How very common,' said His Highness with a sniff.

'Do you want to come with me?' asked Fred. 'We could say the mouse was from both of us?'

His Highness stared at the other cat in astonishment. 'Me visit a cat called Billy? A cat who cost nothing?' He snorted. 'Don't be silly.' And with that he turned round and walked away.

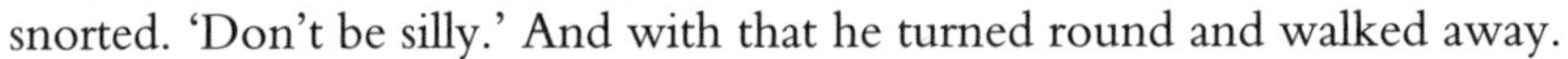

Fred picked up the mouse and continued on his way.

Billy was very pleased to see him. And delighted with the mouse. He told Fred all about his accident and insisted that they share the mouse for tea.

Moral

It's not what you cost that matters. It's what you're worth.